The Carlisle State
Management Scheme:
Its Ethos and Architecture
A 60 Year Experiment in Regulation of the
Liquor Trade

Olive Seabury

Bookcase

Olive Seabury
1920 - 2005

Copyright: Tom Seabury
ISBN 978-1-904147-30-5
First edition 2007
Published by Bookcase
19 Castle Street, Carlisle, CA3 8SY
01228 544560   www.bookscumbria.com

Olive Seabury

Olive Seabury was a Londoner, born and raised in Penge, who lived and worked in London through the Second World War. She moved to Cumberland in 1957 where her husband, the artist Jack Seabury, had taken a teaching post at Carlisle College of Art.

Olive's interests in the arts were not limited to the music education she had gained before leaving London, but included the visual and dramatic arts. As with many of her generation, clothes making and homecrafts were part of the normal mix too. In 1972, a time when mature students were relatively rare, and when university education was open to only five per cent of the population Olive enrolled for the newly launched Open University. She was in one of its key catchment groups, mature people seeking formal but perhaps non-vocational education. As was not so uncommon, higher education was coincident with divorce.

This book can be traced back to the Open University summer school of 1973. The State Management Scheme was in the process of being sold off. One of the summer school sessions, 'Lethaby and the Arts and Crafts. British Architecture 1890 – 1914', was very closely related to Redfern's work, and stimulated Olive's interest.

She was predeceased by her eldest son John, who died aged 46 in 1999. Like John she took pleasure in research and writing. In fact she was so taken with the process of research that she continued it up until her death in 2005 at age 85.

Olive's working life included periods as a comptometer operator, bookkeeper, and a journalist with local Cumbrian periodical Lakescene, who published John Hunt's 1971 booklet on the scheme, 'A City under the Influence'.

In the late 1970s Olive taught General Studies at Carlisle Technical College where she had also herself been a mature student some years earlier in 1969.

Olive's was secretary to the Carlisle Camera Club, and was an enthusiastic chorister in a number of local choirs. She greatly enjoyed the camaraderie of preparation and performance.

An allotment cum flower garden at St Aidan's Road, Carlisle was tended with care and great attention to detail. She also took plenty of exercise as a regular cyclist well into her later years.

Olive felt that this work was 'written as a form of public service'. She wrote: "The history of the Scheme is, in my opinion, a story worth telling and I have striven to tell it with integrity."

Tom Seabury
2007

The Headquarters of The State Management Scheme
at 19, Castle Street, Carlisle.
from 1916 to its final demise.
(Courtesy Tullie House Museum)

CONTENTS

I   DRINK, DRINKING AND DRUNKENNESS :   7
    HADRIAN TO THE CONTROL BOARD

II DRINK, DRINKING AND DRUNKENNESS: 22
    TEMPERANCE AND REFORM

III THE CALL FOR EFFICIENCY   36

IV THE CONTROL BOARD'S CONSTRUCTIVE POLICY   60

V   AFTER THE WAR   78

VI HARRY REDFERN   98

VII THE SCHEME: REDFERN' S MODEL INN   118

VIII MODEL INNS FROM THE 1930s   149

IX ABOLITION OF THE SCHEME by TOM SEABURY   184
    APPENDICES

Royal Commission on Licensing (England and Wales) 1929-31   201

State Management Scheme Acquisitions   201

Table of Preservation Status of State Management Properties   203

The Board's Rules for their Managers   204

BIBLIOGRAPHY   206

Some of the beverages sold by the State Management Scheme

CHAPTER ONE
Drink, Drinking and Drunkenness:
Hadrian to the Control Board

The desire to consume intoxicating liquor is a long-established feature within societies the world over and evidence which has been handed down in stories, writings, and songs throughout the centuries reveals just how pervasive it has been. Its history has been closely linked with agriculture, religion, travel, hospitality, festivities, entertainment, politics, business, and wars.

Throughout time the question of the use or abuse of liquors produced by fermentation or distillation has been the subject of various opinions, attitudes, beliefs and taboos. The ancient Greeks hailed Bacchus, their God of Wine as a promoter of civilisation, a law-giver, and a lover of peace. Amongst the old Indian communities in Canada drinking was controlled as a kind of pleasure. From time to time the hunters were permitted to cease working for a few days and it was presumed that they would get totally drunk, but because it was a controlled activity involving the whole community there was no feeling of guilt attached to it. Drunkenness was seen as a transformation of consciousness. In Judaism there is a liberal attitude to liquor and a joyous use of it as a sacred experience. It is sanctified and given due reverence in the rituals and certain obligatory practices such as the coming-in and going-out of the Sabbath, the redemption of the first-born, and wedding ceremonies. Children are encouraged to participate at an early age secure in the back-up of the Jewish ethic concerning the stability of the family.

The Aztecs of Mexico were at the height of their powers in 1519 when their territory was conquered by Cortes for the King of Spain. Thereafter, on the authority of the first Viceroy (1535-1550), a painted manuscript was prepared in order that the King could form some idea of the nature of his newly acquired land. Known as the Codex Mendoza and written in the indigenous form of pictographs it is now one of the treasures of the Bodleian Library, Oxford. It illustrates many of the contemporary aspects of this Aztec civilisation and fortunately for us includes attitudes to drunkenness. The old people in Aztec society enjoyed many privileges, one of which was the right to get drunk without incurring the wrath of the emperor or the community at large; but for the rest of society, indulgence in the consumption of alcoholic liquors carried a stern disapproval. The Emperor would blame "octli", the fermented juice of the maguey plant for every conceivable vice or disaster whether it be on a personal or a communal scale. The Aztec religion afforded a significant role to the gods of liquor and drunkenness - namely the lunar and terrestrial gods of abundance and good harvests and even to the goddess of the maguey plant itself, Mayauel. However, in the secular field the Aztecs seem to have sensed the dire consequences to their civilisation of the power of "octli" and they consequently initiated formidable barriers to the indulgence in intoxicating liquors. They introduced a kind of safety valve designed to protect the young and able-bodied members of society from this deadly menace. Their defensive measures seem to have been justified for, when the moral and legal underpinnings of Aztec society were eroded, alcoholism spread like camped on the outskirts of the town or village and frequented the tabernae. Surviving fragments of a folding multi-leaved official stores inventory found at Vindolanda and dating from between 80 AD -125 AD mentions three types of drink: vinum (vintage wine), acetum (sour wine), which was the soldier's ordinary drink, and cervesa (Celtic beer) which was by far the least popular.

When the Romans left Britain in 409 AD the roads were no longer defended and the tabernae fell into disuse through lack of customers. As the old order broke down large tracts of land gave way under the Anglo-Saxons to the introduction of small, self-governing areas. These were more conducive to the spread of cottage based alehouses (without accommodation) where the family who owned the land also brewed the ale. The husband took responsibility for the growing and purchasing of the grain while it was his wife who brewed the liquor and stood to suffer severe penalties if her brew was deficient in any way. Her alehouse or tavern became the centre of village life and her ale was expected to be no more than two days old. Her cottage was made distinguishable from others around it by virtue of a projecting pole extended above the door. If she offered wine as well as ale then an evergreen bush was hung at the end of the pole . . . and the "pub" was born! By all accounts the alewife's brew was extremely strong and served many purposes. It was brewed with plenty of herbs as a cure for a fever and to drive out devils in cases of mental disturbance. If the unsweetened ale was mixed with herbs, garlic, and holy water it could be drunk after Mass to cure the fiend-sickness. Pigs were quite frequently fed on her brew to give the meat a distinctive flavour and her ale was often accepted as currency in the payment of debts, rents and tolls.

When St. Augustine arrived in Kent in 594 AD to bring Christianity to the land, he found a people who were worshipping pagan gods of the forest glades and holy wells and sacrificing oxen at their temples. He set about erecting booths close by so that the oxen might be killed instead for the people's nourishment and in praise of a Christian God. These booths quickly became focal points of parish life around which all manner of festivities and money-raising events took place. These money-raising events were called ales to which suitably descriptive suffixes were added such as: church-ale, give-ale, Easter-ale, Midsummer-ale, October-ale, and Scot-ale. The word Scot derived from the Saxon word Sceat meaning part and signified a coin or a portion of payment so that you could pay your Scot and drink your fill. Going Scot-free meant that you made no payment. Ales were sometimes held to help a man to clear his debts even though it meant getting drunk in the process. If an honest man lost money through no fault of his own the law allowed his friends to drink him back to prosperity with a Bede-ale, but in the course of time the practice had to be abandoned because the custom was abused. And so in the wake of brewing came drinking, with drinking came drunkenness, and with drunkenness came legislation.

The question of drunkenness was an issue in Britain even in the sixth century when Ethelbert, King of Kent, while declaring that agriculture was to be the main occupation of the people with sufficient barley being grown for brewing purposes, also had to pass laws regarding drunkenness so that the priests were not too inebriated to discharge their duties. Even stronger measures towards drunkenness had to be adopted in the seventh century when the religious houses were extending hospitality to travellers. The Catholic Church did not classify drunkenness as a sin - not even a venial (pardonable) sin, but it was concerned to contain drinking to a reasonable level. In the eighth century the monk Alcuin reminded his brothers at Jarrow that it was not the use, but the abuse, of alcoholic liquor that made for sin and in 1102 Bishop Anselm decreed that no priest should go to drinking bouts nor "drink to pegs". Previously, during the reign of King Edgar (959 - 975 AD) a scheme had been introduced whereby pegs were placed inside drinking vessels at half-pint intervals in order to restrict the amount of liquor being consumed at one draught. Peg tankards held four pints of liquor divided into eight draughts of half-a-pint so that when it was the custom to pass the tankard from one person to another no-one was expected to take more than one peg. Needless to say, over the course of time it had the opposite effect and led to competitive drinking. Hence, no doubt the origin of the expression "to take your opponent down a peg or two".

Following the Norman invasion in 1066 there was a rise in population and an increase in both trade and travel. The monasteries with their granaries and breweries were able to offer accommodation and medical care to the weary traveller. The infirmerer would attend to wounds and sickness while the cellarer would provide good liquor. Their home-brewed ale was made from the maltings of barley or oats and flavoured with ivy or corn-marigold which was known then as costmary. The monks marked their barrels with the sign of the Cross to denote the strength of the liquor - one cross for the weakest brew, two for a stronger one, and three for the strongest. Later these markings were changed during the reign of Charles II to the form that we still see today: x, xx, and xxx and were used to assess the amount of tax to be paid. The monastic output of liquor at this time was quite sizeable and it is known from the records that Fountains Abbey alone had a brewing capacity of about 900 barrels a year. When wine was introduced by the Normans it was the Saxon over-lords and abbots who drank the wine while the peasantry, monks and priests continued to drink ale. From this time ale became accepted as the people's drink and in course of time became firmly established and officially recognised as a staple constituent of the national diet.

It was not long before legislation and taxation followed. The very first form of taxation levied on ale was introduced by Henry II in 1188 for the purpose of helping to finance a war but it did not take long for the citizens to find a way round it. This they achieved by taking to the forests since the Common Law held jurisdiction only over cultivated or open spaces. The foresters came to the rescue of the good people by providing ale-houses in forest clearings where liquor could be consumed for a modest fee which would have worked out less than the tax imposed. (Perhaps this is what Robin Hood and his band of followers were doing when they took themselves off to Sherwood Forest to get merry, rob the taxman, and help the poor. The Robin Hood is a fairly common name for a public house!). Trade fairs and pilgrimages proliferated to such an extent throughout the medieval period that eventually not even the monasteries were able to cope satisfactorily with the influx of travellers. The outcome was that separate houses were built as lodgings and many great landowners set aside a special house for this purpose which they called an inn, from a Saxon word for chamber. In many instances the arms of the Lord of the Manor were displayed on these houses and thus we see the inn sign beginning to progress from chequerboard to bush-pole to heraldry.

The Church, while stimulating religious fervour in the country was, at the same time also making great efforts to control excessive drinking. A canon law in 1222 required all archbishops, deans, rural deans and priests to abstain from immoderate drinking. They could quench their thirst but were not to over-indulge, nor were they to drink except at certain stated times. A further canon law was instituted in 1236 which forbade the clergy to partake in competitive drinking or to publicise Scot-ales. The Bishop of Lincoln had written to his archdeacons in 1230 saying, "We strictly command that you prohibit in your synods and chapters those drinking assemblies which are commonly called Scot-ales" while the Bishop of Durham was saying, "We adjure all priests, by Him who lives forever, and all ministers of the Church especially those in Holy Orders, that they be not drunkards nor keep taverns".

In 1215, the year of Magna Carta, terms were introduced to standardise the measures to be used for corn, ale and wine. The thirteenth century was about to see another sizeable rise in population numbers and, as ale was by then accepted as a national necessity and brewing was on the increase, the authorities were seriously seeking means by which both agriculture and the brewing concerns could be safeguarded for the benefit of the people. The "Assize of Bread and Ale" was intro-duced in 1267. This assize controlled the prices of bread and ale according to the current prices of corn and malt. Announcements were made by the appropriate civic authorities and it was the responsibility of the brewer to ascertain the correct price for his locality. Failure to do so could land him with a heavy penalty. Juries of six lawful men were appointed to see that the rules were kept and that pots and measures carried the official stamp. Ale-conners or tasters were appointed annually in the Court leet to go round as civic officers testing and tasting the quality and strength of the brews. We do not know the precise extent to which these attempts at regulation succeeded, but it is worth noting the fact that serious efforts were already being made on a local level to regularise the brewing and selling of liquor in the period immedi-ately preceding the introduction of a Representative Parliament. National taxation was controlled by Parliament from 1297, when the Crown lost any personal rights it had previously enjoyed to income from this particular source.

By the end of the medieval period most crafts and trades had formed themselves into guilds and companies which performed a great social function in protecting both the trade and the quality of workmanship, but they did not operate without a considerable measure of faction. The brewers had been grouped together with innkeepers, cooks, pie-bakers, and hucksters but over the years they seem to have suffered from the imposition of many fines for what they considered were but trivial matters. In the end they resented it and retaliated by forming themselves into a separate protective society. During the reign of Henry IV (1399-1413) the brewers of the City of London formed their own mystery - the name given to a specific group of craftsmen or tradesmen. Significantly, they were later granted a Royal Charter by Henry VI which made them a corporate body able to own land and to have the monopoly of brewing throughout the country. The brewers themselves were not slow to appreciate that their own emerging liberty depended upon the ownership of land wildfire among the people.

We do not know with any certainty just when or where the process of fermentation was first discovered, but the early Egyptians in the period 1200 - 1069 BC had found that their bread kept better if it was made from sprouted grains and that when it was soaked for a day or so in an earthenware jar, the liquor which resulted could be drained off and was rather good to drink. The Celts in northern Europe around 500 BC were making their own type of liquor which they called "curmi". and when they later moved across to Britain they found the Ancient Britons making for themselves a mead with water and the wild honey found in the hollow trees.

It was however the arrival of the Romans in Britain which gave the first significant thrust to the long history of liquor in this country. Two significant features emerged from their invasion: they initiated a system of good husbandry and they embarked upon a plan to open up lines of communication. In order that their armies could advance, miles of lonely roads had to be built and maintained. The work was long and arduous and both men and horses needed rest and refreshment. Consequently, the inn began to take its place alongside the stone villa, the temple, the forum, and the baths. Wherever the Romans set up fortifications their military presence afforded the civilian population a degree of security and, as shanty towns began to grow up around the forts, traders were eager to sell to the soldiers. By about the first quarter of the third century AD these shanty towns were expanding and spilling over into an area between the fort and the vallum.

At Housesteads (Vercovicium) one of the buildings closest to the fort was an inn built of wood and stone, one storey high with a stone base and an upper-half with unglazed windows and a pitched roof. The front room which was in the gable end facing the roadway would have been the shop or drink counter while the back rooms would have been the living, and possibly the brewing quarters, with sleeping accommodation in the loft or roof space. These buildings became known as striphouses on account of the inner rooms having been divided off into strips. Customers standing on the roadway would have been served from a counter while others would have been allowed to pass along a passageway to rooms at the rear which had been furnished with benches, stools, and common drinking flagons chained to posts. Facilities would have been provided here for dancing girls, gambling, and games of chess. A chequerboard would have been displayed outside the building giving us our first example of an inn sign. In order that the Roman army could maintain its speed of communication, a kind of postal service was set up staffed by messengers who were capable of riding poste-haste. These messengers thought little of travelling 25 miles a day for an ordinary service, and 50 miles for an express service. It was not uncommon to cover 100 miles in a day and in order to facilitate this, a double system was set up which supplied a fresh team of horses every ten or twelve miles. This was known as a mutatio (change) and this change, in turn, called for a posting-inn a mansio, every 25 miles. It was the responsibility of the local village councils to supply the horses, to keep the mansiones clean, and to keep the fires well-fuelled for the bath suites. The guests at the mansiones would, for the most part, have been officials who would have brought their own bedclothes and food with them while, as an indicator of early social stratification in Britain, the lower orders would have and property.

It was the House of Tudor under Henry VII which introduced the country's first licensing statute in 1495 by which any two Justices of the Peace could "reject and put away common ale selling in towns and places where they should think convenient, and take sureties of keepers of alehouses in their good behaving". This power was further endorsed by Edward VI in the enactment of the Licensing of Tippling Houses Act of 1552 which was the first Licensing Act to be passed, and was the foundation of all our legislation concerning the sale and consumption of intoxicating liquor. The Justices of the Peace were empowered, in the open sessions, to licence alehouse-keepers who were then required to enter into a bond or recognizance for the maintenance of good order and to refrain from permitting unlawful games. Like much legislation in the early history of Parliament the statute of 1552 was vague in many particulars and was itself disregarded in many respects. Many alehouse keepers did not bother to apply for a licence and the original aims were ignored, so that by 1606 a further act was brought in under James I. Parliament sought to restore the principal use of inns, alehouses and victualling houses for the benefit of wayfaring people. It stated categorically that these houses were "not meant for entertainment and the harbouring of lewd and idle people to spend and consume their money and their time in lewd and drunken manner". Prior to 1606 drunkenness had not been an offence although it had been made punishable by the Ecclesiastical Authorities, but the Repression of Drunkenness Act of 1623 then made it a civil offence. Behind the statutes of 1606 and 1623 stood the Privy Council who had consistently in 1599, 1604 and 1608 enjoined upon the justices to suppress unnecessary alehouses but the new spirit that was abroad after the Restoration looked with disfavour upon such restrictions, and dire enactments directed against tippling and drunkenness became almost a dead letter. The supervision of the Privy Council by which the justices had been kept up to the mark, was suddenly broken by the outbreak of the Civil War and no serious attempt was made, either during the Protectorate or after the Restoration, to reconstruct the pioneering, centrally supervised administrative system. The Judges of Assize gradually abandoned interest in the civil administration of the counties in their circuits and by the end of the seventeenth century the Justices of the Peace were left to their own devices. A period of slackness set in just at the time when taxation on intoxicating liquors was found to be an increasing and easy source of revenue for the state.

The three types of establishments which existed for the provision of intoxicating liquor in this period were: the inn which offered stabling, food and accommodation; the tavern which sold ale and wine to all sections of the public; and the alehouse (often referred to as a tippling house) where ale was brewed and retailed on the premises. Coventry in the sixteenth century was a particularly well-administered city and their records of 1544 reveal that they had an excess of alehouses and that many of its citizens had abandoned their usual trades to become brewers and tipplers. The report adds: "Almightie God is highly displeased, the comen-Welthe of this City greatlie decayed". By the year 1547 each alderman in Coventry was required to keep a list of all alehouses and inns in his ward so that licences could be suppressed where the numbers grew to be excessive. It was also required that labourers were not to frequent inns or alehouses on working days. Such rules indicate the early interest taken in the control of the drink trade albeit at a local level and at a time when, because of the risk of disease, no-one was expected to drink ordinary water. Large amounts of ale were being consumed in all strata of society: it was seen as a perfectly normal part of living, and brewing was acknowledged as a legal and justifiable trade. The monastic allowance where it has been found specified in records, indicates that it was seldom less than a gallon (eight pints) of ale a day per head and that a labourer's average intake would have been at least two quarts daily. Since liquor formed such a natural part of the national diet it is not difficult to understand how, in the reign of Elizabeth I, brewers were expected to go on producing quantities of liquor even when, at times, the price fixed by the government was too low. The harsh alternative for them could have been arrest to stand trial as rebels!

The Elizabethans who were great frequenters of inns and alehouses did not however escape censure. An "Anatomie of Abuses" written by Philip Stubbes in 1583 highlights a puritan's opinion declaring that "Every country, city, town, village and other place hath abundance of alehouses, taverns, and inns which are so fraught with malt-worms, night and day, that you would wonder to see them. You shall have them there sitting at the wine and good ale all the day long, yea, all the night too, peradventure a whole week together so long as any money is left . . . swilling, gulling and carousing from one to another, till never a one can speak a ready word . . . and a man once drunk with wine or strong drink rather resembleth a brute than a Christian man. For do not his eyes begin to stare and to be red, fiery and bleared, blubbering forth seas of tears? Doth not his tongue falter and stammer in his mouth? Doth not his head seem as heavy as a millstone, he not being able to bear it up? Finally it maketh him forgetful of himself altogether so that what he doth being drunk, he remembereth not being sober. The drunkard in his drunkenness killeth his friend, revileth his lover, discloseth secrets, and regardeth no man . . . I will not fear to call drunkards beasts, and no men, and much worse than beasts, for beasts never exceed in any such kind of excess or superfluity . . . but measure their appetites by rule of necessity".

Contemporary literature offers some revealing insights into the conditions of a seventeenth century alehouse. John Earle writing in his "Microcosmographie" of 1628 tells us that a tavern "is a degree above an alehouse where men are drunk with more credit and apology. It is a place where they come to make merry but indeed make a noise, and where they come both to quarrel and to make friendships. It is the busyman's recreation, the idle man's business, the melancholy man's sanctuary, the stranger's welcome, the Inns of Court man's entertainment, the scholar's kindness, and the citizen's courtesy". Yet another revealing insight into the conditions of a seventeenth century ale-house is given by Donald Lupton in his "London and the Countrey carbonadoed" written in 1632: "If these houses have a box-bush, or an old post, it is enough to show their profession. But if they be graced with a sign complete, it's a sign of good custom. In these houses you shall see the history of Judith; Susanna; Daniel in the lion's den; or Dives and Lazarus painted upon the wall. It may be reckoned a wonder to see or find the house empty, for either the parson, churchwarden, or clerk, or all, are doing some church or court business usually in this place . . . if either the hostess or her daughter or maid will kiss handsomely at parting, it is a good shoeing-horn or birdlime to draw the company thither again, and sooner. She must be courteous to all, though not by nature, yet by her profession; for she must entertain all, good and bad, tag and rag, cut and long-tail. She suspects tinkers and poor soldiers most, not that they will not drink soundly, but that they will not pay lustily. She must keep touch with three sorts of men: the malt-man, the baker and the justice's clerks".

A brewing revolution had already begun in the fifteenth century when a new ingredient was brought into this country . . . hops. The Romans had previously introduced them to Britain but they had been used as a vegetable, somewhat akin to asparagus. They called them Lupus Salictarius because, as wolves were destructive of sheep, so the hop plants were destructive of the willows growing near to them. Hop growing was known to have existed in Central and Southern Europe as long ago as the ninth century but it was to be the influx of Flemish immigrants into England at the beginning of the sixteenth century which was to result in the actual growing of hops in the warmer, southern areas of this country. By experimentation the Flemish hop growers had produced a liquor which they called bierre, and which was basically ale with the added bitter flavour of the hop. The one overriding factor in its success was that the hops acted as a preservative and the resulting liquor could be stored for longer periods. This brewing revolution was not seen at first as an unalloyed benefit and its introduction was fraught with suspicion and accusation. Many people feared that they were being poisoned, and no fewer than three kings, the Henrys IV, VI, and VIII, are all said to have tried to check the use of hops. Writings of the period speak of the new brew as "drying up the body and increasing melancholy", and a petition was subsequently sent to Parliament by the Common Council of the City of London begging that the use of hops be prohibited on the grounds that they spoilt the taste of the liquor and endangered the people. The argument for and against the new drink waxed strongly throughout the sixteenth century with all manner of essayists, poets and travellers taking up the cry. In 1542 Andrew Boorde in his "Dietry of Health" declared that beer was the "naturall drynke for a Dutcheman, and now of lete dayes it is much used in England to the detryment of many Englisshe people, specially it killeth them the which be troubled with the colyke and the stone, and the strangulation, for the drynke is a cold drinke, yet it doth make a man fat and doth inflate the bely, as it doth appere by the Dutchmen's faces and belyes". Conversely, the medicinal value of beer was lauded in John Gerard's Herbal of 1597 when he said that "the manifold vertues in Hops do manifestly argue the holsomeness of Beere above Ale; for the hops rather make it a Phisicall drinke to keep the body in health than an ordinarie drinke for the quenching of our thirst". The following year Paul Hentzer, a traveller to this country, wrote in his "Journey to England" that, "The general drink is beer which is prepared from barley and is excellently well tasted, but strong and what soon fuddles ". There seems to be sufficient contemporary evidence to indicate that, as early as this, once the initial prejudice to the hops had been overcome, the people began to relish the relatively bitter flavour they imparted to the beer in preference to the sweetness of the country ales. By 1617 Fynes Morrison is telling us in his Itinerary that, "The English beer is famous in Netherland and Lower Germany, which is made of barley and hops. The cities of Lower Germany upon the sea forbid the public selling of English beer, to satisfy their own brewers, yet privately swallow it like nectar".

Crops have been grown not only for brewing by infusion, boiling and fermentation but also to produce liquor by means of distillation.The distillation process extracts the spirit or essence of a substance by first converting it into vapour and then converting that vapour. The exact origins of whisky are not known but it is thought to have been introduced by the Celts, and may have been brought to Scotland from Ireland. It was a combination of home-grown barley and water from the burns which gave it the familiar name of Aqua Vitae, Water of Life. It was made mostly in farmhouse stills for home consumption and the overwhelming number of these illicit stills were in the Highlands of Scotland where life was hard and often lonely but where the quality of the liquor was extraordinarily high. In 1820 one of Scotland's powerful landowners, the Duke of Gordon, sought to get Parliament to legalise the manufacture of whisky to a standard equal to that of the illicit stills, and he promised to use his influence and that of his fellow lairds to repress smuggling as a consequence. Three years later an Act on these lines was passed and one of the first men to go legitimate was farmer George Smith of Glenlivet who, over the next 48 years, was to amass an estate of over 20,000 acres. From this time there was a marked change in the drinking preferences of the Scottish landowners from claret to whisky, yet it was the Lowlanders who were the prime movers in the development of the whisky industry. Unfortunately, with the emergence of the Scottish industrial centres, drunkenness became just as acute and troublesome in some of these towns as in England where the consequences of the demon gin bonanza were being manifested.

It was in seventeenth century Holland that a spirit was distilled from the cereal rye which was flavoured with juniper berries, coriander, and the root of angelica. The habit of spirit drinking did not become common until the end of the seventeenth century and it was first sold in England for its medicinal properties. The supply was relatively small, as the distillation was a monopoly confined to the royal patentees. A petition had been made to Parliament in 1673 requesting that more support be given to the growing of barley for beer and that a restriction be placed on the imports of spirits. The petition failed but seventeen years later the royal patent for the distillation of spirits was abolished and the Act of Parliament of 1690 under William of Orange gave every Englishman the right to distil and retail spirits produced from home-grown malted corn "for the greater consumption of corn and the advantage of tillage". Only a small excise duty was imposed on spirits and the retailer did not require a licence. The twist in the tale came when, in addition to supporting its own agricultural policies, the public at large felt that it was their public duty to drink spirits. Drunkenness became commonplace owing to the cheapness and strength of the liquor, it pervaded all classes, and it took the authorities by surprise. An Act of 1729 then sought to place an extra duty on spirits and required all retailers to take out an annual excise licence, but it met with so much opposition that it had to be repealed four years later. The preamble to this act had stated that, "the drinking of spirits and strong waters had become very common amongst the people of inferior rank", and that the "constant and excessive use tends greatly to the destruction of their health, enervating them, and rendering them unfit for useful labour and service". The accusation of being unfit for useful labour together with the precept of "duty to one's country" was to be heard again most persistently in 1915 at the commencement of the First World War. But the consumption of spirits continued unabated, and fearing that it was tending toward the "devastation and ruin of this kingdom" a further act was passed under George II in 1736 requiring retailers not to sell spirits in quantities less than two gallons. The object of this exercise was to put it beyond the reach of the poor. The retailer, as well as obtaining an annual licence, had an extra duty imposed upon every gallon of spirits sold and this requirement carried a heavy penalty for any breach. It is not surprising that the severity of the act defeated its objective because the duties were regarded as excessive and few licences were taken out. Notwithstanding the penalties, the act was breached more often than it was observed and by 1742 it had to be repealed. Evasion was rife, and the product was being adulterated and put into medicine bottles. The number of gin shops in London alone was truly alarming and some of the adulterations so awful that the victims were more poisoned than drunk. Druggists put up gin in physic bottles and called it cholick or gripe water with the instruction to take it four or five rimes a day or "as often as the fit takes you". It was the poor, both men and women, who had turned to gin as a reliever of misery, wet nurses who needed to drink plenty of fluids were known to be habitual gin drinkers, and even the poor babies who were given gripe water to get them to sleep were really being given gin. A Royal Proclamation against vice and immorality was sent out by the Home Secretary to every bench of magistrates in 1787 and by 1792 the sale by retail of all intoxicating liquors for consumption on the premises had been brought under the control of the justices. Various counties began to admit that too many alehouses had been licensed and the Benches resolved to grant no new licence except where the convenience of the public absolutely required it, or the current number had been considerably reduced. The indiscriminate and illegal sale of liquors was being put down but the number of licensed houses was increasing. Following a movement initiated by John Wesley, a Royal Proclamation against vice and immorality was sent out by the Home Secretary to every bench of magistrates in 1787. The various counties began to admit that too many alehouses had been licensed and the benches resolved to grant no new licence but where the convenience of the public absolutely required it, or until the present number had been considerably reduced. An excise licence could not be granted until the applicant already held a justice's licence. The simplicity of this legislation was not to last long as there was still a certain laxness in granting licences too freely without reference to the needs of the neighbourhood.

At the same time some brewers were supplying poor quality beer to their tied houses and the consumption of gin and other spirits was increasing rapidly. In the parliamentary debate of the 4th of May, 1830 (column 403) it was stated that the consumption of spirits had risen from 12 million gallons in 1818 to 24 million gallons in 1830 and it was alleged that crime had risen in the same proportion. To counteract this situation it was proposed that a free trade in the retail sale of beer would restore the desire for the good old English beverage by virtue of the competition between the brewer and the distiller on the one hand, and the beershop and the ginshop on the other. Another argument was that it would give a "perfect and uncontrollable sale of beer and would break down the monopoly of the publican and brewer". The argument in the debate seemed to go all one way with little being said in opposition. The gut feeling in the country generally was against the bill with 483 petitions against the proposals and only eight in favour. However, within a few weeks of its introduction the bill became law and it meant that in future any person whose name was on the rate book was entitled to open his house as a beer-shop, free from any justices' licence or control, merely by making a payment of two guineas to the Excise. By anybody's standards this Beerhouse Act of 1830 for England and Wales (it did not apply to Scotland) must rank as one of the most extraordinary examples of government legislation in nineteenth century history. It sparked off an intractable problem which was to exercise the minds of statesmen and citizens alike over the years by virtue of introducing bills, passing Acts of Parliament, making amendments to acts, repealing acts, explaining, pleading, cajoling, despairing, hoping, and waiting. If we look back to the general regulations of Parliament in the thirteenth century we see that they took the form of Assizes or Ordinances for Bread and Ale which were directed to securing the purity of bread and ale at a fair price for the citizens. Parliament was concerned with the quality of the product which formed an important part of the national diet, but there is little doubt that by 1643 when Parliament began to impose taxes on liquor in the interests of revenue, it was initiating a process which was to change the aspect of a lawful trade into one that was in danger of being seen to be at variance with the pursuits of a healthy society. Parliament was moving from controlling the quality of the product to controlling the trade in the product, and there started the long and tortuous history of the control of the drink trade with all its daunting complexities.

Within six months of the 1830 Beer Act there were no fewer than 24,342 new beersellers. This figure rose to 45,717 by 1838. Brewers' agents travelled from village to village persuading all and sundry to start selling beer, themselves advancing the excise fee and supplying beer on credit. At the same time the licensed victuallers strove to increase their sales of spirits (which the beer-houses could not supply) by turning their victualling houses into rather splendid, if flashy, gin-shops. The consumption of spirits rose steadily. A Report to the Select Committee of the House of Commons on Drunkenness in 1834 tells how a low, dirty public-house having but one doorway would be converted into a splendid edifice boasting three large entrances and having its doors and windows glazed with large, single panes of plate glass. Costly gas lamps would hang outside to welcome the passer-by and when all was completed placards were carried round the district advertising the premises. By an Act of Parliament in 1869 all sellers of intoxicating drink had, once again to obtain a justice's licence, but for the first time a limitation was placed on the justices in refusing an already existing licence. A sharp distinction was being drawn between the renewal of an existing licence and the grant of a new one. However, the Act of 1869 was a temporary measure for only two years until some more complete measure could be introduced. It was said that the justices had great difficulty in making a proper selection in the absence of any established principle to guide them. In Liverpool where the free-trade principle was being applied they had tried in 1865 to get a bill introduced to define and settle more strictly the considerations covering the granting or with-holding of licences. In 1867 the ratepayers of Liverpool caused a bill to be introduced giving power to ratepayers to veto the opening of public houses in the neighbourhood. Neither of these bills was passed but they certainly served to highlight the unsatisfactory state of the current law as it stood in practice. The struggle to attain a reasonable solution to the nation's abuse of alcohol and deeply entrenched and cherished drinking habits through a programme of sensible legislation persisted to the end of the century and into the twentieth century. The Home Secretary in Gladstone's Government sought to introduce a Licensing Bill in 1871 which would give the justices the power to determine the number of licences in an area subject to a local veto. Licences, or certificates were to be rented out to the bidder of the highest annual rent and then these rents were to be appropriated to worthy public causes. The certificates were to be valid for ten years subject to annual renewal on evidence of good behaviour. Closing hours were specified in the bill and Sunday opening was to be confined to four hours, from 1pm to 3pm and from 7pm to 9pm. Meetings were held throughout the country in opposition to the proposals which it was felt, together with the operation of the tied-house system, was going to make it increasingly difficult for a publican to make a living and keep within the law. The bill was eventually withdrawn.

However, the Government was not deterred by this and after the turn of the century and until the setting up of the Central Control Board (Liquor Control) in 1915 the main statutes of licensing legislation which brought about important changes in the laws relating to intoxicating liquors were the Acts of 1902; 1904; and the Licensing (Consolidation) Act of 1910.

The Act of 1902 gave effect to certain of the recommendations suggested in the Report of the Royal Commission of 1896-99, the most important of which being the requirement of a justices' licence for all "off retail sales of beer, wine and spirits". This measure completed the justices' full control over the retail sale of intoxicating liquor, subject to the exception of "bottle shops". This loophole in the law meant that, despite certain conditions such as the self-contained nature of the premises, persons could carry on a retail sales business in intoxicating liquor without the approval of, and possibly contra to the better judgement of the licensing justices. It presented a frustrating situation by which an area could become over-licensed and the citizens denied their right of expression with regard to the establishment in their localities of liquor retailing businesses.

The Act of 1904 brought in by the Unionist Government of A.J. Balfour heralded important changes in the law. Until then no distinction had existed between the different grounds on which a renewal licence was refused, but from now on refusals were to be divided into two distinct categories, namely, on grounds of misconduct on the one hand, and all other grounds on the other hand. It was this latter category which was to hold such significance since, because of it, a Special Compensation Scheme was introduced. By this scheme all old on-licences (ante-1869) became liable to make contributions on a fixed scale (varying with the annual value of the premises) to a fund which would pay compensation in the event of a renewal being refused on grounds other than for misconduct. This really set the alarm bells ringing. The compensation charge was payable at the same time as the excise duty and the justices, upon the grant of any new "on" licence were bound to exact the monopoly value, they had no option in the matter. The three key issues running through and complicating any discussion of the vexed question of the reduction of licences from now on were to be the tied-house system, compensation, and monopoly value. Great hopes were being expressed while the 1904 Bill was being debated, but by the time the bill actually became law and was put into practice, it was demonstrated how wide of the mark the estimates had been regarding the assessment of compensation. The Government had not adequately dealt with the situation of the increasing value of licences where adjoining licences had been extinquished. If, as the Government had intended, compensation was to be based on market value, then by reason of the extinction on compensation of other licences in the immediate vicinity a "certain betterment" ensued, this should form part of the actual market value and be taken into account when assessing compensation. The Act however did not provide that the charges and awards should be made on the same basis nor had it fully accounted for the risk factor insofar as the liability of a licence to be chosen for extinction was limited by the amount of the premiums paid in compensation charges. This meant that the problem of an excess of licences could only be dealt with according to the funds available via the compensation charges. Two separate authorities were concerned with every operation for extinction, but the licensing justices who might well have wanted to suppress a licence, would have to take into account the willingness of the compensation authority to impose and continue to impose charges at a sufficient rate to cover outlay .This situation compromised the ability to suppress a licence "on merit". It proved to be a serious weakness in the scheme which had been concluded in a rather piecemeal manner and failed to forecast that it would be the smaller and least useful houses that would be chosen for extinction in the first place and that, as the years passed, larger and more profitable houses would be included leading to a possible unfair advantage for the main brewers with their large capital resources. It would also become inevitable that when these more profitable houses were closed, part of the custom would pass naturally to neighbouring houses and be made the subject of repeated payments with the consequence that these houses, because of "betterment" would become more and more expensive to compensate. The amount to be awarded as compensation was subsequently determined in a case in the High Court by the Hon. Mr. Justice Kennedy in 1906 when it was made clear that the award was to represent the market value of the licence at the time of its refusal, and that the sum was to be equal to the difference between the value of the licensed premises and the value which these premises would bear were they not licensed.

Conflict over the issue of compensation had already been foreseen by Arthur Chamberlain, chairman of the Birmingham Licensing Bench, when giving evidence on intemperance before a House of Lords Select Committee in 1877. He had suggested that local authorities might be given the power to close public houses, but the involvement of large sums of money as compensation would be a hindrance and a bar to the prohibition of the sale of liquor. He warned the House that it was a dangerous thing to concede the principle of compensation. One government would start by paying it out of a fund raised from liquor profits while a following government would cancel that out and it would rebound onto the ratepayer. (Parliamentary Papers 1877 (171) XI Q 2294).

The public house was becoming increasingly an issue in party politics, and the money value of possessing a licence was an economic factor which could not be ignored; nor could the indigenous and deeply entrenched appetite for intoxicating liquor be ignored by those who sought to reform and improve the habits and conditions under which it could operate. The Consolidation Act of 1910 brought in under Asquith's Liberal Government dealt with many of the important issues which included compensation, monopoly value, the transfer and renewal of licences, plans for structural alterations and for new buildings, and closing times, as well as many more minor matters such as off-sales to children under the age of 14. Under Section 18 of the Act the justices were given the power to refuse to renew a licence if the licensee had persistently and unreasonably refused to supply suitable refreshment (other than intoxicating liquor) at a fair price. The justices would presume that the premises had been ill-conducted and, under these circumstances no compensation would be payable. A licensee could also be convicted of the offence of "permitting drunkenness" if he supplied more than one drink at any one time to a sober person without having ascertained first that the drink being ordered was not with the intention of it reaching the hands of a person on the premises who was already inebriated, (Section 75). The Act (Section 50 Sub-sect 2) also made it quite clear to licensees that it was illegal to add water to beer and that it was forbidden to mix a stronger beer with a weaker one. No premises would receive a justices' on-licence unless it contained at least two rooms for public use for a full licence, and one room in the case of beerhouses (Section 37). Any structural alteration to licensed premises which would give increased facilities for drinking, or would conceal from observation any part of the premises used for drinking, or would affect communication between where the liquor is sold and consumed was disallowed. Most landlords would not have had sufficient money of their own to purchase houses and they resorted to borrowing money on mortgage from a firm of brewers and tying themselves to that particular brewery for their beer. Brewers were naturally intent upon securing a steady outlet for their product and the tied house system which started in a small way had attained quite large proportions a century earlier. It had been the subject of a House of Commons Select Committee inquiry in 1817. This Committee regarded the system as "a great grievance" which warranted the attention of the legislature in order to "limit its further progress and relieve the public of its mischievous consequences". This did not materialise even despite the introduction of bills in the House of Commons as late as 1905, 1906, and 1907 calling for the abolition of the system. For many years the tied tenancy was carried on as an ordinary business regulated on a commercial basis by which many tenants were subjected to harsh terms and assessing the efficacy or otherwise of the system is not easy. Under the stewardship of a good and careful brewer-owner it was capable of producing some excellent results but there were many drawbacks for both publican and brewer when market forces fluctuated. Notwithstanding individual circumstances a brewery tenant was more likely to have repairs and improvements carried out on the property than would a free publican from a landlord who was not a brewer.

The years from 1876 to 1885 saw a general recession throughout the country and this, together with the growing hostility towards the drink trade by the various temperance organisations, put the brewers on their metal. They realised that if temperance pressure resulted in further government legislation which could threaten the trade then a solution lay in a fervent renewal of the acquisition of tied houses The brewers were propelled into converting to company status and thus their ability to sell shares enabled them to raise the necessary capital to buy property on a hitherto undreamed of scale. An unprecedented scramble for property ensued which in turn led to intense competition, not only between brewers themselves but also between brewers and distillers. In an oblique sense this competition sowed some early seeds of the public house improvement movement by virtue of the breweries wishing to exhibit their own good management skills in an estate of good tied houses. Prosperity returned in 1886 but the public house no longer derived from its surroundings and local customs, but became part of a business ethos, and a large business ethos to boot Prices of properties were soaring during the boom years from 1896 to 1899 and inflation inevitably followed. When the crash came in 1898 the number of bankruptcies escalated with the brewers the main creditors of the insolvent publicans who had no alternative but to part with their mortgaged property. Ironically the value of all this public house property in the major cities had dropped disastrously and by 1915 and the outbreak of the First World War practically no new public houses were being built.

The position was somewhat different in the provinces as many of the brewers were already the owners of the properties in their own regions and they had not succumbed to the enticements of the "Brewers' War" which swept through the urban areas. But they were, nevertheless just as affected by the conditions of inflation and lacked the funds to maintain, yet alone improve their premises.

This was the situation pertaining to licensed premises when the Central Control Board was set up 1915 to take care of the nation's drinking habits during time of war.

Vol. 1. No. 1.]   NOVEMBER, 1889.   [Price One Penny.

CHAPTER TWO
DRINK, DRINKING and DRUNKENNESS
Temperance and Reform

Having given an overview of the efforts of the legislature in tackling the drink problem in the period leading up to the onset of the First World War it would now be helpful to take stock of the various campaigns against drunkenness and the drink trade following the 1830 Beer Act. Of these the four main campaigns were free-licensing; anti-spirits; teetotalism; and prohibition. All in their own way looked for solutions beyond relying exclusively upon legislation. Adherents of free-licensing were seeking temperance by means of education and "moral suasion" rather than through restrictive legislation. The prohibitionists wished to distance themselves from the existing licensing laws in the ardent belief that the drink trade was a most disruptive trade and therefore it was an evil which needed to be entirely abolished - not merely regulated. Temperance reformers rejected the supposition that revenue accrued from this disruptive trade could benefit society in the long term. They wished that the government would distance itself from the policy of free trade in liquor - a movement operating from London at the political level - and concentrate more on the "voluntary abstinence" movement which flourished mainly in the provinces, where it had originated, and was operating mainly at the individual level. Many opinion-formers in both the religious and secular spheres of society were campaigning for sobriety as early as the 1820s with a distinct interest being shown by doctors, industrialists, evangelicals and coffee traders, albeit each from their own specific viewpoint. When the Temperance Movement emerged in 1828 as an anti-spirits campaign it did not initially repudiate free-licensing but sought to achieve its aim of sensible drinking habits through voluntary abstinence - a strategy which it considered to be compatible with the rejection of certain licensing restrictions. It was felt that a considerable number of people would favour temperance in the true meaning of the word - moderation - without having recourse to compulsory absti-nence upon those citizens who use, but do not abuse, alcohol in their lives. Nor was

Above: The banner of The Carlisle Temperance Advocate.

it felt to be right to impose unreasonable interference upon representatives of the Trade who themselves maintained that a licence was given to the public house itself but that too often the property was punished for the faults of an individual manager. Temperance reformers were at all times mobilised into a distinctive unit yet, as can happen when members are forced to struggle with overwhelming perplexities, a split occurred in their ranks with the founding of the United Kingdom Alliance in 1853. The UKA attacked the supply of alcoholic liquor and wanted to outlaw the trade itself. It was the liquor itself that caused people to get drunk more than the external arrangements made for its consumption, and the Alliance maintained that the licensing reforms alone could never get to the root of the evil. This admission divided the temperance movement into two factions - the moral suasionists and the legislative compulsionists. In other words - education versus prohibition: either to avoid the abuse of drink by virtue of the individual's own moral strength, or to remove all temptations to drink so that its use could not be abused. The Trade, naturally, was suspicious and contemptuous of any move which would lead customers into becoming abstainers by virtue of various Acts of Parliament. Adhering to its Christian beliefs as a basis for the social conscience, the temperance movement helped to focus attention on the prevailing level of drunkenness as a serious social evil and to recognise that the cause of the escalating intemperance was the legalised system of temptation itself. It therefore wanted an all-out war on the trade in liquor with unconditional surrender of licences and no compensation. Basically, the Alliance never wanted to see itself as an auxiliary to the legislature and, with hindsight it was a pity that in 1853/4 it declined to take an interest in a government committee recommendation that inspectors might be appointed to supervise public houses. As a consequence of this attitude much expert and detailed knowledge was lost to them in their endeavour.

The industrial revolution had been responsible for plunging nineteenth century society into a state of flux and as Britain was the first modern industrial estate, politicians and reformers alike were faced with the task of achieving some degree of consensus through a process of new and unfamiliar adjustments in order to maintain, or re-establish, social order and acceptable standards. The Liberal Party, the temperance movement, and the evangelicals figured prominently in this cause. It has become an accepted aspect of life for us in the present twentieth century to countenance change after having heard protracted debates between experts both inside and outside Parliament, but many social reform movements in the nineteenth century arose spontaneously in an aura of democratic and semi-religious fervour, often led by individuals of remarkable energy and charisma. It is not possible, due to the lack of firm statistics for the period and the complexities surrounding the issue, to adduce with any certainty that the problem of the nation's drinking habits was aggravated by the effects of industrialisation. Nevertheless the influx of a large migrant population into the cities seeking employment, and the inadequacy of the housing stock to cope with the situation, contributed to the eventual squalor and degradation. The subsequent overcrowding meant that more people were being affected by the behaviour of the drunkards. On the other hand, the newly installed factory system sought to impose regular patterns of labour upon its workforce, and in the cause of both production and the protection of expensive machinery, it was required that the workforce kept regular hours and maintained fitness. This meant that drinking habits and regulations had to change. The terms middle class and working class were just coming into use in the early 1830s as the temperance movement was emerging, but it was the distinction made between the destitute or "rough" poor and the "respectable" poor which was to be politically more important in the cause of reform than the specific division between the classes per se. Liberals hoped that by encouraging the poor to be thrifty and to abstain from strong drink they could reduce the citizen's reliance upon the state which, along with the licensing system, they distrusted anyway. Their declared desire for moral progress eventually led them to uphold a belief in the popular control of the drink trade - a belief which was to be most assiduously fought for in Parliament in the latter half of the century by the Carlisle M.P., Sir Wilfrid Lawson. The temperance movement was mainly a Liberal movement attracting working class support and striving to reach a balance between individual freedom and social obligation. It embraced a formidable body of Anglicans and non-conformists devoted to channelling their religious energies into finding a coherent form of politics, not in order to better their own condition but to improve the lot of the less fortunate in society. It was predominantly an urban movement, particularly strong in the northern industrial towns where it had first gathered support. The formation of the United Kingdom Alliance in 1853 shifted the emphasis away from the crusade for the reclamation of the individual drunkard and towards a demand for group status. Many of the finest minds among liberals were alarmed when moral suasionists thus began moving towards the acceptance of prohibition. They found the rigidity of organised teetotalism repellent and began to veer towards the policy of popular control.

The initial attempts at temperance reform world-wide had originated in America in the early nineteenth century. However, it was slow to spread outside America itself. Surprisingly the first country to take it up was Ireland when the Reverend George Carr founded the New Ross Temperance Society in County Wexford in 1829. At the same time captains of American vessels docking in the port of Liverpool began to distribute tracts to the local residents. This resulted in the Liverpool Temperance Society being formed in March 1830. This was followed in 1842 by the British Temperance Emigration Society. The Glasgow and West of Scotland Temperance Society was also launched in 1829 with William Collins, the printer and publisher, as its vice-president. This later became known as the Scottish Temperance Society. At this time John Dunlop formed the Greenock Temperance Society with several members signing the total abstinence pledge, but by 1834 a gulf had developed in their ranks between those favouring moderation and the teetotalers. The society as a whole then reverted to the moderation principle only. For the next decade the cause of temperance progressed steadily throughout the country and societies were set up in Bradford, Warrington, Manchester, Leeds, Bolton, Birmingham, Newcastle-upon-Tyne, Bristol, London, Blackburn, Preston, Halifax, Southampton, Middlesbrough and St. Ives. The first meeting of the Bradford Temperance Society, founded by Scottish businessmen Henry Forbes, was the real start of the temperance movement in England. Local employers were willing to release their employees early from work in order that they might attend temperance meetings and it was not long before doctors themselves took up the cry to condemn the drinking of spirits. William Collins, the publisher, who had made three attempts to set up a temperance society in London finally succeeded in November, 1830. In July, 1831, it became known as the British and Foreign Temperance Society but ceased to be called this in 1848 after the foundation of the New BFTS in 1836. Cumberland supported a sturdy BFTS membership of 1,524 in 1834 which represented 9 members per 1,000 of the population. In subsequent years only four other areas had a higher ratio of membership per 1,000 population, namely: Gloucestershire at 9.2; Durham at 10.4; Lancashire at 18.8; and Cornwall at 25.1 (figures taken from the BFTS third annual report). The BFTS was based on the tenets of the evangelical reforming movement. The Bishop of London was its president and four peers and four bishops filled the offices of vice-presidents. Wealthy philanthropists involved themselves in the success of the society as did many Quakers: aristocrats and evangelical ladies; and the liberal M.P., the Lord Henley of Scaleby, Cumberland.

The first Parliamentary enquiry into drunkenness had been set up in June 1834, chaired by J.S. Buckingham. Blame for the deplorable conditions was aimed specifically at the level of spirits being consumed, but unfortunately, the enquiry did not take into consideration the troubles which were also being caused by beer drinking. A detailed study of the entire licensing system in existence at the time to include beer would have been most valuable, but instead, the report advocated only the absolute prohibition of the manufacture, import, and sale of spirits and this was to happen only when it felt that pubic opinion was right for such a move. The report, by advocating the right of the state to intervene with legislation to correct the evil in society, was also signifying the weakness of the temperance movement at Westminster and there was to be a gap of another generation before a dedicated parliamentary spokesman arose in its cause in the figure of Wilfrid Lawson.

The emerging teetotal movement however was much more resolute in its methods. By the 1840s many had adopted the long pledge which banned the offering as well as the consumption of intoxicants. The movement originated in Preston. Many of the early tee-totallers were liberal/radical nonconformists who laid great emphasis on self-respect. Their development needs to be set against three other movements which were all concerned with the general concern for social regeneration: Chartism; Owenism; and later, the emerging Labour Party. Many Chartists expressed a considerable enthusiasm for abstinence but their political orientation was disliked by the tee-totalers, while the Chartists for their part disliked the attitude of the tee-totalers in imposing middle class leadership on working men. Overall, the prohibitionist crusade was based on a hybrid form of interventionism insofar as it was trying to combine a strong belief in self-help with a commitment to firm public control. Nineteenth century reformers were falling into separate categories: those who advocated tradition and religion as remedies for society's ills, and those who stressed the importance of reason and the utility of institutions. It was in a spirit of militant nonconformity which was abroad in the land by the middle of the century that radical middle-class and the leaders of the working class found that they could espouse the same cause - the call for sobriety.

The Evangelical Revival, while supporting a new religious seriousness was also instrumental in encouraging the aristocracy to become involved in the moral crusades of the times. The anti-slavery movement had been held in high regard by the temperance reformers who believed following the elimination of the traffic in slaves, there could follow the elimination of the traffic in drink. The intellectual centre of the evangelical movement had been Cambridge University where two of the original chief leaders had been Isaac Milner and Charles Simeon. Milner, president of Queens College, had accompanied William Wilberforce on a continental tour, a consequence of which had been to lead Wilberforce into embracing the Christian faith at the age of 26. Milner was later installed as Dean of Carlisle from 1792 until his death in 1820 and he was affectionately referred to as "the portly dean with the stentorian voice". His widow, in "The Life of Isaac Milner" in 1842, related that her late husband as Vice-Chancellor in 1810 had deplored the behaviour of the Cambridge undergraduates for the "breaking of lamps and windows, shouting and roaring, blowing of horns, galloping up and down the streets on horseback or in carriages, fighting and mobbing in the town and neighbouring villages; in the daytime breaking down fences and riding over cornfields, then eating, drinking and becoming intoxicated at taverns or ale-houses; and lastly, in the night frequenting houses of ill-fame, resisting the lawful authorities and often putting the peaceable inhabitant of the town into great alarm".

Within Parliament the Clapham Sect were the leading evangelicals of their day exercising a profound influence by virtue of the intensity of their belief in putting principle before party or profit. Though few in number within the House, they demonstrated by their own rectitude that there was a substantial body of the middle classes in the country who, though nominally Tory or Whig, were actually independent and operated outside the boundaries of ecclesiastical favour. The Sect which had been formed in 1785 acknowledged William Wilberforce as their leader and laboured wholeheartedly for the reformation of abuses, for the abolition of duelling, state lotteries and brutal sports. Alongside this was the determination to save souls, to keep the Sabbath Day holy, and to overcome ignorance and vice. It valiantly upheld the fundamental principles of the rights of man and was outspoken on the shame of allowing commerce to benefit from measures which were degrading to humanity itself. The campaigns of these pioneers of English social progress survived much of the ridicule directed towards them and lasted about 50 years until the passing of the Emancipation Act in 1833 and the death of Wilberforce. One of the most intriguing members of the Clapham Sect had been Hannah More - the "Queen of the Methodists" and an agent of William Wilberforce. Cobbett called her the "Old Bishop in Petticoats". She was a blue-stocking who moved slowly towards the evangelical position. When in 1789 she and one of her sisters accompanied Wilberforce on an extended tour of the Cheddar area they were horrified and saddened at what they found. Among the poor there was crime, ignorance and illiteracy.

For centuries religion, drink, and agriculture had been closely integrated and parsons, being themselves quite often sons of publicans, had been accustomed to mingling freely with brewers, farmers and magistrates. It was the early evangelicals, however, that began a process of isolating the clergy from the traditional drinking habits of their parishioners in an endeavour to elevate them as a moral exemplar. When Harvey Goodwin was installed as Bishop of Carlisle in 1869 he received many letters, some congratulatory but others commiserating with him for the fact that there was "one great and unpleasant difficulty in the diocese - the prevalence of intemperance among the clergy". By 1869 the clergymen were still too poor to buy books and had no means of visiting outside their parishes except when they went on foot or by a possible lift in a market cart. The incumbent would have been very much reliant on the company of the farmers for his social intercourse and it was not uncommon to find him eking out his slender income by selling ale on Sundays. Until then, drinking of itself, was not considered a sin either in priest or people. Harvey Goodwin was a keen advocate of the temperance cause and instituted a Mid-Lent Temperance Sunday in 1847 together with a Church of England Temperance Society for the diocese in which he urged the clergy to recognise moderation as well as total abstinence. His maxim was to try all things before trusting to legislation. At heart the bishop had always been a builder and restorer of churches and while Dean of Ely he had been responsible for organising the restoration of that great cathedral's lantern, and derived much pleasure in watching and encouraging craftsmen at their work, including the young wood and stone carver James F. Redfern - a relative of Harry Redfern - as he worked on the numerous items of statuary. He also maintained a deep interest in scientific matters and it seemed fitting that it was he who undertook to preach the funeral sermon on Charles Darwin in Westminster Abbey on 1 May, 1882.

Towards the last quarter of the nineteenth century, the temperance cause began to owe much to the dedicated work for the advancement of sobriety made by two renowned personages of Cumberland, namely Sir Wilfrid Lawson, Bt., and Rosalind, Countess of Carlisle. Wilfrid Lawson, the elder who was granted a baronetcy in 1831, was a devout evangelical and a total abstainer at a time when total abstinence was commonly denounced as un-patriotic; un-gentlemanly; and un-Christian. His wife was the sister of Sir James Graham, the Liberal statesman responsible for the Municipal Corporation Act of 1835. This act gave birth to the modern town council system and among the provisions of the measure as it was presented to the House of Commons was a clause seeking to transfer the licensing power in the boroughs - at least concerning ale-houses - from the magistrate to the town council or to a committee of the council. With hindsight this can now be seen as a more momentous proposal than was realised at the time. Had this clause been enacted the subsequent course of liquor legislation could have been markedly different, and it is conceivable that the temperance movement might well have been able to work away steadily through local channels to achieve the changes which Parliament and the country wanted to see. As it was, the Bill went to the House of Lords and returned a shadow of its former self with this clause falling victim to the Lords's disposition. Wilfrid Lawson, the elder, died in 1867 and was buried in the grounds of the little Congregational Chapel at Aspatria.

Wilfrid Lawson, the younger, was born in 1829 and took the first step in his political career at the age of 28 when the Friends of the Liberal Cause in West

Cumberland adopted him as the Prospective Parliamentary Candidate in the General Election of 1857. He was a man of independent spirit and all his life he wished to be accepted in an independent role which he considered to be the only position worth having. "Our children", Lawson wrote in his memoirs, "can have no conception of the wild excitement of the days on the hustings and of open voting. It seems to be a point of honour that nobody should be heard. Non-electors were not expected to vote but to show their patriotism by pelting their fellow citizens". It was little wonder that Lawson was defeated by a majority of 271; however, he stood again two years later but this time for Carlisle, and together with Sir James Graham the Liberals polled 1054 votes against the Torys' 475.

Lawson had always held in high esteem the statesmanship of his maternal uncle, Sir James Graham, and it was under his wing that Wilfrid entered Parliament on May 22nd, 1859. Palmerston was Prime Minister and Gladstone was Chancellor of the Exchequer. The following year he married Mary, daughter of Joseph Pocklinton-Senhouse of Netherhall, Cumberland, and, in 1861, he became closely associated with the United Kingdom Alliance which had been set up in Manchester in 1835 by men who believed that the benevolent efforts of the temperance societies could never be realised until the influence of legalised temptations to drunkenness had been abandoned. Lawson saw the drink situation as "a national crime and a national disgrace of the first magnitude", adding that, "It has always been a great mystery to me how the people who are called professing Christians can sustain and support our liquor laws which are nothing more or less than a gigantic network of temptation". His first speech which was delivered at the A.G.M. of the Alliance at the Free Trade Hall, Manchester in 1861 served as a public profession of faith to which he steadfastly adhered all his life, both inside Parliament and outside in the community. "I, for one, am prepared to support the principle of the UKA. I take that principle to be that the people are the best judges of what is for their own interest. I think they know better what is their good and what are their wants than any set of magistrates than ever existed". In 1860 when the Chancellor of the Exchequer had announced in the House of Commons that there was growing dissatisfaction with the trial of free trade following the 1830 Beer Act, Lawson had entered a plea to allow the inhabitants of a parish to decide on the number of licences to be granted. Thus he had formally enunciated in the House the possibility of popular control over the liquor traffic. The theory was not exactly welcomed with a chorus of alleluias: in fact only one member spoke in favour of it and the debate was short and apparently unproductive. It did however have one significant spin-off insofar as it established Lawson's position as a rather novel type of democratic reformer. He was seen as a courageous and able advocate of social reform who was determined to keep the urgent but prickly problem of drink traffic before the eye of the legislature. He, along with his fellow temperance reformers, wanted to see the day when Parliament would be compelled to deal trenchantly with the drink problem and eventually give the people the supreme controlling power over the question. This was advanced thinking for the time but it was unfortunate that the strength of the temperance party in the House was weak compared to its strength in the country at large. In 1862, when the Customs and Inland Revenue Bill which dealt with the granting of "occasional" licences was being debated in the House, Lawson took the opportunity to advance the cause of curtailing licences and adopting the choice of local option. He maintained that the magistrates had duties imposed upon them which it was impossible for them to discharge and that the 1830 Beer Act had failed to give working men good beer and the kind of public house where they could enjoy themselves.

On 10th March, 1864, Lawson sought leave to bring in a bill to enable owners and occupiers of property in certain districts to prevent the common sale of intoxicating liquors within such districts. He was not criticising the magistrates who granted licences, nor the owners of the properties, nor the publicans or beer house keepers, but he was most certainly criticising the system. "My bill", he said in his memoirs, "simply provided the machinery by which a neighbourhood might inform the magistrates - or the licensing authority - that their requirement was - 'no drink-shops in that neighbourhood' - when that really was their wish. I provided that the statement of desire should be made a very large majority, so that there might be no mistake. This bill, one would have thought, was as simple as it was just". Notwithstanding petitions carrying 327,000 signatures being delivered, the bill which came to be known as the "Permissive Bill" found little favour and the second reading was defeated by 292 votes to just 35. The successful brewer, M. T. Bass (M.P. for Derby, 1848-83) who was a good friend of Lawson, good-humouredly offered to settle a pint of beer a day on him if he would give up the bill. As time went on the bill came to be called "Local Option" and then later "Local Veto" but the policy remained constant, i.e. no forcing of liquor shops into unwilling areas.

Lawson, a high-born gentleman with the common touch, was clearly aware that the kind of reform he was espousing could not possibly be accomplished until the franchise had been extended to include more representation of the working classes insofar as it was the under-privileged who suffered most sorely from the ravages of liquor abuse. He admitted in his memoirs that, "I certainly would not have taken the part which I did if anyone else would have undertaken it. But having no axe to grind, and nothing in the world to gain by politics, it seemed to me the right thing to support any policy which would provide the greatest good for the greatest number". He himself would have appreciated that in the world of politics the adjustment of interests is rarely, if ever, fully achievable, but that social order is better established and maintained within a continuing process of adjustment. Patient persuasion together with a degree of consensus could ultimately culminate in a measure of legitimate authority.

His first Permissive Bill lost him his seat for Carlisle in 1865. He was, however, returned again to Westminster as M.P. for Carlisle three years later in 1868 when Gladstone became Prime Minister for the first time. Carlisle was the only constituency in the country at the time to return a United Kingdom Alliance supporter. Albeit that the following five years of this new parliament were full of reforming zeal, it seemed that the House could not devote sufficient attention nor feel sufficiently convinced to support a second reading of Lawson's Permissive Bill in 1869 when half the members abstained and only 87 voted in favour with 193 against. Undaunted, Lawson brought the bill forward again in 1870 with slightly better results - 90 in favour and 123 against, but again with a high abstention rate and much absenteeism. The bill was becoming a hardy perennial and despite his engaging style, he was unable to achieve the triumph of the cause he most sincerely advocated. He was careful at all times to maintain his own independent stance and was happy to have it known that he considered the House of Lords to be a trade-union of Tory landowners. He told his constituents in Carlisle in 1872 in his accustomed genial but frank style that he was no House of Lords reformer, but an anti-House of Lords reformer. He wanted to do away with it altogether as a political absurdity believing that if the House of Commons properly and adequately reflected national thought across all sections of society then it would have no need of a correcting authority. By 1879 the Permissive Bill had been taken to division in the House of Commons nine times and the highest vote in favour had never seen more than 115. Obviously if the cause was still to be pursued then a change of tactics was called for and it was decided to proceed by a resolution rather than by a bill. A resolution would simply lay down a principle for action and if this was accepted by the House then a bill could follow to carry the principle into effect. Hansard (11th March, 1879) records Lawson's resolution asking for "a legal power of restraining the issue and renewal of licences which should be placed in the hands of the persons most deeply interested and affected - namely, the inhabitants themselves and this to be achieved by some efficient measure of 'Local Option' ". Gladstone, nominally opposed the Resolution but was, in reality, in favour of the cause which it represented and wanted legislation on the issue. So now with the back-up of the PM's declared interest in legislation the House affirmed the principle of "Local Option" three times: in 1880, 1881, and 1883, with majorities of 26, 42, and 87, respectively. In addition to this, the Queen's Speech of 1884 contained a promise to deal with the issue. Liberal ministers however had never been comfortable with the Permissive Bill because they felt it went beyond the opinion of the general public who wanted a reduction in licensed premises but not a complete extinction of the liquor trade. Prohibition was not, and never had been, an option to court public favour in Britain.

With the Reform Act the following year, 1885, the franchise was widened to include agricultural labourers and the existing constituencies were re-organised on a more equitable basis. Carlisle was reduced to a one-member constituency and Lawson stood once again for the Cockermouth division, losing by 10 votes on a poll of 7,600, but winning with a majority of 1,004 in 1886. During the next five or six years controversy raged in Parliament over the issue of Home Rule for Ireland. It sapped the energies of many politicians and tested to almost breaking point many political friendships. Gladstone took complete charge of the legislation dealing with Ireland while other great reforms were deemed to be mainly departmental matters and the concerns of the relevant ministers. Lawson, for his part, adhered firmly to Gladstone's endeavour to confer full powers of self-government on the people of Ireland as a step to the attainment of democratic ideals. He travelled the country, from platform to platform, trying to win sympathy for the demands of Ireland, but his stance in championing an unpopular cause possibly rebounded on the very cause he felt most strongly about and his personal influence with a section of the temperance movement suffered to some extent.

Almost a generation passed before the House of Commons under a

Conservative Government finally conceded the fundamental principle of "local option" in its Local Government Bill of 1888. The County Councils which it created were given powers to set up Licensing Authorities who in turn could suppress licences. But one serious flaw in the Bill as far as the Alliance was concerned was that it provided for compensation to be paid from the rates to enrich publicans and brewers. There is no doubt that the brewers were by this time well established as successful capitalists but they were facing an increasingly hostile world as the temperance movement gained momentum and they decided to resort with renewed vigour to the tied house system. The Bill was subsequently dropped, but a further "local option" Bill was presented by Lord Randolph Churchill two years later which also foundered on the principle of compensation. This finished the short-lived alliance between the tee-totalers and the Conservatives and the local option principle was left to be accepted finally as official party policy by the Liberals in 1890. Sir Wilfrid died in 1906 having had to accept a series of crushing defeats for the cause to which he felt so keenly committed. In a sense he had been in permanent opposition and in his memoirs he admitted of himself: "There is no man in the kingdom who has advocated more questions that were in the minority, or were more unpopular at the time than I have". Despite this, his cheery optimism never failed him and he maintained his political integrity - never jesting with a principle nor offering a jest instead of a principle. Some seven years after his death the government actually passed some "local option" legislation - on this occasion, for Scotland in the Temperance (Scotland) Act of 1913. The Act, however, had been rushed through both houses after invoking the Parliament Act and the House of Lords had been deprived of its absolute veto over legislation. This Act offered the possibility of the partition of all Scottish territory into "licensed" and "non-licensed" areas and gave localities the power to suppress licences in specific areas. It would not come into operation for the purpose of "local veto" polls until eight years from June 1912. Significantly there had never been a vested interest in the renewal of a licence in Scotland as there had been in England under the Balfour Act of 1904, and the Trade criticised the bill bitterly saying that it was full of absurdities which represented neither the wishes of the people of Scotland, nor of the House of Commons, nor the opinion of the Upper House. It was a useless victory of the prohibitionists and by 1939 the Scottish Licensing Commission was led to conclude that the limited experience had not justified this particular "experiment".

During Gladstone's premiership the prohibitionist movement had become a flourishing organisation and while Gladstone himself was never a teetotaller, his views on some form of public management of the drink trade were taking shape by 1894 when he was of the opinion that the Gothenburg Scheme offered the best chance of escaping from the country's disturbing predicament. Nurtured by the strong evangelicalism of his family background and his intensely religious upbringing in the Liverpool of his day, he viewed his own political career as a second best choice to that of a priestly vocation. Wilfrid Lawson, in his memoirs, had written of Gladstone: "Brilliant as he was as Chancellor of the Exchequer, more brilliant would he probably have been as Archbishop of Canterbury - but whether the Church of England could have survived him in that capacity is another question. But wondrous were his powers of exposition and explanation". For all his reforming zeal Gladstone never quite enunciated where he stood on the drink question, but he admitted in 1880 that, "We have not yet got out of the stage of experiment in this matter". (Hansard Parliamentary Debates, (third series, Vol 251 cc470-l. 5 March, 1880). The Gothenburg Licensing Company was formed in Sweden in 1865 and sanctioned by its government in an attempt to alleviate some of the deplorable poverty, distress and misery amongst the working classes. The object of the system was to take away all private interest in pushing the sale of liquor. A salaried manager was to be installed and encouraged to make his profit from the sale of food and non-alcoholic drinks, and/or on billiards, stabling and accommodation. The income, after certain expenditures had been taken into account, was to be put into the hands of some responsible people and expended for the purposes of the public utility. Originating in an attempt to check pauperism the system failed to remove the root of the evil and only alleviated temporarily, and in some degree, the distress caused by strong liquor. It operated mainly in the towns. Its companies only took over the management of the meaner taverns and public houses while selling the licenses for the larger premises to keepers of the hotels and drinking saloons. Many temperance reformers in this country were urged to take an interest in the experiment and give it a fair trial. Prohibitionists strenuously opposed the scheme together with any idea of the nationalisation of the drink trade. They contended that either system would implicate all citizens in the wicked trade.

However, by the 1880s, there was a distinct change of character in the drink trade due to the position of the brewing industry itself. With the temperance movement in full swing the brewing industry was forced into the limelight of national politics in order to preserve its interests. The general recession of 1876-85 hit the industry hard and it decided that a renewed programme of acquisition of tied houses was the best form of protection against an uncertain future. Brewers were convinced that if they could maintain first-class houses with good tenants and respectable customers, then they would be more likely to survive the onslaught. Such a response to the pressure of the temperance organisations and the effects of the nine-year recession actually marked, in its way, the beginning of the "improved public house movement". Breweries converted to company status thus enabling them to sell shares and raise enough capital to buy property on a scale never before envisaged. This scramble for property in the two periods from 1886-90 and 1895-99 attracted increasing attacks upon the monopolistic nature of their business interests. Gladstone, himself, in 1885, considered that the large introduction of brewers as capitalists represented a most threatening circumstance.

The temperance crusade now moved into new areas by opposing the compensation of the dispossessed publicans; the municipalsation of the drink trade; and the treatment of drunkenness as a disease rather than a moral failing. The fact was, however, that after years of teetotal advocacy the drink problem was still a serious issue of moral and political concern and, as the century moved towards its end, people began to feel that they were inevitably moving into new times. Many of them could not remember a time when Victoria had not been Queen, or that either Salisbury or Gladstone had not been Prime Minister. Victorian imperialism was on the wane, and sharp distinctions were all too obvious between Britain's pride overseas and the dreadful squalor and degradation at home. An enormous amount of drinking was going on, and the environment was acting as a constant incentive to the behaviour under condemnation. Temperance reformers were coming under specific ideological attack for having lost contact with political realities and were forced to face the full implications of the debate between a temperance remedy and the emergent labour movement. Many pioneers of the labour movement such as Keir Hardy, Tom Mann, Richard Pankhurst and George Lansbury had themselves been temperance reformers, but they began to question the whole policy of isolating the "drink problem" from all other social problems. By the turn of the century the idealism of the temperance reform was no longer being seen as avant garde and, in 1901, Philip Snowden was advocating an attempt to try to combine the temperance and the socialist movements behind a policy of municipal action and "local veto". Socialists wanted to see an improvement in the management of the public houses but did not want to see them abolished altogether. As the early twentieth century progressed the Labour Party declared its rejection of prohibition and interpreted "local veto" as including the right to regulate and control the drink trade, but with the caveat that there should be no firm commitment to any one panacea if this excluded other remedies. It was felt that all approaches might be required to a greater or lesser degree before the drink problem could be solved. This was indeed a broader outlook than the temperance movement, for its part, had been in a position to embrace. By 1900 there was a steady build-up of the declared differences between temperance and the socialist principles on the question of insobriety in society. Socialists were now seriously challenging the narrowness of the temperance movement's radical attitudes and were insisting that it was short-sighted to continue to isolate the drink question from other social issues. Victorian opinion could not be neatly classified as either in favour, or against the public house, for a broad section of the citizens were neither teetotal, prohibitionist, nor out-and-out drunkards. At this time there was a growing apprehension of the commercialism within the public house trade. The Licensing Act of 1902 had not helped the situation in that it gave powers to the authorities to restrict proposed improvements in existing premises for fear that it would encourage even more drinking. The temperance lobby accepted the fact that many citizens in humble circumstances often needed to frequent a public house in order to pass a sociable hour, and they consequently came up with an alternative suggestion in the form of coffee public houses. These were designed to have the social attributes of the public house but with the alcohol left out, and aimed at providing good food together with non-alcoholic drinks. Many of the premises provided a reading room; a social or functions room which could accommodate musical events or debating societies; and they provided billiard tables and bagatelle boards. It was intended that they should have the atmosphere of a well-conducted club, but despite the fact that this movement was given the full support of many well-intentioned Victorians, including Gladstone himself, it did not succeed. It was criticised for its lack of good manage-ment skills and practical experience, and while it might have been able to operate in parallel to the public house, it could never have replaced it in a society already vitiated by strong drink.

There were so many problems in this expanding industrial society - real struggling poverty; destitution; hunger; ill-health; drunkenness; brutality and crime. Writers and social reformers were all too aware of the enormity of the task ahead of them in recording the facts so that solutions to these problems might be found. In 1852 Henry Mayhew's valuable survey of the conditions of "London Labour and London Poor" was published, and this was followed by a translation of Friedrich Engel's "The Condition of the Working Class in England" in 1885 in which he too discussed the drink problem. The following year, 1886, a Liverpool ship-owner, Charles Booth, decided to make his own street to street survey of the lives and occupations of all the inhabitants of London. It took him seventeen years to complete and filled seventeen volumes with the last volume being published in 1903.

He had to establish his own precedent as his only guides had been occasional reports from factory inspectors, the census returns or the Royal Commission reports. He began by soliciting the help of school attendance inspectors to categorise the standard of living in the various streets and localities. Empiricist that he was, Booth did not want anything to stand between the observer and the facts which he strove to gather with an impartial mind. The facts had to speak for themselves and when they were finally publicised the middle-classes were shaken by the stark reality of the harrowing details. Many children had rickets and many young men suffered from stunted growth through lack of nourishment. There was much evidence of bad eyesight, few teeth, shocking skin conditions through lack of hygiene facilities, high levels of infant mortality, and an earlier death rate. Booth saw with his own eyes the degree of moral decay and destitution attached to much of the domestic life of the poor and the oppressive conditions of the workplace. He reckoned from what he was observing that families on the poverty-line could survive with a measure of luck if they disciplined themselves to live frugally and have few vices. Below the poverty line there was little hope - it was a sub-culture of the very poor who were for various reasons in perpetual want. Sadly, old age was a primary cause of pauperism with a high percentage of old people ending up in the workhouse in certain areas of London. As a result of his investigations Booth concluded that the cause of poverty in about 85 per cent of the cases could be categorised under three headings: employment, circumstances, and habit. Both lack of work and low pay together with large families and much sickness accounted for about 70 per cent of the cases. Only 15 per cent was due to illness, drunkenness, or lack of thrift. This signified a distinctive shift in opinion: the drink problem was removed from the centre of the poverty debate. Primary poverty was due to inadequate income, while secondary poverty emanated from inefficient expenditure. Many people had become poor first and then taken to drink to relieve their misery. But, of course, when it was the breadwinner who was alleviating his misery in this way, it only added to the pitiful state of his family. Many families were brought to ruin and destitution because most , if not all, the money had been spent on drink. Booth was saying that the responsibility for obtaining and maintaining a higher standard of living rested on society at large. This conviction was readily echoed by moderate socialists such a Beatrice and Sidney Webb who were convinced that the sporadic reforms of the past now needed to give way to a re-organisation of society as a whole. It became obvious that there was a change taking place in middle-class attitudes to poverty and this was accompanied by a growing political campaign for reform. The Prevention of Cruelty to Children Act passed in 1894 had enabled magistrates to commit to Inebriate Homes the drunken parents of ill-used children. The tragic over-conception of babies by drunken parents was due in part to an excessive intake of liquor, and in part to the lack of adequate family sleeping quarters. Such tragedies were becoming intolerable and there developed a general move by social reformers to improve domestic conditions. But in order to bring about change it now required, more than ever before, the backing of politically experienced individuals who were sufficiently indignant with the status quo to take a lead in crusading against it. The new name of the game was to be - indignation coupled to modern methods of agitation. The year 1908 saw the beginning of a period of great Liberal social reforms with Lloyd George, supported by Winston Churchill, ready to espouse the cause of the poor.

When the First World War broke out on 4 August, 1914, the country was already in an unsettled frame of mind. Seamen, transport workers, and railwayman had been on strike in 1911 and a million colliers had been on strike for a month in the following year to secure for themselves a minimum wage. The cost of living had been rising steadily while wage rates remained stationary and this led to a sense of grievance which smouldered away in certain of the great trades, while the relations between capital and labour was growing ever more fractious. Added to this, all the tensions concerning the question of Home Rule for Ireland were still present and the militant women's franchise movement was gathering momentum. The gravity of the war with Germany quenched internal controversies and subdued contentions. Resolutions in favour of industrial peace were adopted by a joint meeting of the Parliamentary Committee of the Trades Union Congress; the Management Committee of the General Federation of Trades Unions; and the National Executive of the Labour Party. The governing clause was: "That an immediate effort be made to terminate all existing trade disputes whether strikes or lock-outs, and whenever new points of difficulty arise during the war period, a serious attempt should be made by all concerned to reach an amicable conclusion before resorting to a strike or a lock-out". Imprisoned strikers and suffragettes were released by order of the Home Secretary and national unity became the supreme need.

CHAPTER THREE
THE CALL FOR EFFICIENCY

The drink question almost alone among social issues gained in importance with the conflict: it came to be seen as the "enemy within". It was tied to the overriding call for efficiency. A long and tortuous history was attached to the trade in intoxicating liquor and there were still many residual complications which had baffled politicians again and again. Reformers of all persuasions were aware of the struggles that other overseas countries were having with their own "internal enemy". A prohibition had been placed on the sale of vodka in Russia by decree of the Czar while France, Italy and Egypt had all found it necessary to suppress the traffic in absinthe. Norway had, by the end of 1916, prohibited the sale of spirits. Henry Carter writes of this country: "It is interesting to speculate what would have been the situation in 1914-15 had the Licensing Bill of 1908 become law. Under this Bill one-third of the "on"-licences were to have been suppressed with compensation within fourteen years. In 1915 half the term would have gone and presumably the closing of public houses would have been most general where they were most numerous, namely near large works and factories and in the poorer residential districts. As it was, public houses abounded where industries congregated; along the roads to work; and hard by the workers' homes. It remained for the War to show how heavy was the price to be paid for the rejection of the Licensing Bill of 1908". (The Control of the Drink Trade in Britain. 1915-1918. ppl02/3).

Immediately upon the outbreak of war the first Defence of the Realm Act was passed on 8 August, 1914. It gave power to the competent naval or military authority

Above: Dwellings for workers at the munitions factory near Gretna.
(Gordon Routledge)

to close licensed premises within, or in the neighbourhood of, any defended harbour except during such hours as may be specified in the order (by these authorities or the Ministry of Munitions). Regulation 17 of this Act stipulated that no person shall give or sell to any member of H. M. Forces employed in the defence of any railway, dock, or harbour any intoxicating liquor when NOT on duty with the intent to make him drunk. The competent naval or military authority or the Minister of Munitions was enabled to make such provisions as was thought necessary for the prevention of the practice of "treating" in any licensed premises within any area specified in the order. This was a bold step to take especially when it is remembered that for centuries past convivial drinking had become deeply rooted in the English tradition. The prohibition was first applied to the treating of service men in an attempt to stop civilians from plying them with excessive amounts of liquor. The same restriction soon had to be implemented in a general manner to prevent workmen who, because of war work and the additional money in their pockets, were being drawn into the habit of each "standing a round" of drinks as a point of honour even when they had already consumed sufficient. The treating of a drink was permitted only when a meal was ordered at the same time. While some men found relief from what had become the somewhat burdensome convention of "standing a round", a great many people considered the ban was unnecessary and a nuisance. Clearly it was a case of having to make a general regulation for the many, to halt an abuse by the few which was interfering with the prosecution of the war. It came in for a fair amount of ridicule during the prosecution of the war and was finally withdrawn on 3 June, 1919, seven months after the Armistice. An Intoxicating Liquor (Temporary Restriction) Act was also quickly passed on 31 August, 1914, to enable licensing justices for any licensing district, if they thought fit upon the recommendation of the chief officer of police that it was desirable for the maintenance of order or the suppression of drunkenness in any area, to order the suspension of a licence to sell and/or supply intoxicating liquor on any premises or in any registered club in a given area. The Act was intended to remain in force during the continuance of the current war and for a period of one month after the cessation of such a war.

Captain Greatorex, R.N., Director of Naval Equipment reported to the Third Sea Lord on 4 March, 1915, that: "The condition of labour is deplorable, and the men are in a most uncertain and undependable state and this is so serious that at any time the whole of the shipbuilding work on the Tyne may come to a standstill. Sunday work is of little value as the money paid for Sunday work leads to abstention from all work for often two days and a Sunday worker will frequently not return until Wednesday". The only approach that he could see was to partially or totally close all public houses. Again on 2 April, 1915, the Third Sea Lord, F. C. T. Tudor sent reports to the First Lord of the Admiralty, Winston Churchill, showing the effect of excessive drinking on the output of work with regard to shipbuilding, repairs, and munitions of war being carried out under contract for the Admiralty; and of a similar effect on transport work. It was claimed that the work put in by workmen in the Clyde, Tyne, and Barrow districts was much less than might be expected under normal peacetime conditions. The Captain-Superintendent on the Tyne, which included the North-East coast and Barrow, reported that it was the early morning drink that was responsible for a great deal of the short time, and that it would be a great help if the public houses were closed until 10 a.m. An officer overseeing the construction of vessels being built by a firm on the north-east coast reported on the poor time-keeping of some of the men who, by virtue of their own absence from work would thwart the productive output of whole gangs: "The firm was of the opinion that the remedy lay in the prohibition of all spirits". A further report from the Director of Naval Equipment after a visit to the Clyde suggested that much greater restrictions should be imposed on the hours in which liquor may be sold and that these restrictions should apply to all classes equally and have reference not only to the large shipbuilding yards and engineering works but should also embrace the firms manufacturing munitions of war which were also being adversely affected by the drink question. Total prohibition, even with all its attendant objections and disadvantages, it was suggested, would at least have the general effect that all classes would at last realise the existence and seriousness of the war and that they themselves were personally involved in its consequences. These reports illustrated two salient points. One was that a case was being made at this early stage against drink in that it impaired efficiency; and the other was that some form of prohibition was still lingering in the mind and being considered as a suitable remedy for this "industrial drinking". A basic week's work for most of these workers in heavy industry was around fifty-three hours to which was added overtime. Reformers were aware that fatigue and a lack of canteen facilities subscribed quite significantly to habitual drinking.

The dreadful result of the first three days of the Battle of Neuve-Chapelle from 10 March, 1915, presented Asquith's government with the wake-up call that was so desperately needed with regard to the armaments situation. The casualties at this battle amounted to 12,992 of which 583 were officers and 12,309 were other ranks. All this sacrifice was to gain an area of ground that was less than one square mile. Sir John French, Commander-in-Chief of the British Army in France, had alerted the War Office that if the supply of ammunition could not be maintained on a considerably increased scale then the offensive efforts of the Army could only be spasmodic and separated by considerable intervals of time which meant that they could not therefore lead to decisive results. The following month witnessed, at Ypres, the first use of gas by the Germans. "Our army found itself deplorably deficient in artillery ammunition with which to extricate the doomed infantry from the death-cloud that was annihilating them. . . . a feeling of anger and horror ran through the whole nation". (War Memoirs of David Lloyd George 1933/4 p117). Lloyd George was at this date the Chairman of the Munitions Committee when he discovered that information from the front line complaining of the uselessness of shrapnel in attacking barbed-wire entanglements coupled with the desperate call for high-explosive shells was not reaching the committee. "The War Office had failed to keep abreast of modern development in pattern of munitions and machinery for munitions production . . . and of bringing munition production up to the standard demanded by the actual conditions of warfare. . . modern warfare was to a far greater extent than ever before a conflict of chemists and manufacturers. . . troops, however brave and well led were powerless unless equipped with adequate and up-to-date artillery (with masses of explosive shells). . . against enemy machine-gun posts and wire entanglements the most gallant and best-led men could only throw away their precious lives in successive waves of heroic martyrdom". (ibid pp77/78). Sir John French became tired of remonstrating with the War Office over the shortage of ammunition, particularly shells, and he finally decided to appeal to the politicians and the press. On 14 May, 1915, The Times published a damning article under the headlines: "Need for Shells: British Attacks Checked: Limited Supply the Cause". The newspaper's military correspondent, Colonel Repington, went on to summarise the concerns of Sir John French in that although the British attacks were well planned and valiantly conducted, the conditions under which the troops had to fight were too difficult. The want of an unlimited supply of high explosive was a fatal bar to success and until they were comprehensively equipped for this type of trench warfare they would continue to have to attack under grave disadvantages. This was the first time that the reading public had been informed in such plain language from the front line of the serious situation concerning the shortage of munitions. Lloyd George could see that, at this stage in events, there was little prospect of rectifying the situation under the existing methods of organisation. As Chairman of the Munitions Committee he wrote to Prime Minister Asquith with details of the information he had received regarding the crisis in the supply of ammunition and explained that, although full reports had been sent to the War Office, they had not been shown to the Munitions Committee. Consequently Lloyd George felt that he could no longer preside over this Committee under such conditions. He was aware that what he urgently needed was executive power in order to take rapid action, and that only a government department could deliver this. And so, after some internal organisational manoeuverings Lloyd George left the Treasury in May, 1915, to become Minister of Munitions and there followed a Ministry of Munitions Act which created a new department and received the Royal Assent on 9 June, 1915. His own reactions to the change were set down in his memoirs (ibid p143): "It was a serious decision for me to make. As Chancellor of the Exchequer I had been holding the highest and most responsible office under the Prime Minister. . . and in that position had been initiating and carrying through schemes of social amelioration which were very genial to my disposition and upbringing. I was exchanging all that for the terrible task of manufacturing engines for human mutilation and slaughter. . . I was leaving a well-established and well-organised department, staffed by some of the picked men of the Civil Service and directed in all its ramifications by well-defined rules and traditions which worked with perfect smoothness. I was taking in hand a department with no staff, no regulations, no traditions. Politically it was for me a wilderness of risks with no oasis in sight. . . . in many ways the creation of the Ministry of Munitions was the most formidable task I ever undertook". Fortunately, the job of the new ministry in the tasks it was to set in motion was not defined by Act of Parliament but was left to be fixed by Orders in Council which meant that valuable time was not taken up by Parliamentary procedure and the minister could adopt the power he required which was best suited to his needs as they arose. The new ministry made a resolute start to speed up delivery of existing contracts for war material, and put its energies into opening up fresh sources of supply by organising both outside firms for munition production and by establishing new government factories.

A Bill had already been laid before the House of Commons on 9 March, 1915, while Lloyd George was still at the Treasury, to amend and extend the provisions of the Defence of the Realm Act (DORA) to give the government the power to take over and use any factory or workshop, and to control its processes and output, and to remove its plant elsewhere if necessary. This Bill was quickly passed without any division or challenge. (The second Defence of the Realm Act of 28 August, 1914, had already given the government powers of control over armament factories and their workers). In April, 1915, a report was presented to both Houses of Parliament by the Advisory Committee set up by the Liquor Trade Finance Committee (England and Wales). This committee was chaired by Herbert Samuel.Hartley Withers was secretary and the other members were Cunliffe, John Simon, John Bradbury, Ed. F. Coates, J. S. Harmwood-Banner, William Plender, Philip Snowden and Thos. P. Whittaker. They were appointed to advise the government, even at this early stage, on the financial arrangements that would be necessary if it should be decided by the State to PURCHASE the whole of the Licensed Liquor Trade in the country. The Committee was not expected to enter into the broad area of policy-making, either general or financial, but was asked to view the possible purchase quite simply as a commercial transaction without prejudice to the issue of how far a licence to sell exciseable liquor could, or could not, be regarded as property. After taking into account the current position of the trade and considering the prospective future trends, and in the realisation of the compulsory nature of any proposed purchase, the committee were of the opinion that the property to be acquired should be bought by the exchange of £1.00 of Government 4 per cent stock for every ascertained £1.00 worth of liquor securities or property. It would therefore be necessary to appoint commissioners to determine values and to transact the transfers, while at the same time instituting an authority to conduct the trade on the state's behalf.

As some of the brewery companies issued shares quoted on the Stock Exchange and operated in an active market while others were not so quoted and acted in a restricted market, the committee recommended that each class should be purchased from the holders separately and undertakings should not be purchased as a whole. Any liabilities on mortgages and loans entered into by the brewery companies would be taken over by the Authority, which would also hold or realise the collected assets of the purchased undertaking. Allowances were to be made to local authorities in lieu of rates, and compensation was to be paid when property ceased to be used for the sale of intoxicating liquor or where licences were suppressed with loss of livelihood. The Authority would collect the assets of the purchased undertakings and hold or realise them at its discretion. It was foreseen that some properties would need special consideration. The creation of a very large amount of new government obligations could not fail at any time but to have an effect upon government credit even when, as in this case, they would be issued for the purchase of a revenue-producing undertaking, and even when it was not a question of going to the market for new capital, but of substituting capital in one form for capital already existing in another. In this instance, however, it was considered crucial to avoid causing a general depreciation of government stocks. The government, therefore decided that the creation of a new government security with unrestricted liberty of sale upon the market could not be contemplated during the continuance of the war. On the strength of the available information it was difficult for the committee to forecast accurately the amount of capital needed for such an unprecedented enterprise. It did, however, indicate, according to estimates submitted to it, a figure approximating to £250 million for England and Wales with an allocation to a sinking fund of not less than one-and-half per cent on the amount of stock issued which would become an additional charge against profits. Any pension liabilities of the brewery companies would be taken over by the state and it was recommended that, pending new legislation for the regulation of the supply of alcoholic liquors, Parliament should prohibit the starting up of new breweries, the granting of new retail licences, and the opening of any new registered clubs. On balance it was felt that the financial prospects of the trade under state monopoly would depend significantly on efficient business management and economy in the conduct of the undertaking. (PRO/HO 185/273).

This report with its assessment of the financial considerations inherent in any proposed state acquisition and management of the trade in liquor suggested that it could be economically advantageous by virtue of the elimination of redundant breweries, by the concentration of the distribution and sale of liquor; by brewing a lighter beer; and by savings arising from the lack of strenuous commercial rivalry. Set against this would be the possible drop in turnover resulting from the system of "disinterested management" in which the publican would not be required to push sales and would become, in essence, a civil servant. Right away, it was only to be expected that the Treasury would be looking to secure an adequate financial return on the capital involved, so that it was incumbent upon the management of any scheme adopted to pursue a sound business policy. The estimated sum of £250 million mentioned in the report represented the value of all brewery property - tied houses, free houses; and other various on-licences but did not include the value of distilleries. Many politicians felt the estimate, in these circumstances, was too high and the time was completely wrong to embark upon such a heavy financial commitment. The Conservative leaders intimated that they would offer no opposition if the Government decided that it was essential as a war measure. However a number of influential politicians and businessmen who favoured the principle of "local option" brought great pressure to bear on the Prime Minister that he feared serious trouble within the Party. "I decided for the time being to proceed with a more limited form and abandon the attempt to purchase the whole of the liquor trade. I prepared a measure to secure its more effective CONTROL - a measure which further enabled the experiment to be made of State purchase and management of the liquor traffic on a small scale in particular areas". (Lloyd George War Memoirs pp 198/200). On the 30 June, 1915, Lloyd George having moved from the Treasury to become the Minister of Munitions, appointed twelve members of a government authority to be known as the Central Control Board (Liquor Traffic). Members of the Board were: The Lord D'Abernon (chairman); Major Waldorf Astor, M.P.; Mr. Neville Chamberlain; Mr. E. R. Cross; Mr. John Denny; Mr. John Hodge, M.P.; Sir William Lever, Bart.; Sir George Newman, M.D.; Mr. John Pedder, C.B.; Mr. R. R. Scott; Mr.

Philip Snowden, M.P.; and Mr. W. Towle. The Board was established on the responsibility of the Cabinet by an Order in Council under the statutory powers and the appointment of its members rested with the Minister of Munitions, but beyond that he had, under the Order in Council, no control over the proceedings of the Board. Lord D'Abernon as chairman at the age of 58 brought to his task valuable experience in financial matters and a wide knowledge of public affairs. As Sir Edgar Vincent he had been financial adviser to the Egyptian Government for six years and Governor of the Imperial Ottoman Bank for the following eight years. For seven years until 1906 he had been M.P. for Exeter as a Unionist Free Trader. The Secretary of the Board, J. C. G. Sykes, C.B. was an established civil servant on loan from the Board of Education. Two assessors were appointed. Edgar Christian Sanders, an acknowledged authority on licensing laws and their administration, was the assessor for England and Wales. He was appointed General Manager of the Board's "present and future undertakings"in June 1916, and for Carlisle, specifically, in December, 1917. He was credited with having drafted the financial and administrative details of the Carlisle Scheme. Sir Thomas Munro, Clerk to the Lanark County Council was appointed assessor for Scotland. Of the other members of the Board, Major Waldorf Astor was a teetotaller dedicated to temperance reform and an advocate of prohibition by "local option". He had served as an inspector of ordnance factories and was a Unionist M.P. for Plymouth. He was a founder member of Lloyd George's Secretariat in 1916, and was made Parliamentary Private Secretary to Lloyd George in 1917 to take charge of drink control, Parliamentary Secretary to the Ministry of Food in 1918, and then of Health in 1919. Neville Chamberlain was Lord Mayor of Birmingham, 1915-16. He resigned from the Board in 1916 prior to becoming Director of National Service in 1917. He was a member of the War Cabinet 1916-17. E. Richard Cross had been President of the Justices' Clerks Society. He brought to the post an expert knowledge of licensing but was drowned while bathing in the Lake District in August 1916. The two industrialists on the Board were the soap magnate Sir William Lever, Bart., and John Denny, C.B., Director of a Dumbarton engineering firm. W. Towle as Manager of the Midland Railway Company's hotels contributed expert knowledge in hotel management. John Hodge was Labour M.P. for the Gorton Division of Lancashire. He became Minister of Labour in 1917 and then retired from the Board. George Newman, C.B., M.D. (later Sir George Newman, K.C.B.) was Principal Medical Officer to the Board of Education. He remained with the Control Board during the war period but resigned in 1919. Philip Snowden was the Independent Labour Party M.P. for Blackburn. He became Chancellor of the Exchequer in the first two Labour governments. He too resigned in 1919. (In 1901 he had wanted to weld together the socialist and temperance movements behind a policy of local option and municipalisation). John Pedder (later Sir John Pedder, K.B.E) was leased from the Home Office, and R. Russell Scott, C.SI. was leased from the Admiralty and became chairman of the Advisory Committee for Annan as part of the Gretna Scheme. He returned to the Admiralty in 1917 and was replaced by R. S. Meiklejohn, C.B., Principal Clerk at the Treasury. This proved to be a Board with an efficient man at the top supported by a team of dedicated, knowledgeable and energetic staff. They received no remuneration from public funds as members of the Board.

Appointment of new members to the Board took place from time to time and these were always publically notified. lt had been suggested to Lord D'Abernon in May 1915 that the Board should include one first-class brewery manager. In reply Lord D'Abernon had said, "On the whole I am against a brewery manager on the Board - at any rate at the moment because if you give representation to "interests" you get advocates - and long discussions unsuited to our administrative body. . . we can always take a first-class brewery manager later as a paid agent". (PRO/HO 185/231). In January 1916 two new members were taken onto the Board, one of whom was Sir William Waters Butler who had been born in a public house and was the chairman of brewers Mitchells & Butlers of Birmingham 1914 -39. He was one of the leading brewers of his day and a pioneer of the "improved public house" campaign. He remained a member of the Control Board until 1921 . The other new member was the Reverend Henry Carter of Carlisle, Secretary of the Temperance and Social Welfare Department of the Wesleyan Methodist Church. A further brewing representative was brought onto the Board in July 1917. Sir Sydney Oswald Nevile was managing director (later director) of brewers Whitbread from 1919, and was a firm advocate of the "improved public house". And then in November, 1917, the Hon. Hugh Godley, a permanent civil servant at the Treasury was invited onto the Board, as was J. H. Thomas, M.P. (Labour) and former railway worker who was president of the Amalgamated Society of Railway Servants and became general secretary of the National Union of Railwaymen from 1918. Lloyd George had already stirred up public opinion against the menace of excessive drinking during time of dire peril for the nation in his speech at Bangor in Wales in February, 1915. He warned the people that the government had great powers to deal with drink and that they meant to use them. He added that they would be used discreetly in a spirit of moderation and used wisely, but that they would be used quite fearlessly. He felt sure that the nation's needs demanded it and the country would support their actions. "It is futile to legislate far in advance of popular opinion or the public conscience. RESTRICT!ON and LIMITATION the nation would accept, and a considerable degree of reform could be achieved under State CONTROL where the element of private profit and exploitation was eliminated. I confined my objective to this practical programme". (ibid p202). Whereas state intervention in the nineteenth century had been a close liaison between social reformers and religion, now the awesome remit for this newly-formed Central Control Board was to ensure efficiency and economy for the sake of social cohesion and survival.

Apart from the fact that the Ministry of Munitions appointed its chairman and members, and the size of its staff was subject to the approval of the Treasury, the Central Control Board was in all other respects an autonomous body. lt possessed a legal entity and was capable of suing or being sued, and of acquiring property which would be vested in trustees appointed by the Board from its own membership. The powers conferred upon it were wide and varied but it was unable, of itself, to schedule any area for control. This would require an Order in Council. The Statutory Rules and Orders permitted the Board to close any licensed premises or club, to regulate hours of sale, prohibit the sale of any specific liquor, impose its own conditions of sale, establish satisfactory supervision of premises, establish the right of inspection of licensed premises and clubs, prohibit the custom of treating, and prohibit the sale and supply of liquor by any person other than the Board. This last rule was capable of creating a monopoly and, together with the other extensive and drastic powers conferred upon it, the Board was laying itself open to quite a considerable degree of risk. In addition, its agents were exempt from the licensing laws and the police were at their disposal to see that the regulations were enforced. There was no appeal against their decisions which were not subject to public revision. As Lloyd George had already intimated, the Board moved carefully, proceeding step by step and doing nothing in haste, so that public opinion and acceptance of the measures were not seriously compromised.

No area could be scheduled without an Order in Council and there was no arbitrary imposition of the control system. Applications were made in the first instance by those authorities responsible for maintaining efficiency for the prosecution of the war, and the Board's first step after receiving a request was to hold a local inquiry and take cognisance of the conditions which prevailed in the area. They would confer with all concerned: with the many representatives of the local authorities; with the army, the navy and the judiciary; with employers and municipal, and trade union officials; with licensed traders and with temperance organisations - in short with anyone who could furnish them with relevant information. The Board had to satisfy itself that the conditions were such as to justify the imposition of control and then to decide what restrictions would be best suited to the needs of the particular case. The Board also needed to come to an agreement as to the extent of the area to be so circumscribed. It did not assume as a matter of course that any given application, of itself, proved the need for control, and no order was made without due consideration of the rights of licence-holders and the convenience of the public. After scheduling an area the Board would send, via the police, a copy of the regulations to be applied to all concerned and to the central organisation of the trade and to all licensed premises and clubs. A copy was also published in the London Gazette which could then be reported by the local newspapers. A circular letter sent out with the order specifying the regulations to be imposed explained that the Board had acted with the desire to meet public opinion insofar as it was consistent with an effective result, and with the necessity of treating the various areas over which their powers extended with some degree of uniformity. A period of ten days was then allowed before enforcement to enable the authorities, the trade, and the consumers to prepare for the change.

The first Order issued by the Board in this way was on 26 July, 1915, and applied to Newhaven on the south coast. Others quickly followed, many being seaports, shipbuilding centres and commercial ports and the Channel ports directly engaged in war transport. Control then moved inland to the industrial areas and, by the end of 1915, almost half the population of Great Britain was living under the new control conditions. At the end of 1916 when the whole of Wales and almost the whole of Scotland, including the Orkney and Shetland Isles were added, it was estimated that, of the total population of 41 million, at least 38 million were living under control. Eventually the whole of Great Britain, with the exception of a few purely agricultural areas was scheduled. This process of extension was due mainly to the ongoing establishment of many air and naval bases, army camps, and new munitions factories. The whole process was based on the principle of necessity.

As well as the powers of control, the power to purchase and conduct the business of licensed premises had also been conferred upon the Control Board. The Board remained restrained in the use of this power of state purchase and only took over the trade in three significant districts which were deemed vital to the war effort.

The first was at Enfield Lock in Middlesex at the request of the Ministry of Munitions. The problem here at the Royal Small Arms Factory was a need to supply the requirements of a greatly increased workforce engaged in munitions work at an isolated government factory. The men themselves, particularly those employed on night-work, were asking for a readjustment of opening hours. On further enquiry the Board learned that the works canteen and the accommodation provided by the four adjacent public houses were quite inadequate and unsatisfactory with regard to the provision of meals and shelter for the workforce. The Board decided that a unified system of management and the provision of canteen facilities would best be accomplished by taking over the four fully licensed premises and the one house with an off-licence. They came into the possession of the Board on 2 January, 1916, and two of the best placed houses, the Greyhound and the Royal Small Arms, were selected for reconstruction. This was the earliest example of a practical application of state ownership.

The second instance of state purchase concerned Invergordon and Cromarty on the north-east coast of Scotland which was the site of an important naval base and dockyard. The first move came from the Admiralty who suggested that the Board should take over the licensed premises in these two villages on the grounds that, "notwithstanding the special measures that had been taken by the naval authorities and the police, a state of drunkenness still existed which required a prompt remedy in the interests of the naval service". Consequently thirteen premises, including four inns, were taken over by the Board in April, 1916.

The third acquisition was on an altogether larger scale. It involved Gretna-without-the-Township on the Scottish side of the border between England and Scotland. Carlisle and district followed a little later, mainly from August to November, 1916, with an urgent appeal to make progress as rapidly as possible. Although for administration purposes the Gretna and Annan district on the Scottish side was later divided from the Carlisle district, it is essential to recognise that the origin of the Carlisle undertaking was due to, and its development influenced by, the proximity of the national munitions factory at Gretna. This huge enterprise straddled the English/Scottish border and occupied a strip of land nine miles long and almost two miles wide.

The first drafts of construction workers arrived in the early autumn of 1915 to start work on the two large distilleries. One, for glycerine, was at Dornock between Eastriggs and Annan. The other, which distilled ether, was at Mossband and Longtown in the county of Cumberland. These distilleries were for the production of cordite, a smokeless propellant of guncotton, nitro-glycerine, and vaseline which had to be shaped into "rope" and pressed into rods of varying lengths and thicknesses.

This highly explosive paste was mixed by hand in great vats by the women munition workers. Conan Doyle when he visited the factory described it as the "devil's porridge". The factory produced 1,000 tons of cordite per week . This was more than the total output of all the other existing plants in the country. Drying the nitro-cotton was an especially dangerous task since the material became very unstable if the temperature rose above 80 degrees fahrenheit. A girl would watch the thermometer and open the door if the temperature rose too dangerously. The girls wore no special protective clothing, and it was quite common for acid to splash onto the skin and cause burns. One of the workers recalled that, "The particles of acid land on your face and make you nearly mad - they make brown specks on your clothes - they rot your handkerchiefs - they get up your nose and down your throat and into your eyes. My gums were all poisoned by the acid and I had to have all my teeth taken out". Lloyd George in his War Memoirs (p352) saw fit to mention similar hazards faced by other munitions workers nationwide who were working with T.N.T. (trinitro-toluene) and suffered from toxic poisoning as a result: "faces bright and a repulsive yellow . . . a blotching ugliness. . . a peril which tested their courage perhaps even more than the risk of explosion. In 1916 there were 181 cases of toxic jaundice of which 52 ended fatally".

The building of the Gretna factory was graphically commented upon by Sir Arthur Conan Doyle in an article reported in the "Annandale Observer" of 1st December, 1916. The site was referred to as "Moorsidc" for security reasons. "It is perhaps the most remarkable place in the world. Only a little more than a year ago it was a lonely peat bog fringing the sea, with a hinterland of desolate plain over which the gulls swooped and screamed. Then the hand of the Minister of Munitions was stretched out to this lonely and inhospitable waste for it chanced to lie with good rail and water connections and not too remote from centres of coal and iron. No money and no energy was spared and half a dozen master hustlers took charge of the whole scheme. It is a story which is more characteristic of Western America than of our sober British methods. The work went forward by day and by night. The place grew and grew and is still growing. In the daytime there are at least 25,000 inhabitants - the greater part are the builders who still extend the township - the smaller are the munition workers who will occupy it all when it is finished. It is not fully manned - or shall I say "girled" - but when it is, not less than 12,000 munition workers will be running the miles of factories which overlie the peat bogs of last summer. . . to say nothing of the military guard of over 1,000 men; factory police; workmanlike women police; central bakeries with 400 loaves at a baking; central laundries; central kitchens with 8,000 meals a day going out; and cashiers who pay away £800 an hour in wages. And all this with the primaeval ooze lying in stagnant pools around". The factory had its own large power station, water treatment plant, telephone exchange and its own railway with 125 miles of track. Because of the dangerous nature of the materials which needed to be transported around the plant, special tyreless locomo-tives had to be used which dispensed with the usual firebox and ran instead on cylin-ders of steam which were kept topped up.

As well as the extensive factory complex, two new residential townships were erected four miles apart, one at Gretna and one at Eastriggs. They were laid out on model "garden city" lines by the renowned architect Raymond Unwin with C.M. Crickmer as his assistant. Three hundred dwelling houses were built. Detached; semi-detached; and terraced houses stood in attractive avenues and terraces on wide, well-formed metal and tarmacadam roadways. Unwin based his housing scheme for Gretna on a new theory of simplicity, and restricted his designs to unbroken hipped roofs and plain facades of brick or roughcast blockwork. All the residential roads Umwin planned for Gretna ended with a view of Skiddaw in the Lake District, 40 miles away. (From 1916 Raymond Unwin became one of the chief government advisers on working-class housing). The two townships were provided with many essential public buildings including institutes, hostels and bath-houses, cinemas, dance-halls, banks, post offices, telephone exchange, police barracks, fire station, police station, rail stations and engine sheds, hospital, and five churches - two Anglican; two Catholic; and one Presbyterian. All public buildings had electric light and were serviced with a public water supply and a main drainage system. The overall supervision of the work was entrusted to Lord Cowdray's firm of S. Pearson & Son under the personal supervision of his brother Edward (later Sir Edward Pearson). The work was divided between five construction firms with a substantial share of the work for the new township including hospital and medical facilities being awarded to the builders John Laing & Son of Carlisle. On 13 August, 1919, the Secretary to the Minister of Munitions, Mr Kellaway, in replying to a question in the House of Commons, said the cost of the residential buildings, hutments and amenities in connection with the Gretna factory was £1,237,000 and the average number of persons employed from September 1916 to the end of September 1918 had been 18,117. (The total capital expenditure including equipment as reported in The Times on 9 August, 1919, stood at £9,184,000). With the cessation of hostilities in 1918 the need for a huge, high-powered armament industry thankfully came to an abrupt end. Gretna's workforce dropped to around 1,000 and Unwin's garden city became a virtual ghost town. Because of its isolated position it failed to appeal to alternative industries and in 1920 responsibility for the site passed to the War Office and then to the Disposals Board who advertised it for sale. 600 lots were put up for sale by auction by the Carlisle estate agents, W. L. Tiffin & Sons in conjunction with W. P. Gibbings & Son, in the County Hall, Carlisle from 22 - 25 July, 1924.

The factory on this 9,000 acre site with its 17 miles of perimeter fencing had gone into production while the township was still being built. In all about 20,000 people were employed including many thousands of navvies. The whole complex was built in under two years in the most trying conditions. Heavy Scottish mists alternated with a drifting sea wrack and this weather took the heart out of the men. Their clothes would get wet early in the day and having no change to call their own, the same damp clothes would be worn again the next morning. These men were separated from their families but they were earning big money. Carlisle was the only city of any size within 50 miles of the factories and it is not surprising that a large contingent of the serious drinkers among them crowded into Carlisle in the evenings and at weekends to drink their fill as quickly as possible before boarding their return train. They joined the thousands of navvies who lodged in Carlisle itself and together they filled the public houses to overflowing.

Many of these houses, because of their position or structure were quite unsuitable for so much trade, being situated in narrow lanes or alleys where supervision was impossible. When the Western Border Area Order had been applied in November 1915 with Gretna roughly at its centre, the usual restrictions had been imposed. Hours of sale were cut to five and a half per day; off-sales of spirits were limited to the mid-day opening periods on five days a week only; "no treating", no credit, no hawking of liquor, no "long pull" were all introduced. There was a compulsory dilution of spirits, and Sunday closing was imposed in the part of the area nearest to the border so as to prevent the migration of drinkers. But this Order had little or no effect and Longtown and Annan had found itself unable to cope with the drunkenness and disorder in its midst. It was not long before the same troubles on a larger scale and in an aggravated form developed in Carlisle for which the current machinery of control was confessedly inadequate.

The convictions for drunkenness in Carlisle which had stood at around 250 in 1914/15 had risen alarmingly to 953 in 1916. They represented the highest rate of 85 county boroughs in England and Wales in respect of the ratio of convictions to population. These figures confirmed the notion that the storm centre was now Carlisle. The Rev. G. Bramwell Evens, a Wesleyan Minister who had been resident in Carlisle since 1914, described the position in the city in his booklet "The Truth about Direct Control in Carlisle."(p4). "Into this quiet city of 50,000 inhabitants . . . there poured 10,000 to 12,000 of the navvy class whose hard-drinking propensity is proverbial. In addition to these, 2,000 to 4,000 more took up their abode in the Gretna hutments and neighbouring hamlets making Carlisle, especially on Saturday nights, their drinking rendezvous. . . The housing problem at once became acute. Small houses were simply stacked with men. Every available room was commandeered for sleeping purposes. Hundreds were compelled to board out. At night these men were practically turned out into the street until bed-time. Their landladies did not want them inside the house; their money was wanted but not their company. . . The cafes and places of entertainment were crowded, and after these there only remained the public house as a place of refuge. Here then were thousands of men wandering aimlessly about with no home ties, with plenty of money and with public houses at every few yards inviting them to conviviality and seeming comfort. It is not to be wondered at that scenes of the most nauseating and degrading character became a common occurrence. Men fought like beasts; fierce fights raged round the doors of public houses. The diminished police force was unable to cope with the situation. Almost every alley was littered with prostrate drunken men. The main thoroughfare of Carlisle was Bedlam".

What was to be done? Prohibition was out of the question. Local prohibition of liquor would have been bitterly resented and the government had already decided that prohibition on a national scale was impracticable. It was not deemed essential for the conduct of the war, and if adopted for the war period, would be likely to lead to violent reaction when the war was over. There remained the consideration of the earlier possible expedient for which the government had previously made a feasibility study, albeit for the whole country at the time; namely, that of state purchase. In June, 1916, the Central Control Board held a series of conferences in Carlisle with

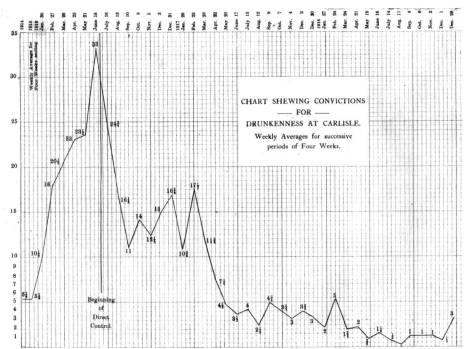

Chart of convictions for drunkenness taken from the General Manager's Report, 1918. The weekly average came down rapidly from a high of 33 convictions in June, 1916, just before the introduction of Direct Control, to settle at a low number in 1917 and 1918.

representatives of the civic authorities; the licensing justices; the brewers; the Licensed Victuallers' Association; and eight local registered clubs. Following these discussions a special meeting of the Board was held in London on 21 June, 1916, with Lord D'Abernon as chairman, to consider the report of the Board's delegates who had recently visited Carlisle to negotiate the purchase of licensed premises. The proceedings of this special meeting were held in private and no report was issued to the press. It transpired that a decision was confirmed to place the whole of the liquor trade in the city and part of the surrounding country district, under the direct management of the Board, and that the licensed premises and other businesses which would be taken over should be purchased outright and acquired permanently. Without this, the Board felt that the necessary speed and full control would not be attainable.

The decision was put into force immediately. Without any delay the Carlisle and district undertaking became a working reality. In July, 1916, the first group of public houses in Carlisle came into the possession of the Board. The Board was anxious to make it clear from the start that licensed premises were being acquired with neither a commercial nor a philanthropic objective, but solely for the purpose of giving proper effect to the control of the liquor supply as an aid to the successful prosecution of the war. There was little doubt that the current very serious war situation contributed an added impetus to the decision. The Board was fortunate in obtaining the support of local opinion at this stage for its policies. The local newspapers - the Liberal Carlisle Journal and the Unionist Cumberland News were both initially in favour of the Board's work. (Nonetheless, the Cumberland News remained critical of some aspects of the Board's policies and after the war by 1921 was actually suggesting its abolition).

The scheme, later to be generally referred to as the Carlisle "experiment" was gradually extended to cover an area stretching from Ecclefechan in Dumfriesshire to Maryport in Cumberland. This amounted to some 500 square miles which supported an estimated population of 140,000. Carlisle itself had a population of 52,000, and the small town of Maryport to the south west, a population of 10,000. But the term "experiment" is somewhat misleading if it is to imply that the Government deliberately set out on a social experiment per se. It became obvious as time went by that this previously untried expedient was indeed a social experiment with significant national possibilities in which Carlisle played a unique role. The Carlisle and District Direct Control Area consisted of the city of Carlisle and the north-western portion of the county covering an area of approximately 320 square miles with a population of approximately 120,000.

When the Board commenced its operations in the area in June, 1916, there were in total 339 licensed premises. 119 and a further seven registered clubs were in Carlisle and the remaining 220 were in the county area. By the end of October, 1916, the bulk of the city houses were either under management or had been closed. 65 houses were under management with one pending; 53 had been closed, and three new licences had been granted (Gretna Tavern; London Tavern; and the Citadel Station Refreshment Rooms). Her Majesty's Theatre had an excise licence but this was discontinued at a later date and is not included in these figures. At the same time the Board took the opportunity to end the joint use of premises for the sale of groceries and intoxicants. Nine off-licences and one full licence had been held in connection with grocers shops but in seven of these the Board closed the premises for the sale of intoxicants while in the remaining three the sale of groceries was given up. In the early part of 1917 the Gretna navvies were still present in undiminished numbers and it was deemed unwise for the Board to close any more public houses in the city for the time being. The houses were uncomfortably crowded, especially on Saturday nights, and any further closures would only have increased the congestion. In the country districts outside the city, besides two licences which had been allowed to lapse by the owners, 23 houses which appeared to be redundant had been closed by the end of 1917.

Over and above this the Board became aware that the inconvenient and uneconomical way that the wholesale spirit trade of Carlisle was being conducted at a number of different places in the city prompted them to concentrate the trade at one central store. A lease was taken out towards the end of 1916 from the North British Railway Company for what was formerly a goods store. Built on two levels the building proved to be admirable for adaptation to the Board's requirements for housing the washing, bottling, corking, capsuling, and labelling machines, together with a spirit filter, and adequate storage racks. The vats used had a total capacity of 13,520 gallons and the bottling machine could fill 140 dozen bottles an hour. All this was ready for use by July 1917.

The Board had found itself practically compelled to take over the whole of the properties of the Maryport Brewery which owned a considerable number of houses in Carlisle and district in order to avoid the payment of heavy compensation for "severance". The business done at these houses formed a significant proportion of the brewery's profits and the company's future status stood to be seriously jeopardised by the Board's action. Protracted negotiations finally reached a satisfactory conclusion with an agreement dated 19 June, 1917. Under this agreement the Board had become possessed, as from 11 November 1916, of the whole of the assets of the Company which included the brewery, bottling stores, spirit stores, mineral water factory, 21 licensed premises and some unlicensed premises in the town of Maryport, together with 84 licensed premises and a certain amount of cottage and other property in the surrounding countryside. In addition the Board acquired 20 public houses, cottage property, offices, and stores in Carlisle itself. A large number of houses overall were owned by the five brewery companies (four in Carlisle and one in Maryport) which found themselves involved in the Scheme, and compensation was paid both to the owners and the licensees of the premises which were taken over or closed.

On taking over licensed premises under their own compulsory powers the Board was conscious of the interests of all the parties concerned with the properties, and endeavoured to safeguard these interests, but they were sailing in uncharted waters in this unique and urgent experiment. In the absence of any existing foundation on which to base their procedures, the Board was faced with some degree of difficulty regarding the manner and amount of compensation to be paid in settlement. This is how they went about it: - a statutory notice of acquisition was served personally on the occupier of the premises with copies being served on each of the other interested parties. The Board appointed a well-known valuer to act for them, and negotiations would follow with the interested parties, but before any sum was finally settled the details were submitted to the Board in a written report. This report was then submitted to the Treasury with any comments the Board wished to make appended, and once it had been approved by the Treasury it formed the basis of a formal agreement under the Defence of the Realm Losses Commission which had been appointed as the guardian of the public funds. In the case of owners of property, the next step was that they should furnish evidence of title in the ordinary way to the Board's solicitors so that the money could be paid over. The solicitors' and valuers' costs were paid by the Board according to a scale approved by the Treasury. The procedure was much the same for tenants except that no documentary proof of title was called for and therefore the payment was somewhat quicker and, as in the case of owners, interest at five per cent per annum was paid on the amount from the time the property was vested in the Board. The tenants' stock, trade utensils, furniture and fittings were paid for immediately. A serious endeavour was made to assess the amount of compensation at a reasonable sum which was fair to both the interested parties and the Exchequer. In fact the Board felt that in some cases, due to the fact that the acquisition had been compulsory, they had leaned slightly to the side of generosity.

Notwithstanding this, there arose dissatisfaction with the time involved in referring all claims to the Defence of the Realm Losses Commission. Some cases were settled in this way within a reasonable time and without difficulty but in others there was delay and friction. This irritation came to a head when a case elsewhere in the country was taken to the High Court by the Cannon Street Brewery Company of Enfield in which an important decision defining the basis on which compensation was to be paid was given by Mr. Justice Younger in August, 1917. The case was given a fair and comprehensive coverage in the Cumberland News. Its report stated that the Board had taken over a public house at Enfield belonging to the Brewery Company who were claiming compensation under the Land Clauses Act. The Control Board however held that they had no legal entitlement to any compensation, but only to such as the Defence of the Realm Losses Inquiry Commission recommended as an act of grace. The Company then, while reserving all their legal rights, applied to go before the Commission, but their case would only be considered if they waived their legal rights. This they refused to do and instead gave the Board notice under section 68 of the Land Clauses Act to have the compensation payable to them assessed by a jury. The question before the High Court was whether, where the Board took over licensed premises, the owners were entitled to claim compensation of right under the provisions of the Land Clauses Act, or whether they were to accept the Losses Commission's act of grace. The case for the Board was argued by the Solicitor-General, but, in March 1918, Mr Justice Younger decided against them on all points and gave the Brewery Company the declaration which it claimed. Mr Justice Younger held that the Land Clauses Act was incorporated with the Acts and Regulations from which the Board derived its powers, and consequently that the method of assessing the compensation payable by the Board for premises permanently acquired in pursuance of those powers was the method laid down by the Land Clauses Act. Following the judgement, the reference of claims to the Royal Commission was suspended and outstanding claims were, as far as possible, settled by direct agreement. As the Board had taken up the same position with regard to compensation at Carlisle as it had at Enfield, the decision held great local significance. The settlement of a number of the larger claims had been deferred by claimants pending the progress of the Cannon Brewery case and until these claims had been resolved it was not possible to prepare an estimate of the Board's capital expenditure upon the acquisition of properties as would justify the publication of a balance-sheet. (HO/190 405). The Cumberland News had already suggested that the Commission had "freely upset agreements and thus created misunderstanding and friction, and considerably embarrassed the local work of the Board. . . the Board and its officials have, so far as we can gather, endeavoured to settle fairly and equitably with those whose businessess they have acquired". Once it was decided that the Commission had no jurisdiction in the matter, the subsequent system of direct agreement between the Board and claimants, subject to Treasury sanction, speeded up the process considerably and the total amount paid in compensation increased considerably in 1918/19. In the Carlisle area compensation had been pending for two years in some cases where owners had been holding out for exorbitant terms and resorting to threats of instituting legal proceedings to compel certain payments of compensation on a Land Clauses scale.

As a corollary it is interesting to note an article on the Board's policy which had appeared in the Financier as early as 27 June, 1916: "The problem is not an easy one to solve and those who have tentatively undertaken its solution are not to be envied. . . . there is a strong desire to see the experiment given a fair trial under such conditions as will enable safe conclusions to be drawn from it. The area selected is a good one for the purpose . . . From the standpoint of the brewers the scheme is quite unobjectionable as long as they are afforded reasonable compensation for the expropriation of their properties. Provided their claims in that respect are met they will probably be glad to be freed from the possibility of harassing legislation in the future. . . . The brewery shareholder need not be alarmed as long as it is not shown that the authorities are animated by any vindictive desire to penalise a certain class of property owners and to embark upon a policy of spoilation. There is little likelihood of grossly unfair terms being imposed upon brewers and owners of licensed property with a government in power which is representative of both parties, and with bitter domestic controversies for the time being at an end".

At the outset of their proceedings the Board decided that the excessive number of licensed premises in the city of Carlisle, together with the unsuitable situation and unsatisfactory internal arrangements of many of them had, in part, been contributing to much of the drunkenness and disorder. A dual plan was conceived and adopted to run in parallel, namely that of restrictive and constructive policies.

In August, 1916, the secretary of the Central Control Board wrote to the Carlisle City Council Watch Committee intimating that the Board proposed appointing a local committee for the City of Carlisle and the Petty Sessional Divisions of the Cumberland Ward and Longtown with a view to securing local assistance in the management of the Board's scheme. The function of the committee was to liaise between management and local opinion in an advisory capacity. The City Council was invited to nominate two representatives to serve on the local committee, and the first meeting was held on 6 September, 1916, with the Earl of Lonsdale as President taking the chair.

As early as October, 1915, the Board had inclined to the view that much excessive drinking may be traced to the want of adequate facilities for food, refreshment and recreation, particularly in conjunction with long hours of work and overtime. It was convinced that the improvement of public houses and the provision of canteens could do much to render less necessary the imposition of purely restrictive measures. Various voluntary bodies such as the Young Men's and Young Women's Christian Associations, the Women's Legion, the Church Army, the Salvation Army, and the British Women's Temperance Association had set up numerous canteens throughout the country by public subscription but before long the flow of money became exhausted. The secretary of the People's Palace Association, P.W. Wilson had written to Lord D'Abernon in July, 1915, complaining that 150 of the 200 firms which his Association had approached had ignored or refused its request to be allowed to establish canteens on their premises. Wilson urged that "a little tactful pressure by the Board would greatly hasten the extension of this work". The Board responded with enthusiasm. (PRO/HO 185/242). A Canteens Committee of four members was formed under the chairmanship of Sir George Newman, and the Treasury agreed to provide up to 50 per cent of the capital required by any voluntary society to establish a works canteen allowing employers to set the cost against excess-profits tax. An ancient link was thus reinstated between the supply of food and the sale of liquor. It was, however, on the question of the financing of the canteen schemes that friction developed. The Finance Department of the Ministry of Munitions held that canteens, once established ought to pay their way. Consequently the Ministry set up a separate Canteens Finance Committee to carry out close financial scrutiny of canteens in national factories. The Control Board itself did not escape the Treasury strictures over canteens policy. In 1918 it was severely reprimanded for "establishing five canteens between 1915 and 1917 on their own initiative when they could find no employer or voluntary organisation willing to bear or share the cost. About £12,000 had been spent, it was alleged, without Treasury approval having been sought. Lord D'Abernon indignantly defended his department, maintaining that in two cases prior sanction had been obtained whilst in the others the urgency of the situation precluded any delay". (PRO. T/112). There were the anticipated warnings from the Treasury of the need for financial retrenchment and by February 1918 responsibility for the establishment and the supervision of industrial canteens was temporarily transferred from the Board to a new department of the Ministry of Munitions. Once the war was over however, the Board bid for the re-transfer of canteen administration to its own charge since it was "an integral factor of their system of liquor control".

The restrictive measures of the Board's dual policy of control were imposed within a few weeks of the influx of the navvies into Carlisle and had come into force in November 1915. The hours for sale of intoxicating liquor were reduced to five-and-a-half a day for on sales, and four-and-a-half for off sales. At the same time off sales of spirits were limited to two-and-a-half hours a day Monday to Friday, with no off sales at all during the week-end, and all off sales at railway refreshment rooms completely forbidden. Added to this there was to be no "treating"; no credit; no "long pull" (an old device used by some publicans to overstep the authorised measure in order to attract custom); no hawking and canvassing; and no "bona fide" traveller's privilege to buy liquor during closing hours. All these conditions were applicable to the registered clubs as well as the licensed premises. Although the clubs would not be taken over they would nevertheless be subject to the same regulations as the public houses - selling at the same strength, and not selling at a lower price. They would also have to close at the same times and would not be permitted to obtain liquor from outside sources without the permission of the Board.

The position of clubs was anomalous - their trade was with a quasi-domestic consumption of liquor - they did not carry on a business and could not be categorised as licence-holders. There was therefore no going concern for the State to acquire and control and there was no extinguishment of licence for which the Board was duty-bound to pay compensation. Nevertheless clubs had to adhere to the same regulations set out by the Board for licensed premises. Scotland was already operating a policy of complete Sunday closing and the Board found it wise to impose a similar restriction for Carlisle and those areas adjacent to the Scottish border in order to prevent a general exodus across the border in pursuit of liquor.

On the question of the prohibition of "treating", a report by Edgar Sanders, general manager of the Carlisle Scheme, dated 19 February, 1917, illuminates the local reaction to the imposition. "It is quite clear that the general public dislike the Order, evade it whenever possible, and put pressure on the managers and their assistants to induce them to evade it. . . . Sometimes personal resentment against the manager himself is experienced, particularly if men wish to buy their wives a drink, or their female friends. . . . Most of the managers were emphatic that treating was part of the social habits of the drinking public in Carlisle to be stamped out. All agree that treating in large groups by each member in turn is a thing of the past". (This was partly due, no doubt, to the rise in prices.) "Managers are split on the issue between those who try, and those who say it is pointless. The majority try although they do not like the Order or the extra work. 'No treating' also means paying for only one drink and this makes too much work for staff giving change etc. at busy times. Treating since July 1916 is no longer done openly but managers know that it goes on extensively and most of them believe themselves powerless to stop it". (The Local Advisory Committee in February, 1919, recommended that the Order be discontinued on the grounds that the differentiation of the district from the rest of England was no longer necessary owing to the cessation of hostilities and the consequent partial closing down of the Gretna factory. The Order was finally revoked in June, 1919)

Another bone of contention was the Sunday Closing Order. This had been imposed on Carlisle and district as early as November, 1915, because of the area's proximity to Scotland where Sunday closing for intoxicants was already operating under the ordinary law. Thus, the necessity of including Carlisle in the Order had arisen before the institution of the Board's scheme of direct control for the Gretna district as originally defined. In May, 1917, the Board found it necessary to extend the Sunday closing area to include Maryport and its immediate neighbourhood notwithstanding a plea earlier from the Cumberland & North Lancashire Federation Board representing coal miners, steelsmelters, blastfurnacemen, and winding enginemen who opposed Sunday Closing on the grounds of the hot and strenuous nature of the work for which they were in need of liquid refreshment of their choice. Five months later the Local Advisory Committee, at the behest of some of the local Trades Unions, and by a narrow majority, recommended that the Board be requested to modify the Sunday Closing Order and permit the sale of beer and wine on Sundays for two hours at midday and another two hours in the evening. The Board, after careful consideration, decided that it was not desirable to alter the existing regulation. The Order was not finally revoked until 9 February 1919 on the recommendation of the Local Advisory Committee.

The Board also decided to try an experiment in prohibiting the sale of spirits on Saturdays throughout the area. This decision came about as a sequel to a successful trial carried out over the Christmas season of 1916 and the following New Year's Day when the sale of spirits was stopped, resuiting in a marked drop in arrests for drunkenness. The "spirit-less" Saturdays Order, on the approval of the Local Advisory Committee, took effect as from 22 February, 1917, and the Chief Constable's report for the end of that year stated: "arrests for drunkenness on Saturdays, which formerly was the heaviest day, have become practically nonexistent, and this is the more remarkable when it is remembered that Saturday was always market day in the city". For the eight Saturdays preceding the Order, 45 arrests for drunkenness were made, whereas there were only 24 arrests for the whole of the following 44 weeks of the year. The ban continued throughout 1918, but was finally revoked for the same reasons as those pertaining to the Sunday Closing Order.

One of the earliest reforms instituted by the Board was an 80 per cent reduction in the number of houses under their control at which spirits could be sold for consumption off the premises. Experience had shown that many persons on leaving the public house at closing time in the middle of the day were tempted to take away a bottle of spirits for drinking in the afternoon, either outside or in the home. The number of houses at which spirits could be bought for off consumption was reduced from over 100 to just 18, and a little later to only 15, but the Board were careful to select such houses so as to meet the convenience of the public in various locations. A further instruction was given that only one bottle at a time was to be sold to any customer at any of these fifteen houses.

Each and all these measures put the Board in the exceptional position of being able to regulate the sale and supply of spirits for home consumption within the city. Because of the war situation, power had been vested in the Board giving it the freedom to act in the public interest unfettered by private enterprise. No body of licensing administrators in the country had previously been in such an exalted position and it is only in retrospect that all the problems confronting the Board can be expounded and evaluated. Certain aspects were far from clear when the Board began its work. In this sense it was an "experiment" and the Board harboured no desire to impose unnecessary arbitrary restrictions on personal freedom but faced each problem as it arose. The practice of ordering beer and spirits at the same time was known locally as a "heater and a cooler". The spirits were drunk neat and then washed down by the beer. This practice was discouraged by the Board and a definite instruction was issued that spirits and beer were not to be sold at the same time. Instructions were also issued forbidding the sale of spirits to any young person apparently under the age of 18. All advertisements for the sale of liquor were removed from the exterior of the premises and bottles were no longer displayed in the windows.

The public generally could understand and accept the rationale behind many of the control restrictions of the Board, but it was the rationing of liquor which seemed to cause the most discomfort among the drinking public. Control was one thing, but limitation was hard to bear.

By the beginning of 1917, there were real shortages of staple foods and fuels in the country. Enemy submarines were taking their toll of the shipping available for imports and the situation was fast becoming a crisis. A new government department had been promptly created for the purpose of controlling the food supplies of the country. Lord Devonport, who had been Parliamentary Secretary to the Board of Trade, was put in charge. A War Cabinet meeting was called for 23 January, 1917, to discuss the restriction of liquor traffic. It was decided that the Food Controller should restrict the supply of brewing materials so as to reduce the output of beer by 25 per cent on the 1915 standard in addition to the existing 15 per cent on that standard, making a total of 40 per cent. (A further reduction of 30 per cent was made in February, 1917, under the Output of Beer Restriction Act.) It was decided that there should be a simultaneous and similar reduction by the Chancellor of the Exchequer in the quantities of wines and spirits released from bond. The Food Controller was authorised by an Order and Defence of the Realm regulations to stop further malting as soon as a sufficient amount had been produced at the reduced quota for beer. Food stocks had to be used sparingly and used for the essential requirement of feeding the nation and so the number of standard barrels of beer brewed dropped steadily from 26,000 in 1916 to 12,600 in 1918/19.

But it was with the arrival of summer weather that discontent at the shortage and high price of beer began to manifest itself among land workers and munition workers. The government decided to try to allay this irritation by brewing a light beer and permitting a third more production for the following three months from June 1917 on condition that its alcoholic strength was reduced and the price modified accordingly. At the end of the three months this increase in brewing was allowed to continue provided the specific gravity was kept at the reduced rate. In July Edgar Sanders, general manager, wrote to Henry Carter saying they had experimented with the 2 per cent or non-intoxicating beers but that they were not popular despite the low price. "The working man who is in the habit of taking beer does not merely regard it as a thirst quencher but, to some measure it takes the place with him of solid food . . . conversion is not likely unless the process is gradual and uniform in all districts". (HO190/490). Ultimately in March, 1918, it was decided that all beer brewed in Great Britain should be of a specific gravity not exceeding 1030 degrees. "Although the innocuous but insipid character of this light beer was the source of a good deal of grumbling at the time, it unquestionably helped to wean millions of workers in Britain from their pre-war proclivity to unduly heavy drinks. The old habit of stupe-faction by strong ales, which led to many being not perhaps drunk but fuddled, was permanently broken. So was the habit of men getting drunk on Saturday nights which was so prevalent amongst a section of the wage earners before the War. This is one legacy of good from the wartime work of Food Control". (Lloyd George, War Memoirs p792/3). One of the snags which had to be resolved was the mistake of including the light beers with the general quota. A memorandum from twenty firms in the Midlands requested the government to issue certificates sanctioning the brewing of the light beer in addition to the standard barrelage. "In all these works the men work under great heat or conditions of exceptional stress and the employers foresee a considerable reduction in their output unless supplies of beer are maintained. Men cannot obtain supplies to bring into the works with them (also made worse by lack of sugar for other types of drink). . . The working classes resent keenly the Food Controller's restrictions on the supply of beer at a season when the need for it is most severely felt". (HO 185/266). It was also foreseen that there could well be difficulty in obtaining labour for haymaking if the usual allowance of beer was not forthcoming. In Carlisle the Control Board had found that the light beers had been acceptable when ordinary beers were in short supply but recommended that light beers be excluded from standard barrelage. The average drinker in Carlisle knew that his beer and spirits were expensive and weaker than he liked and made the connection between the advent of the Control Board and this sorry state of affairs. In reality, these conditions obtained in other parts of the country also and the Board were not, and never had been responsible for these measures which were entirely the result of the Food Controller's orders.

After careful consideration the Board had decided that it would employ managers on a fixed salary so that the liquor would be sold by persons having no pecuniary interest in the amount sold, added to which, as paid servants of the Board their duty would be to see that the Board's instructions were strictly carried out. The existing licensee was given the opportunity of continuing to occupy the premises (if the licence was to remain) but on quite different terms which required him to prevent any undue consumption of alcohol upon his premises and to do all in his power to curb excessive drinking. If drunkenness should be traced to his house he would be held to account, and increased sales of intoxicants would not be deemed to be meritorious. Instead he was to be encouraged to promote the sale of food and non-intoxicants by a system of liberal commission of 75 per cent of the gross profits on the sale of everything but intoxicants. All his goods would be supplied from the Board's breweries or spirit stores for which he would be held accountable by means of a periodical stocktaking. He was also subject to a rigid system of inspection. For a while some of the Board's critics suggested that the previous tenants would have made fortunes from the influx of the Gretna navvies had they been left alone, but by the time of the general manager's report of December, 1919, he was able to offer a word of praise to the managers. "They have well discharged a very difficult task. It has needed, especially on the part of those who were licensees under the old conditions, a considerable amount of tact and forbearance to accommodate themselves to the new method of trading, and they have loyally served the Board in this capacity".

The opinion of the general public and the degree of social improvement was difficult to measure with any certainty for a period prior to the development of the sophisticated methodologies which exist today, but the convictions for drunkenness go some of the way towards providing an index of the prevailing situation to the end of 1919. The average number of convictions pre-war had been around 250 per annum and for the following years from 1915 to 1919 they stood at: 277; 953 (when the number of navvies was at its height); 320; 80; and 78. The dramatic drop in 1917 from 953 to 320 was due mainly to the "spiritless Saturdays", the scarcity of liquor, and the changing nature of the male population in the city as the navvies began to leave. The Chief Constable for Carlisle in his report for 1919 felt able to state that the orderly condition of the streets to date showed that the latest figures were a fair index of the sobriety of the city. "There can be no question in the minds of careful and impartial observers that the direct management of the licensed trade by the Control Board has been of great benefit to the city". The Carlisle Journal also wrote that, "Whatever the critics may say, the Control Board has demonstrated that State Control of public houses leads to a reduction of drunkenness and if the State had the whole of the trade in its hands still more could be done". At the same time the Cumberland News was saying that, "Both socially and financially the Carlisle 'experiment' has been fully justified, and there is a growing consensus of opinion that the only satisfactory method of carrying on a necessary trade which is liable to abuse is for the State to become entirely responsible for its conduct". The general manager's Report for 1918 concluded that: "Whatever be its fate the 'Carlisle experiment' will have left its mark on the social history of this country. It is the first piece of constructive licensing reform undertaken with the prestige and authority of a government department. It has shown that the liquor trade can be carried on, subject to reasonable regulations, without detriment to the well-being of the community, and without undue interference with the liberty, tastes, and preferences of the large mass of the adult population. It has shown that the transfer from private ownership to public control can be carried through without undue friction and without loss to the national exchequer. Above all it has offered a new solution to the problem of intemperance". The Local Advisory Committee unanimously passed a resolution in August 1919 to ask the Control Board "to urge upon the government that the system of State Management which has proved such a success in this area be maintained with adequate powers to complete and continue the work. In November, 1919 a conference of delegates from the Trades Unions of the district was held representing some 15,000 workers at which a resolution was passed by a majority of more than 200 to 1 urging the government to continue the present control in Carlisle and to extend it to the rest of the country.

The general manager, in his report to the Control Board for year ending 31 December, 1919, sought to express the response of the ordinary drinker: "All that can be said is that if there were any real signs of discontent they would soon be apparent. Those who use the houses are not behindhand in complaining if there is cause for it. But the fact is that very few complaints of substance are made, notwithstanding that interested parties are continually trying to persuade the public that they are being badly treated. And the managers who naturally hear all there is to be said, assert that whereas there was loud grumbling when it was necessary to curtail the supplies so drastically under the Food Controller's orders, now that the supplies are adequate the amount of grumbling is negligible. On the other hand the customers appreciate what has been done for them in the way of improved conditions. . . What appears incontrovertible is that any proposal to hand back the licensed trade to private interests would be received with dismay by the great majority of the inhabitants".

CHAPTER FOUR
THE CONTROL BOARD'S CONSTRUCTIVE POLICY

From the outset it was the Control Board's policy to encourage the provision of food to accompany the intake of liquor and they did their utmost to give practical effect to this side of their policy which was compatible with the war-time conditions and limitations. A serious and sustained effort was made to encourage the supply of food in 26 of the ordinary type of public houses in the city and in the two auction marts. These houses were kept open on weekdays from 10a.m. to 9p.m. (with a 30 minute interval at 2.30 p.m. for the purpose of cleaning and ventilation). On Sundays they were open from 12 noon until 2 p.m. and then again from 4 pm to 6 pm. Freshly baked meat pies were delivered daily and the managers were given facilities for the supply of light meals, sandwiches, and snacks. A commission equal to 75 per cent of the gross profits on the sale of food and 25 per cent on the sale of non-intoxicants was allocated to these ordinary houses where food was supplied by the Board. In cases where the demand for food was only small the manager provided it himself and was permitted to keep all the profits. The system was given a prolonged trial but eventually it was found that the demand just wasn't there, and that only if the public house was in a district where the workers were some distance from their homes would the premises be regarded as places for obtaining anything but liquid refreshment. It also needed to be born in mind that the general shortages of food at the time and the consequent lack of variety on offer at a suitable price did little to attract the ordinary customers at this type of house and the attempt under war-time conditions to resuscitate the functions of the old victualling houses of the past proved somewhat of a failure.

More successful however was the Board's experiment with the food taverns which it constructed as model refreshment houses. The policy was to have not only fewer but better houses which meant remodelling old premises or building new ones. This, of course, entailed the use of labour and materials which were both in short supply at the time and in consequence the Board's programme had to be strictly limited until the situation improved. Nonetheless, it was able to undertake staggered reconstruction projects at seven premises in Carlisle and one in Longtown during the war years. In all but one of these projects provision was made for the supply of cooked meals alongside adequate kitchen arrangements and easy access to the dining areas. The first two reconstructions were the Gretna Tavern opened in July, 1916, and the London Tavern opened in the following November, with five more to follow namely: the Pheasant Inn; the Albion; the Goliath; the Irishgate; and the Citadel - all in Carlisle; followed in June 1917 by the Globe Tavern, in Longtown. The Citadel was the only reconstruction which aimed at catering for customers other than those from the working classes and for whom the prices charged were on a higher scale than those at the other taverns. There was much criticism of this at the time on the ground that such status was not necessary to the promotion of the Board's objective which related to the efficiency of the Gretna munition workers and an increase in output of shells at the factory. The Board however saw it as an integral part of its general duty to cater for people of all classes - professional and business as well as wage-earner, and a catering superintendent was appointed to take charge of the supply of food to both the taverns and the hotels. While endeavouring to provide typical refreshment houses for the various localities, the Board was always conscious of the fact that each of its reconstructions was in the nature of an experiment, and that it would strive with each new design to embody the virtues of its predecessor and avoid its faults, matching the alterations and adaptations to the needs of each particular district. Some structural difficulties were encountered on the way since many of the old public houses in Carlisle (as in the country at large) had been poorly constructed and sited.

The persistence of the mere drink shops had been aided by the fact that there was a greater profit to the brewers in the sale of beer than of food and, since the introduction of the tied house system, it was much less trouble to sell. The proliferation of drink shops after the 1830 Beer Act had meant that many of the older cities had insufficient trade to support all the licence holders and the old, stuffy, and sometimes ramshackle premises could well be closed down and the trade diverted to premises that were altogether larger, lighter and more airy . The Board was free to close those houses which were least suited to its purpose regardless of the amount of trade they did, but it chose carefully those public houses which it felt should and could be closed without causing congestion for those that were left. The choices were on the grounds that their position in narrow streets and lanes and their structure made supervision difficult and sometimes well nigh impossible. The seven premises chosen for conversion into food taverns were conveniently situated to serve as centres for different parts of the city, and well suited structurally for the requisite adaptation and reconstruction. Snugs were removed and practically all the back door trade entrances were closed, and since, as the industrial canteen movement and the improved public house movement advanced in step, the lighting. heating, ventilation and sanitary arrangements assumed a significant role in the planning and execution of the work undertaken.

The first two premises chosen for reconstruction were the Gretna Tavern in Lowther Street and the London Tavern in London Road. Both opened in 1916. A further five, the Pheasant, Albion, Goliath,Irish Gate and the Citadel,opened at various dates between May and October, 1917. Each of the last five formed a reconstruction of one or more public houses which had formerly occupied the site. All these taverns were of a similar general type in that they all contained spacious accommodation for both standing and sitting drinkers. The Board aimed at providing an alternative to the ingrained habit of standing at the bar counter to drink and as a consequence it took the bold step of shortening the length of the counter. The drinking rooms themselves were generously supplied with seats, tables and chairs round an island or projecting bar counter, and a well-equipped kitchen was able to offer substantial meals with or without drink in a comfortable dining room. The Board's aim was to ensure that drinking, even if was to be drinking only, should be conducted in conditions of decency and comfort with the additional option of food for those who wanted it. Previously in Carlisle there had been little if any provision of a similar nature. Because of this, and the extraordinary increase in the population at the time, the Board was convinced that these factors prevented any case of hardship arising from competition between the state and existing private interests. By the time of the General Manager's report in December, 1918, it was clear that the Board had quickly recognised that the provision of food in the selected houses, was and would continue to be, one of its main duties. Here the demand for food exceeded all expectations and was, to all appearances, new trade. It seemed to show that dining rooms in selected public houses had been needed and what is more they were appreciated. During 1918 the takings for food at the seven taverns amounted to no less than £16,370 representing 33.3 per cent of the total takings from all sources at such houses. The Caterer and Hotel Keepers' Gazette was able to report in March, 1917, that The Gretna Tavern had become a catering success: "On Saturdays it is usual to sell about 200lbs. of cooked meat, 40 stones of potatoes, 16 gallons of soup, and proportionate quantities of other food".

Another constructive element in the Board's work was the arrangement at four of the taverns in Carlisle - the London, Pheasant, Goliath, and Irish Gate - and the Globe in Longtown for the off sales of cooked food. (Government "takeaways"). The idea at its inception was a novel one and in adopting it the Board anticipated the Food Controller's scheme for communal kitchens. This measure was particularly timely in respect of supplying hot soup and food for children to take away since there was a considerable demand for female labour at the large factories in the city and it was difficult for the women to provide adequate meals at midday. The part of the premises allocated to the off sale of food was distanced from the bar areas with a separate entrance, little shop, or hatch so that customers had no need to enter the public house at all. Meat pies always proved exceptionally popular and the Board had found it necessary to construct a special venue to bake meat pies alone. By the end of the war years the conclusion was reached that, while as yet there seemed only a lukewarm response to the provision of food in the ordinary public house, in special cases a food trade could be developed as a profitable enterprise with public benefits.

Two of the minor steps taken by the Board for the supply of food and non-intoxicants during these difficult years are worth recalling. Many hundreds of Gretna workers were arriving at, or departing from, Carlisle station by the late night or early morning trains when other refreshment places would have been closed and so for their convenience the Board, by courtesy of the railway authorities, provided coffee carts at the station entrances. Large numbers of munition workers took advantage of this facility. Also, in November, 1916, a coffee house was opened in Longtown by converting portions of the outbuildings of the Graham Arms Hotel into a coffee tavern in order to provide regular meals and non-intoxicant drinks for the Gretna workers during 1916 and 1917. The dining hall was provided with ten tables each capable of accommodating six persons while to the side of this main room was a reading and writing room and space for a piano and games. Lithographs had been donated by the manager of the London Underground to adorn the walls. Because no intoxicants were sold the house was able to open daily including Sundays, from 12 noon until 9 p.m. Once the Globe Tavern opposite was opened this supply of meals was discontinued. However, at the request of the Local Advisory Committee, the premises continued to be kept open for light refreshments. The hotel itself, which had previously enjoyed a considerable reputation among fishermen, was then refurbished as a first class residential hotel, but without a bar. Its only public drinking room was virtually detached from the hotel with its entrance in another street.

The country inns also had to be considered in order that food might be available at suitable premises should the demand arise. The Board therefore provided and furnished a special room at certain houses where teas and light refreshments could be served but it did not itself provide the food. The catering was undertaken by the manager himself who then qualified to take the whole of the ensuing profit. The general manager's report in December 1918 was able to confirm that the country inns had done quite a considerable trade in food and while there was little demand for meals in the winter months a total of 4,856 meals had been provided during September, 1918, at the 62 licensed houses (excluding hotels) lying outside the city. All this endeavour was laying the foundation for what was to develop later in the post-war years.

The war years had been desperate times for the architectural profession and some of the country's best architects and designers, who, by reason of age, did not qualify for call-up, were grateful for the work offered them by the Ministry of Munitions. The Ministry itself also stood to benefit greatly from their employment since men like Harry Redfern, George Walton, and C.F.A. Voysey all brought with them a previous background of high-class work for prestigious clients. Working for a government department may not have been a natural choice into which to channel their talents of quiet refinement but, as they were all members of the Art Workers' Guild, it at least offered them an opportunity to do something for the war effort in congenial company. Harry Redfern was appointed chief architect to the Central Control Board with George Walton, his junior by six years, as his assistant.

Walton was delegated to undertake much of the surveying work which he found rather tedious, but he had the sympathetic support of the architect, Basil Oliver. Oliver had taught at the Central School of Arts and Crafts and had recently been elected to the Art Workers' Guild. He was currently based in an office in Carlisle. The architectural work on reconstruction and improvement fell to Redfern. He brought to the task a long and successful career in conserving and restructuring old buildings. At a later date, when the national situation began to improve, he was able to design and build new model public houses for Carlisle and district. Walton's remit was with the interior decoration and furnishing of the premises, while Voysey designed the Board's badge and contributed graphics, posters, and framed pictures for the walls. He would take himself off to the London Zoo with his sketch pad or would contribute a sketch of some country activity such as freshwater fishing. Unfortunately these and similar contributions are now hard to trace since there had been no concern at the time to credit the work of individual designers. George Walton was a colourist of great subtlety but he quickly learned that much of his usual elegant and sophisticated approach to design would have been out of place in his new assignments for the Central Control Board in Carlisle. The rigours of the situation in these war years led him to find alternative adequate solutions to urgent requirements.

The first of the food taverns to be provided at short notice was the Gretna

Tavern in Lowther Street. It was opened on 12 July, 1916, by Lord Lonsdale with Lord D'Abernon, chairman of the Control Board, in the chair. The dignified, solid stone building (now Lloyds T.S.B. bank) occupied a commanding position in a main thoroughfare and was formerly a Post Office but had been made available to the Board by the Postmaster General when the new General Post Office premises in Warwick Road was built. The conversion was skillfully planned by Harry Redfern with J. F. Genders of London as clerk of works and J. & R. Bell of Carlisle as contractors. A long open stand-up bar was provided from what had been the old selling counter, while the old sorting room at the rear was turned into a large dining hall with a low platform on one side to accommodate a piano and a gramophone. There was a small newspaper stand in one corner and a writing desk in another, and three rows of tables with sturdy Windsor wheel-back chairs ran the length of the hall. Adjoining this spacious, lofty and airy room, Redfern had provided a well-equipped kitchen, store rooms, lavatories, and rooms for the manageress and attendants.

The national newspapers immediately began to take a keen interest in the work of the Control Board and this first state-controlled public house. Four days after its opening the Sunday Chronicle of the 12 July, 1916, printed a fairly lengthy article describing, praising, and criticising various aspects of the enterprise. It found the dining room a charming room where "pretty girls in black dresses and white caps and aprons flit about to supply your needs". The article was not so enamoured of the long, stand-up bar. "On one side of the long high bar is a cold and comfortless flagged

Gretna Tavern interior.

floor . . . customers cannot sit down except at their own risk on the hot air radiator. . . . more could be looked for if the stand-up bar was made as comfortable and satisfactory to the senses as is the refreshment room. All men do not like music, and some don't care for the hustle of a restaurant and the sight and smell of food except at mealtimes. Such men will not go to the Gretna Tavern for their beer. If this experiment at Carlisle does not turn out well and State control of drink is a short-lived idea, it will be buried under the cold flags of the stand-up bar in the Gretna Tavern".

Several alterations however were put in place early the following year when, because of the growing success of the enterprise and the decision to open at 7 30 a.m. each weekday in order to supply breakfasts to the men who could only find sleeping accommodation, it was found that a considerably larger space could easily be utilised at busy times. There followed an extensive enlargement of the kitchen and significant alterations to the bar area where an oval counter was erected in the middle of the long bar. Red leathered seats were introduced; and the floor was covered with linoleum. This all resulted in a considerable increase in the receipt from the sales of beer. In a letter to Rev. Henry Carter, (appointed to the Board 23 May, 1916), the general manager, Edgar Sanders, wrote on 2 July, 1917, that: "The current percentages were: food and minerals 55 per cent; beer and wines 43 per cent; and tobacco 2 per cent. but it was necessary to remember two important points - that the Food Controller's Orders which had come into force on 16 April, 1917, had compelled them to limit the cost of any meals served at the Gretna Tavern to 1/3d. This meant that £100 taken in food now represented a greatly increased number of customers". (PRO HO/19O/490). Conversely the price of ale and beer had been increased by 2d a pint.

Smoking was allowed in all parts of the Tavern. Opening hours were: Monday to Saturday inclusive, 12 noon to 2.30 p.m. and 6 p.m. to 9 p.m. with an extension of 30 minutes drinking-up time during which no intoxicants would be sold. No intoxicants would be sold on Sundays but the Tavern would be open from 12 noon to 9 p.m. At the opening ceremony on 12 July, 1916, the Mayor of Carlisle, W. P. Gibbings, in his vote of thanks to Lord Lonsdale, felt it was his duty "for the fair fame of their ancient city to point out that the present condition of affairs was one for which they were in no way responsible. . . They were very jealous for the reputation of their city". He thought, "The Board could rely on the hearty co-operation of the Council and the citizens generally in any steps which they might consider necessary to remove the reproach which had lately rested on it. He would be lacking in his duty if he did not make it quite clear that the necessity had arisen from circumstances over which they had had no control whatever".

On 18 May, 1917, King George V and Queen Mary visited the Gretna Tavern. As the Cumberland News commented the next day: "The city in which a Plantagenet King held Parliament, in which a Stuart Queen was imprisoned; and in which a Pretender to the throne had his headquarters has not been visited by a monarch of the realm for exactly 300 years". The weather for the occasion was not at its best and most of the day's events took place under lowering skies. The royal party arrived by road from the north at 4.45 p.m. and were met by Mr. F. W. Chance, chairman of the Local Advisory Committee; Mr. Waters Butler, member of the Central Control

Board; and Mr. B.C. Sanders, general manager of the Board's Carlisle scheme. Invitations to the ceremony had been extended to 75 Carlisle licensees and about 25 other employees from the Board's offices and brewery. Their majesties saw the tavern under normal working conditions and appeared to have been favourably impressed. "It was," the King remarked to one of the party, "a modern clubhouse for the working man", and the Queen expressed her pleasure that the munition girls were using the tavern.

A variety of problems and decisions were exercising the talents of the Board throughout this early period. Not the least of these was the ever present question of conscription to the armed services. A first Military Service Act in January, 1916, imposed conscription on unmarried men between the ages of 18 and 41 and this was quickly followed in May of the same year by a new military service law extending conscription to all men up to the age of 41. Two examples in August, 1916, illustrate the point quite succinctly. George W. Ellis, painter and decorator, a married man of 37 with three children, appealed for exemption from conscription on the grounds that he was doing government work for the Liquor Control Board. He had been decorating the Gretna Tavern and Redfern had written to the relevant authority saying that his services were of value to the Board. This was at the time that the Gretna Tavern was nearly finished, but there were some alterations pending, and there was soon to be another big job in Castle Street. The appeal was dismissed. The other plea for exemption from military service concerned John Edward Bell, a brick-layer and a married man of 27. Mr. Bell had already been subject to a conditional exemption, but the local tribunal had not been unanimous on the decision as the marriage was only recent. The firm of Messrs J. and R. Bell said that the man was doing very special work for the firm and was, with only one other man, inspecting boilers and flues for most of the important firms in Carlisle. Only vigorous young men could perform this work and the replacement of men in the building trade was now almost impossible. Before the war Messrs. Bell had 153 employees. They were now reduced to between 50 and 60. Of their former employees, 41 had gone into the Army and 88 to the Gretna factory. The appeal was dismissed.

At this same time the Board, which was occupying first floor premises at 28 Castle Street, close beside Tullie House, was seeking more suitable accommodation in which to transact its ever increasing business. The Board was in negotiation to convert 19 Castle Street into offices and notice was duly served on the owner. The building occupied an extensive site stretching back to Fisher Street. It had once been the residence of a Mr. Slater, manufacturer. More recently it had been Devonshire House School for Girls, a private school conducted by a Miss Reynolds. At this time the Board took over the premises of Hope & Bendle, wine and spirit merchants in Lowther Street. The intention was to make it the chief distributing centre for the bottled trade. The premises were just a few yards from the Gretna Tavern and the Board thus acquired a large block of property with an imposing frontage. Negotiations had also been started for the acquisition by agreement of the premises of the unregistered South End Unionist Club in London Road which was situated in a well-populated working-class residential district close to some large engineering works and a railway goods yard. The ground floor was adapted into two large public rooms. One became a dining area with a kitchen and a bar. It was provided with chairs and tables and served alcohol with or without food. The other became a spacious reading room. Food and non-alcoholic drink were served upstairs where long tables were provided. There was also a billiards and recreation room. The house had hot water in the bar, but there was no hot water or bath in the domestic quarters. The tavern opened on 15 November, 1916, but it was found to be too far from the centre of the city to do a large trade in food since the majority of those employed at the neighbouring works and yards lived near at hand and had their meals at home.

A complaint was made to the Board when Carlisle City Council's Health Committee held a special meeting in November, 1916, and passed a resolution in protest against "the Board's attempt to set at defiance, and evade compliance with, the provisions of the Acts of Parliament and bye-laws with respect to public health and good government". The Board was to be requested to discontinue the works in progress until plans of proposed alterations and additions had been submitted for the approval of the committee. It was felt that an important question of principle was involved and the committee was duty-bound to safeguard and maintain whatever legal rights and powers the Corporation possessed in the matter. The Board replied to explain that it was not in a position to compromise the principle of the Crown's immunity from local regulations relating to building. It maintained, however, that it was always prepared to consider representations made by the proper local authority as to buildings in progress or in contemplation.

There was a great urgency in these early years to ensure that the process of reconstruction and reconditioning should proceed with as much speed as possible under the difficult war-time strictures. The Central Control Board exhibited a marked tenacity of purpose in 1916 when it put the improvement of the public house in the forefront of its policy. When it started to abolish the snug and discourage "perpendicular drinking", it was running somewhat in advance of the conservative opinion of the time. These initial prejudices steadily disappeared, and as the years went by the majority of Carlisle consumers became well satisfied with the service generally on offer.

When the First World War broke out public house improvement was in its infancy. An early start had been made by the Public House Trust Companies, and the Trade had conducted experiments in various directions. However, it was the Central Control Board in its unique capacity in Carlisle and District that was able to forge ahead towards significant reform. The Board's work was the subject of visits and investigations by a large number of observers. While its business was always carried out in the limelight of publicity and its management was always liable to be challenged by questions in the House of Commons, there was actually comparatively little Parliamentary criticism over the years.

The Lion and Lamb, an old and poorly constructed public house situated in one of the narrow lanes leading out of Scotch Street in the centre of Carlisle, was closed as licensed premises by the Board in April, 1917. For the convenience of the large number of farmers and others attending the market, the stabling and market room at ground level were retained and the whole building was placed in charge of a resident caretaker. It was a roomy building ad it was decided, at the suggestion of the National

Health Insurance Joint Committee, to utilise the space as committee rooms for meetings by any friendly society or trade union at a small charge per evening. The name of the premises was changed to the Trades Hall and it proved to be a useful facility over the ensuing years.

After the Gretna Tavern the next of the five premises to be reconstructed as food taverns was the Pheasant in Caldewgate. The building work was again carried out by J. & R. Bell. The Pheasant incorporated a former public house and an adjoining property. It was designed to meet the needs of a "poorer class of custom". The ground floor, which was entered directly by two doors leading from Church Street, was arranged for the sale of alcoholic beverages with or without food. This room extended the full width of the building and was served by a comparatively small U-shaped bar. There was a parlour at one end and a partly screened-off dining room at the other. A rest room and writing room lay to the rear. It was situated opposite the large works of Carr's flour mills which employed a considerable number of women. The Board decided to create a special room on the first floor of this public house for the provision of cooked food without intoxicants. A separate side entrance, quite apart from the ground floor bar, was provided in Rigg Street and the Board made this room as bright and cheerful as possible. In addition to this extensive room, with its numerous tables and chairs, there was another room at one end where the girls could rest, read, or write. Redfern is reported as having said at the time that he wanted "to make a pretty room for the girls - a room that would make them happy and bright". The Pheasant was the first serious attempt by the Board to include an off-sales food shop in their reconstructed premises. A shop, where cooked food could be bought and taken away, was opened at ground level on one side of the building with an entrance from Queen Street. Customers could take away jugs of tea, coffee, or cocoa and purchase soup, stew, beef pie, bacon and egg, steamed pudding and plate-cake. All the food was well-cooked in the spacious kitchen on the first floor and was conveyed downstairs by a lift. It was sold at the lowest possible price. Another praiseworthy facet of the Board's policy from these early days and throughout its existence was the provision of proper living accommodation for the manager and his family. At the Pheasant the original manager's house was converted from a cottage into superior accommodation with three bedrooms, one reception room. There was also a garage, and a garden. When all was ready, the Local Advisory Committee decided that there would not be a formal opening for the ground floor area which was opened for business on 26 May, 1917. Instead, the Mayoress was invited to open the first floor reconstruction on 31 May, 1917.

The Albion Tavern in the busy thoroughfare of Botchergate, was opened on 7 June, 1917. It occupied the site of the old Albion and half the site of an adjoining public house, Deakin's Vaults. The remainder of Deakin's Vaults was turned into a shop. The bar was on the ground floor. It consisted of a large open room instead of the four small rooms which existed in the old house, and was furnished with seats, tables and chairs. There was a dining room on the first floor which could be entered by a separate door from the street. It had formerly been a billiard room. The facilities available in the dining room took some little time to become known, but once known, they were very well patronised and the Albion generally did a large trade.

The Pheasant Inn, Caldewgate

Before the advent of the Control Board, the Goliath in Crown Street, a poor part of the city, was patronised largely by coal carters and railway workers. It was notorious as one of the worst houses for factions and brawls. The Board surveyed it in August, 1916, made improvements, and re-opened it in the following December. Development of the food trade was delayed since the shortage of labour meant that the kitchen arrangements were behind schedule. However, a small dining room was provided and the Goliath eventually opened as a food tavern on 18 June, 1917. The dining room was not greatly used at first but the food trade gradually improved.

A queue of children buying lunch at the Food Shop at The Pheasant Inn, Caldewgate, Carlisle in 1933 during the economic depression.

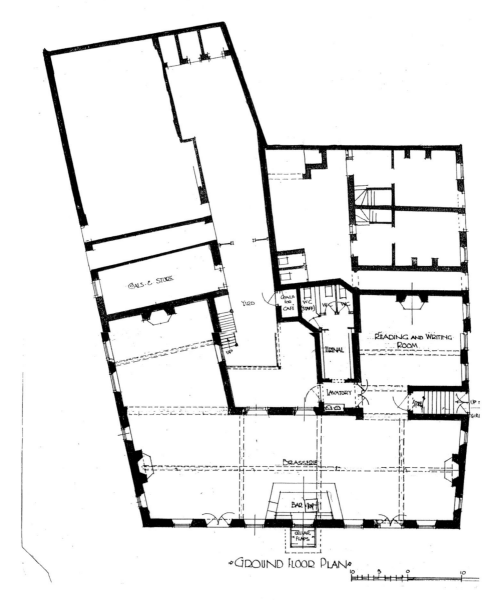

THE PHEASANT INN · CALDEWGATE · CARLISLE ·
· PLANS· SHOWING ALTERATIONS·

COALS·&·STORE

YARD

COALS FOR CAFE

W.C (STAFF)

W.C

W.C

READING AND WRITING ROOM

UP

URINAL

LAVATORY

STORE

UP ↑

GIRL

BRASSERIE

BAR

CELLAR FLAPS

·GROUND FLOOR PLAN·

The Pheasant Inn, Caldewgate. Ground Floor Plan.
Note the Reading and Writing Room and the Brasserie.

70

It was becoming ever more urgent for the Board to bring workmen to Carlisle from other parts of the country to work on the reconstruction schemes. The problem of accommodating them was solved to some extent by converting the malting floor of the disused Iredale's Brewery into dormitories.

The next project to be completed was the Irish Gate Tavern in Annetwell Street close to the Castle. Two older licensed premises near the railway sidings were merged into a single house. They opened for business on 1 October, 1917. The Board's aim at first was to have a large open hall, furnished with tables, chairs and seats, with a small service bar. This arrangement however proved unacceptable to the clientele at the Irish Gate. They preferred a room of moderate size in which to sit with their friends. Drinkers had become accustomed to the long bar on which they could lean and rest their glasses. The original plan was modified and the large open space was divided into sections, each about the size of an ordinary bar parlour and separated by latticed partitions. These afforded a sense of privacy but were easy of supervision by the manager and his assistants. A billiard room led off the bar. An entrance from the street led to a small dining room. The off-sales of food were made from a hatch which communicated directly with the kitchen via a passage leading from the street. No meal cost more than the 1/3d stipulated by the Food Controller.

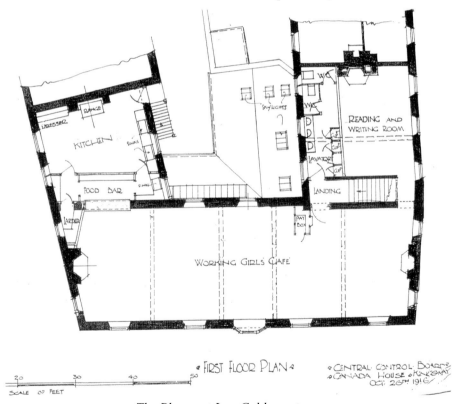

The Pheasant Inn, Caldewgate.
First Floor plan, showing the Working Girls' Cafe, Food Bar and a second
Reading and Writing Room

This house proved exceedingly popular.

The site of the CITADEL Tavern was in the centre of the city and involved the acquisition of two large adjoining public houses, the Three Crowns and the Wellington in English Street. The Board took the opportunity to make better use of the valuable property by converting the frontages into two handsome shops (which readily found tenants at remunerative rentals) and transforming the rear portions into a licensed restaurant. A wide entrance led to the dining room and bar on the ground floor and two rooms of moderate size became restaurants on the first floor. The Citadel was designed to meet the trade usually found in the centre of a large town. Meals here were served at a higher price although they were kept strictly within the rations imposed by the Food Controller. A sample menu for 1917 offered lunch at 1/6d. with a choice of lentil or chicken soup; lamb cutlet or minced steak; college pudding or prunes and rice; biscuits and cheese; tea or coffee. Dinner at 2/6d offered a more sophisticated menu of kidney or julienne soup; fillet of haddock; timbales of chicken or roast lamb; college pudding or French sago pudding; biscuits and cheese; tea or coffee.

However, yet again, all was not sweetness and light for the Board. On 20 November, 1917, the Carlisle Journal printed the contents of a letter from the Hon. R. D. Denman to Mr. Kellaway who represented the Control Board in the House of Commons. The letter deplored the Board's entry into the high class refreshment business. It declared that, "It has no substantial relation to the real objects of the Board, which is the control of liquor or the supply of solid refreshments to munition workers. The table d'hote meals offered by the Citadel restaurant are appropriate to, and consumed by professional, business. and well-to-do classes. I have no objection

The interior of one of the Scheme's restaurants. The Hon. R.D. Denman, M.P., felt the provision of "table d'hote meals" had no relation to the objects of the Board. (Courtesy of Tassell Carlisle Ltd.)

to the state deliberately undertaking an enterprise of this character though it is absurd that it should be done in the name of temperance or the welfare of munition workers".

To this early phase of the improvement programme of public houses in Carlise should be added the Joiners' Arms in Caldewgate. The Joiners' was first surveyed in December, 1916, and was reconstructed and re-opened for business on 22 October, 1918. It had been a low, ramshackle house in a bad state of repair and was immediately adjoining another public house in a similar condition. This last house, the Queen's Head, was closed on the re-opening of the Joiners' Arms. It was not turned into a food tavern as it faced the Pheasant Tavern and there would have been insufficient custom to satisfy both houses.

In March, 1916, the Board had decided to take over control of all the licensed premises in the Gretna area. It purchased all the houses in the burgh of Annan and in the villages of Springfield and Kirkpatrick Fleming. In July the houses in Ecclefechan, Kirtlebridge, Canonbie, and Powfoot were added to the Board's holdings. Annan contained three hotels, six public houses and six licensed grocers shops. The Board at once abolished all the grocers' licenses and confined the sale of beer and spirits to just one shop in which the sale of other goods was discontinued. Only one public house was used for off sales. The owners of the extinguished licenses received compensation. In June the sale of spirits was discontinued completely in Springfield and Kirkpatrick Fleming. Soon after the acquisition of the Annan houses, the number of labourers lodging in hostels in the burgh increased rapidly so that by July, 1916, the total had risen from 460 to just over 1,000. There was a further 500 men in private accommodation. With 1,000 extra men joining the normal population of 5,200, the potential drinkers had increased by about 150 per cent. At weekends the figure would have been considerably higher. The congestion in the hotels and public houses presented a serious problem and it became necessary to regulate admission. The doors were closed as soon as the house was full and fresh customers were only admitted as others left. It was a constant complaint that drinkers had been unable to get refreshment at all on a Saturday evening.

Owing to the congestion in every house, it was unthinkable that any one of them could be closed for alterations or enlargements. The Board decided to build an entirely new public house, and that food and non-intoxicants should form part of its provision. This new tavern in Annan, known as Gracie's Banking, was opened to the public in November, 1916, and two of the old houses, the Alexandra and the Albert were closed at the same time. Harry Redfern, the Board's chief architect, was prevented from being present at the opening by other duties, but George Walton and Basil Oliver were both able to attend. It was the intention of the management that the tavern should run as much in the nature of a club as possible, but local sentiment was quick to point out that an experiment in liquor control in Scotland which leaves out spirits is only half an experiment. In Scotland in cold, inclement weather the men, especially the older men of ingrained habits, would want to order spirits in preference to beer even if the beer was offered in more attractive and comfortable surroundings. It was decided from the outset however that beer and wines only would be sold in Gracie's Banking - with no spirits - and no stand-up bar.

The L-shaped, one-storey building with a verandah was designed on graceful lines using timber on a brick base with an exterior colour scheme of black and white and an interior scheme of green and white. The main building containing the restaurant, beer hall, and billiard room was 160 feet long. It was partitioned off with glass screens to give a capacity of 300 in the beer hall and 100 in the restaurant. A cinema, accommodating 300, stood at right angles to the main building. It enjoyed an enclosed verandah so that it was able to be used as an auxiliary tea-room for 40 persons. Admission prices were 6 pence and 9 pence. The tavern stayed open all day until 9 p.m., the cinema was open until 10 p.m. There was also a balcony at the far end of the main building fronted with white, ornamented woodwork, which could also be used as a tea-room and could accommodate a modest sized orchestra. The kitchens and scullery were fitted in the most modern fashion and a hot plate was provided under the counter next to the restaurant. Redfern, in his customary style, did not neglect to provide satisfactory lavatory accommodation. The beer hall which adjoined the restaurant was a handsome room, cosily furnished and with a bar running almost the length of its wall. At first it was intended that it should be an open bar with the usual counter, but on reconsideration the bar room was completely detached from the beer hall by a partition fitted with numerous sliding panels. From here the waitresses in their blue and white check dresses and white aprons and mob caps would serve any liquor required while the customers remained seated. There were twelve assistants on the payroll in the bar and restaurant. With the cooking and general kitchen staff, there was a complement of 30 staff overall. At the far end of the beer hall were two full-sized billiard tables and, with dominoes, draughts, and chess in constant use, according to the general manager's fourth report, there was practically no drinking in the billiard room. The immaturity of the turf at first restricted the use of the bowling green but the two pitches for quoits were in great demand from the first. A Post Office official would attend the premises on Fridays and Saturdays in order to run a savings bank, attend to registered mail, and sell stamps, and a pillar box had been provided on the verandah outside.

Gracie's Banking had been designed primarily for the navvy population. When they left the area the interior was re-arranged by moving the partitions and extending the billiard hall and restaurant at the expense of the beer hall which, being reduced in size, became more comfortable and homely. The plan of this tavern, built at the back of the main road on an acre of land which was once an auction mart, illustrates clearly the principles on which the Board had embarked. The drinking facilities had been placed in the background. They could only be reached after passing through grounds and premises devoted to recreational activities.

As a postscript to the developments at Gracie's Banking the provosts of the other districts, having found the results so satisfactory, asked the Control Board to extend state purchase to the whole county of Dumfriesshire. The fact that this request was not acted upon by the Board rather proves the point that liquor control was inaugurated primarily in those areas where there was a pressing need for war-time efficiency.

On 21 June, 1917, a few days after the Goliath in Carlisle had extended its business as a food tavern Lord D'Abernon opened the Globe Tavern in Longtown.

This tavern was built on the site of the outbuildings and stables of the old Globe Inn which in turn was converted into shop premises. The new building was a handsome structure of local red sandstone. It consisted of three main rooms. The beer hall and refreshment room stood at right-angles to each other with the kitchen and bars for drink and food occupying a space at the angle. Over the kitchen was an attractively appointed room for reading and writing. Over the refreshment room was a billiard hall with a modern new table. The beer hall contained four open fireplaces with inglenooks and being the principal room was large enough to be used for meetings or entertainments. The gallery over one end of the hall sported a decent piano, and settles were placed back to back along the side walls with tables and wheelback chairs placed between. Adjoining the large hall was the dining room which had a separate entrance from the street. Ample kitchen accommodation had been provided. There was a steady trade in food including afternoon teas and a considerable custom for off sales. A small bowling green was laid outside. The opening of the Globe Tavern with its ample accommodation made it possible to dispense with three other public houses in Longtown which were closed at approximately the same date.

Redfern was praised for his planning skills and good taste. A Times correspondent found the Globe an ideal building fit for its purpose - simple and practical, yet extraordinarily tasteful and attractive. In his speech at the opening ceremony Lord D'Abernon reminded his audience that the establishment of Government wartime works had given rise to local liquor problems of extreme difficulty for which the ordinary machinery of control was confessedly inadequate. Gradually, however, experience was showing that it was possible to reorganise the trade in liquor without causing public friction or inconvenience. On the whole he thought people were prepared to give the experiment a fair trial. All the Board asked for was patience.

The Board's newest venture was on a smaller scale and somewhat unusual in character. It involved the conversion of the village reading room at Rockcliffe, which was about four miles from Carlisle in the direction of Gretna. The old Ship Inn had been closed some months previously in December, 1916, and the accommodation at the Crown and Thistle was not considered satisfactory for development. Consequently, when the village reading room was offered on a lease of seven years at a nominal rent by the widow of the local squire, the late Mounsey-Heysham of Castleford, the Board was pleased to accept. The Crown and Thistle was closed. Its licensee, Mrs Waller, was appointed as manageress of the new premises to be known as the Mounsey Arms. Only a few structural alterations were needed which, together with refurnishing from stock, incurred little expense. The premises comprised one large room with an inherited billiard table and a piano provided by the Board. The small extant library was retained and the usual games, newspapers and periodicals were provided. The smaller room was reserved for non-intoxicants during the day but beer and porter were available during permitted hours in the evenings. The opening ceremony was carried out on behalf of Mrs Mounsey-Heysham by her daughter on 24 August, 1917. By the following February the Board's general manager, Edgar C. Sanders, was already questioning whether such an innovation in the style of a village public house would be a success. The closing of Rockcliffe station on the Caledonian Railway as a wartime economy measure and the absence of the young men of the district on military service was already having a prejudicial effect on its viability. However, it was felt that it was only by trying experiments of this nature that light would be thrown on the subject of the improved public house for which Bills had already been presented to the House of Lords on Public House Improvement by Lord Lamington as long ago as 1909 and 1911. Others followed in 1918 and 1919. Bills had also been presented to the House of Commons by Mr (later Sir) W. Rutherford in 1908, 1910, 1911 and there was a later one in 1919.

In the course of taking over the licensed premises in the controlled area the Board had also acquired a number of hotels as distinct from the ordinary public house or inn. These were placed under the direct management of the Board but no change was made in their status except by way of redecoration, furnishing, and equipment. Among these were the Crown at Wetheral, a popular fishing hotel on the river Eden; the Victoria in Carlisle, a commercial hotel close to the railway station; and, in 1919, the Red Lion, also close to the station; the Solway at Silloth, always well patronized because of its proximity to the golf course; the Marine, a first class residential hotel at Skinburness; and the Waverley at Silloth. The Golden Lion at Maryport and the Grapes at Aspatria had both been in decline and were both redecorated. The Kildare at Wigton was in a different category since the old posting hotel, the King's Arms, was in a very poor condition and had not been conducted as a residential hotel for some time. It would have involved a lot of expense to make it fit for its former use and the Board decided to look elsewhere. It was fortunate in finding, and being able to purchase at a reasonable price, a house which had been constructed for use as a club, and this suited the Board's outlook to perfection. It was then handsomely furnished and equipped by the Board and stood comparison with any principal hotel in a small country town.

Overall, there was still much to be done generally by way of structural improvements especially in the country districts but this was going to have to wait until the scarcity of labour and materials became less marked and the dreadful, draining war was at an end. When the announcement was made on the 11 November, 1918, that an armistice had been concluded with Germany, it came as a surprise to the nation. The struggle for victory had been so arduous and protracted and the nation was, by this time, desperately weary and sorrowful. Hardly a family in the land had been left untouched by events, and the numbers of dead and wounded had been terrible to contemplate, - three quarters of a million had died and nearly two million more had been wounded. As if all this was not enough to bear, the blind waste and brutality of the war was compounded by a particularly virulent type of influenza which swept across the country and peaked a week before the armistice. The final wave of the epidemic subsided in February, 1919. Byy that time the national figure of deaths had totalled 151,446 of which 140,989 were civilians. Once the armistice had been declared, Parliament was dissolved on 25 November, 1918, and an election - the "stampede election" - was called for the 14 December. The speed with which it was called meant that only about a quarter of servicemen were able to vote, even though counting was delayed until after Christmas, and, in consequence, 107 seats remained uncontested. The Representation of the People Act of February, 1918, had given the vote to all women householders and wives of householders over the age of 30. When the election was called at the end of 1918 the electorate had increased from the pre-war number of about eight-and-a-half million to over 20 million. As a result, almost as many women were entitled to vote now as comprised the whole electorate before the Act was passed. To augment this development a further Act was rushed through Parliament in November, 1918, making women eligible to stand for Parliament.

Lloyd George decided to fight the election in partnership with members of the war-time coalition. Labour members wanted none of this and seized the opportunity that the women's vote offered them. They decided to withdraw from the Government and fight the election as a separate unit. Lloyd George and Bonar Law issued their joint manifesto on 22 November, 1918, intent upon getting the nation back to some degree of normality. This was to include a "proper adaptation to peace conditions of the experience which during the war we have gained in regard to the traffic in drink". Reconstruction was to become the buzz word of the day, but a hard battle was going to have to be fought against the industrial dislocation which had taken place. It was not a question of rebuilding a society as it had been before the war, but of moulding a better world out of the social and economic conditions which had come into being during the war. "The war has brought a transformation of the social and administrative structure of the State, much of which is bound to be permanent". (Report of the War Cabinet 1918. Cmd 325 pp 214/5).

CHAPTER FIVE
AFTER THE WAR

If the war had brought a transformation of the social and administrative structure of the state, the coalition government which emerged from the 1918 election was far from being a homogeneous entity yet it had to contend with the aftermath of a devastating war. In November, 1918, it was agreed that the Control Board's policy should be maintained for the period of the armistice and for one year following. Already the Treasury felt constrained to warn the Board of the need for financial retrenchment (PRO T/112) and it refused permission for the purchase of two hotels in Carlisle, "having regard to the general financial position and to the present state of uncertainty as to the future of the Central Control Board" (PRO T/147). For the time being at any rate, reconstruction was of necessity, going to have to give way to retrenchment.

Nevertheless, there was one area of progress which was by this time unstoppable. Without doubt the war had brought into play a new situation for women and an era had begun which was to change significantly the mores of their society for the future. When, at the beginning of the war, Lloyd George had realised that only 15 per cent of the country's factories were working night shifts, and that, in order to overcome the munitions crisis, work had to be continuous, he decided in October, 1915, to introduce a programme of "dilution". In essence this programme stipulated that in any trade for which there was a shortage of manpower, the deficiency was to be made good with the labour of soldiers invalided home, men unfit or over age for military service, and women and juveniles, all of whom were to be known as "dilutees". It was this crusade for munitions which indirectly improved the lot of women for the foreseeable future. Emmeline Pankhurst had led a demonstration of 30,000 women in July, 1915, to demand of the Minister of Munitions, not this time the right to vote, but the right to serve. In the Munitions of War (Amendment) Act of 1916, the Minister was given the power to control not only the wages of the dilutees but also their conditions of work. A new welfare section of the labour department was created, with B. Seebohm Rowntree at its head, to steer a course which would merge the old Liberal tenets of social reform with the more recent principles of state control. The dilution programme had given women the opportunity to prove their worth in many fields which were new and challenging for them. As a result they had been able to demonstrate to society that they were quite capable of handling responsibility in a spirit of self-reliance and dependability. When the war ended few of them had any desire to return entirely to the roles that had been allocated to them prior to 1914.

The Ministry of Munitions had taken care to provide temporary hostels for its female dilutees. They were watched over by government welfare supervisors who were responsible for investigating complaints and keeping an eye on the condition of canteens, dining areas, and lavatory accommodation in the factories as well as organising nurseries for working mothers. The Women's Police Service was also formed during the war, and when production began at Gretna in 1916 the WPS was employed by the Ministry of Munitions to police the girls working in the factory. A grant of £850 was received from the government, but this had to be augmented with donations. By June, 1918, there were 167 WPS members employed at Gretna. This was, at the time, the largest force of police women in Britain. Their duties at the factory included checking all passes and searching for any hazardous materials such as hairpins, matches and cigarettes. They were expected to keep a lookout for any "slackers or shirkers" and would patrol the streets and parks and watch the hostels for any potential immoral behaviour. It was also their duty to meet girls arriving at the railway stations and to see that they used the "women only" compartments when departing.

The ground for women's advancement in society was already being prepared before the onset of war. One of the country's most colourful and determined feminists was Rosalind, Countess of Carlisle of Naworth Castle and of Castle Howard in Yorkshire. (Naworth is eleven miles east of Carlisle and two miles from the small town of Brampton) Known as the Radical Countess, Rosalind was a dedicated liberal and a social reformer of extraordinary dynamism who worked continuously for temperance and women's suffrage. Born in 1845 she was the daughter of the second Baron Stanley of Alderley. In 1864 she married George James Howard, a descendant of one of the great Whig families of England who inherited the title of ninth Earl of Carlisle in 1889. Rosalind campaigned for her husband when he was elected unopposed as Liberal M.P. for East Cumberland in 1879 and re-elected in 1881. It was in that same year, when she had already given birth to eight of their eleven children. that she began her temperance work in Cumberland. Temperance reformers had at all times been concerned with the sufferings of women, and through them of their children. They had tried to lure husbands away from the sanctuary of the public house and encourage them back to their own domestic quarters. But such was the economic situation of the working classes in nineteenth century Britain that it would have been well nigh impossible for many of them to have had the resources to provide a comfortable and pleasant home environment. In a public house the men could at least find a kind of collective camaraderie with the opportunity to air their grievances. Victorian women, on the other hand, had far less chance of airing their grievances in public for fear of shaming their menfolk on whom they were economically dependent and subject to their authority. Women were expected to accept their lot without complaining and the temperance movement was well aware of this. It started to rectify the exclusion of women from discussions on social issues by inviting some articulate women onto its platforms. The very act of joining a teetotal society was for many women an early, if modest, form of feminism.

A certain mixture of intellectualism and eccentricity had existed in the teetotal leadership through the years and some of this was reflected in Rosalind's own resolute adherence to the notion of prohibition. In 1883 she took over a small public house in Brampton on a seven year lease to turn it into a working man's coffee-house. She knew it was not going to pay its way, but she was not prepared to extend unduly the power of the state. She would have nothing to do with the notion of disinterested management or nationalisation of the liquor trade. She wanted the power to be placed in the people to protect themselves from the greed of publicans. Such views were endorsed by the secretary of the Boilermakers' and Iron Shipbuilders' Society speaking at the National Prohibition Convention in Newcastle-upon-Tyne in April, 1897. He stated that self-reform was the most needful and practical solution to the drink problem: "It works automatically; the mind supplies the motive-power, there being no complex State machinery required to put it into operation, and its effects are immediate". And what was the Central Control Board's motto on its badge designed by Voysey? . . . SE-COERCERE! To restrain or control oneself.

When Waldorf Astor became a viscount in 1919, his wife Nancy campaigned for his vacated seat in the House of Commons and was returned by the working class constituency of Plymouth with an overwhelming majority. She was the country's first ever woman M.P. and during her 25 years in office she worked untiringly for women's rights, world peace, and prohibition. She chose "Temperance and State Purchase of the Liquor Traffic" as the subject of her maiden speech in the House on 24 February, 1920, on the motion of Sir J.D. Rees against the continuance of the Central Control Board in time of peace. She clearly understood that in the new postwar society politics was indeed coming into the home, and home matters were to be the proper concern of politics. . . so where better to start than with the liquor trade? The House was crowded and listened to her speech with the keenest attention. Speaking in Manchester a month before making her maiden speech Lady Astor had made her position on the drink question quite clear when she told her audience that she didn't trust any man where drink was concerned. Reform would/could not come from men but it must come through women, and if the country did not get State purchase it would be because the Prime Minister, the Cabinet, and the House of Commons were afraid of the Trade.

In the early post-war years the Government had been confronted and preoccupied with two important matters, foreign affairs and reconstruction, and as part of the reconstruction programme the future regulation of the traffic in intoxicating liquor was unavoidable in the circumstances. Licensing arrangements were in suspense and the emergency regulations of the Defence of the Realm Act 1915 would need to be modified or in some instances revoked. The authority and powers of the Central Control Board would automatically expire within twelve months of the armistice and all extant regulations and restrictions would lapse failing new legislation from the government. Declaring an armistice on 11 November, 1918, was one matter, but the official termination of the war could only be ratified when the Peace Treaty with Turkey had been signed and this could be delayed for some time pending negotiations with Greece. State purchase had been an emergency measure in Britain's licensing history when the CCB had possessed the power to act with sole regard for the well-being of the public without the hindrance of private interests. Would the permanent transfer of power from the trade to the state to control the traffic in drink result in a progressive advancement to sensible drinking? The Board had always maintained that control was impossible without ownership because ownership determined management and management determined results. In addition, the elimination of private profit through the establishment of state control would possibly effect a divorce between politics and the drink trade. No action was taken during the first three months of the armistice and licensing arrangements were left in suspense, but the wartime emergency regulations brought in under DORA were going to have to be revoked or modified within twelve months when the authority and powers of the CCB automatically expired.

The experience of the wartime liquor control measures had created an opportunity which was unique in the country's history, and Carlisle had held its own unique niche in this history by setting new standards and pointing the way to a better future. The years from 1919 to 1921 were going to be crucial for the government in the task of forming new legislation which would appeal to general opinion and contain the promise of progressive advancement. The controls imposed by the Board and the objective manner in which they had been introduced were generally accepted even by the working classes who were most affected by them. Any grievances which had arisen over drink had been more concerned with the lower gravity and short supply which had been the consequences of the Food Controller's edicts. As long ago as 26 August, 1916, an editorial in the Cumberland News, stated that: "The selection of Carlisle for this vast experiment in nationalisation is in many ways unfortunate because it is being made in abnormal times on an abnormal population. . . but the selection having been made it is the duty of all citizens to give the Board a fair field and not to judge them hastily". By 1919 much of the heat had been taken out of the drink question nationally and it was unlikely to rouse such political storms as it had done in the nineteenth century.

Nevertheless, the war was no sooner over than a general clamour broke out fuelled by the trade and the newspapers against the restrictions and control which had been borne for the duration but, according to its critics had been disliked. The complaints came from different quarters. They were inspired by different motives but focussed mainly upon wanting to see the end of the Control Board to which was attributed the bulk of the unpopular measures. What many of the newspapers failed to distinguish was the parts played by the Treasury and the Food Controller, as well as the Board, in the restraints imposed upon the trade. Lord D'Abernon, chairman of the Central Control Board, writing a preface to Henry Carter's book, "The Control of the Drink Trade", 1917, pointed out that no scheme for the future regulation of the liquor traffic would be satisfactory to public opinion at large unless it failed to maintain the current level of temperance and ensure that the nation did not relapse to the level of alcoholic excess which prevailed before the war. In a postscript added eighteen months later in April, 1919, he posed the essential question: Can alcohol be controlled or not? To which he himself declared that it depended upon the good sense of the public and the wisdom of parliament, and that in order that the modifications and adjustments to suit the conditions of peace might be properly effected, a new departure would have to be made and a new commission issued. A return to prewar conditions could not be contemplated with equanimity. Already in the early stages of the peace, voices were being heard urging the politicians that any future organisation for the control of the traffic in liquor must be answerable to Parliament.

On 26 October, 1916, during the debate in the House of Commons, Colonel Gretton, Conservative M.P. for Rutland (1895- 1943) and member of the brewing firm Bass, Ratcliffe, and Gretton, had moved the important motion: "That in the opinion of this House, the Central Control Board (Liquor Traffic) should no longer be independent of the control of Parliament and that its proceedings and expenditure should be made subject to the control of a minister responsible to Parliament. The House was never told that the Government intended to set up a Board which was independent of the control of Parliament. . . and has unknowingly surrendered to this independent Board complete powers which are exercised so drastically over so wide an area. . . . The Board at the present moment is going far outside what was intended by Parliament when the Act (1915) was passed and Parliament never realised that the Board intended to purchase licensed property over a complete area and it never realised that the Board intended to acquire breweries as well as licensed properties, and to effect control at the national expense over an area so large as Carlisle. . . Where do the Treasury get the money? There is no vote in Parliament. They can only get money out of the Vote of Credit which is voted by Parliament for the conduct of the War and not for the purchase of private property in this country. . . Whether the proceedings of the Control Board are good or bad they should be under the control of Parliament and the Government have no right and are exceeding their duty when they hand over the uncontrolled expenditure of public money in this way to this body". In reply the Minister of Munitions, Edwin Montagu, informed the House that, "Members of the Control Board have laboured so ungrudgingly without remuneration on work which is unpopular. . . The Treasury controls the expenditure. The Ministry of Munitions defrays the expenditure out of the Vote of Credit, and the Vote of Credit bears upon its face the statement that it is applied to given purposes. . . Through the Vote of Credit, through the Treasury and through the Ministry of Munitions there is ample control in regard to the Control Board - more than was contemplated by this House when the Bill was passed. . . we deliberately made this Board independent of Parliament so that it might act quickly". It was felt that under the current circumstances the Board should be independent of the daily cross-currents and influences which existed in the House and the constituencies, and that it should not be subject to daily interference. The Minister then informed the House that: "At the time the Liquor Control Board was set up we agreed that it was not to apply to Ireland until a Member representing Ireland was added to the Board, and no such member has been added to the Board". (Hansard VoLLXXXVl col. 1363 - 1406).

In May 1917 a proposed Bill was being debated which would include a clause extending the area under the Liquor Control Board so as to cover the whole of the United Kingdom. The War Cabinet met prior to the discussion to take place next day in the House of Commons. It was decided that: subject to his approval, a definite statement should be made by the Prime Minister announcing that the Government had decided in favour of the State Purchase of the Liquor Trade. lt was felt to be of great importance that the statement should provide an indicator of the Government's policy as a whole so that the qualifications with regard to local option and prohibition might be made known at the same time. The Chief Secretary for Ireland and the Minister of Munitions were instructed to take part in the debate. (PRO HO 185/266). A strong case for this suggestion was submitted in a memorandum by Thomas O'Donnell, M.P. in which he said: "The drink traffic as it exists in Ireland today is one of the most serious hindrances to national progress. To lessen its ravages, to confine and limit its evil influence in the manner suggested in the alternative scheme would be such a great national blessing that nothing should be done which could even remotely arouse fears of injustice, or unfair treatment in the minds of the publicans. The human wrecks, physical and moral which one sees in our cities and towns; the ruined homes; the squalor, poverty and decay; the neglected, underfed and diseased children, all present a spectacle calling for immediate and radical treatment by a drastic extinction of small, badly kept, isolated and remote public houses, and by a proper supervision and management of those that remain. To achieve any great reform we must carry public conscience with us". An immediate response came from John Curry, chairman of the Irish Licensed Trade in a telegram to Lord Milner: "View with alarm the proposal of State Control. Unsuitable to Irish Licensed Trade interests. While ready to consider any reasonable scheme of State Purchase we will not under any circumstances agree to any form of State Control of Liquor Trade for Ireland. Controlling our own business should be left in the hands of an assembly of Irishmen and we claim exemption from any scheme brought forward for State Control". An equally vociferous reaction was received from Scotland albeit from a somewhat different perspective. It pointed out that: "Any measure which deprived the localities of the powers of 'local option' won for them under the Act of 1913 (Scottish Local Veto Act known as the Temperance (Scotland) Act) would be a public wrong. If drink businesses were set up in localities from which the direct veto of the people had excluded them, there would be added a great cause of social irritation. 'Purchase' to block 'Prohibition' would be widely, vehemently, and properly resented". The argument went on to point out that: "The Trade in Scotland is highly organised and its interests in Scotland which appear to be amply equipped with means, are defended with vigilance and vigour and with great ability. . . There is a personal and sympathetic feeling towards members of the Trade". It was felt that if their influence was taken away the vote would veer more towards prohibition and it would follow then that State Purchase would hasten prohibition, and prohibition was not within the realm of practical politics.

Countless opinions surfaced during the immediate postwar period as to the future of the liquor trade. These were given ample coverage in the national newspapers. Sir Edgar Sanders, general manager of the Carlisle undertaking in a letter to Arthur Sherwell, M.P. in March, 1919, forecast that, as it appeared to him, "The financial part of it at the present moment is of most weight as I think we have shown that the profits, due chiefly to concentration, are sufficient not only to put the trade on an entirely different footing but to return to the State a very handsome profit as well as to repay the capital cost in a comparatively short period". There followed a meeting of the Carlisle Advisory Committee of the Control Board in August when they passed a resolution to the effect that having regard to the improvement in the conditions in the Carlisle district under which every branch of the licensed liquor trade was carried on with advantages to the public in increased sobriety, the Board be asked to urge upon the Government that whatever course was to be taken on the licensing question generally, the system of State Management in the Carlisle area be maintained with adequate powers to complete and continue the work. When Lloyd

George in 1915 had asked for a feasibility study to be made for a scheme of nationalisation of the liquor trade for the whole country, Labour had withheld its approval, but by 1919 it was in a very different frame of mind. A Trades Union Conference on State Purchase was convened by the Carlisle Trades and Labour Council in November, 1919, which was attended by J.H. Thomas, M.P., President and Arthur Greenwood, M.P., Acting Secretary to the Labour Party Committee in favour of State Ownership and Control. A resolution was passed by 274 votes to one, urging the government to continue and extend the Scheme to the whole country. Mr. Thomas had said that at such an important time in the nation's history if we wanted a thinking nation, it was essential that we had a sober nation.

It is often assumed that members of the brewing industry were unanimous in opposing any scheme of state purchase. The chairman of the large Birmingham brewery Mitchells & Butlers was also a member of the Control Board. Speaking to a representative of the Westminster Gazette in October, 1919, William Waters Butler declared quite openly that he supported state purchase in the conviction that the state alone could carry out what was necessary for the public's needs and afford to give adequate compensation to the dispossessed. He thought it a pretension to think that the Trade alone could put to rights the abuses and the evasions of the law that creep into management, and with the best will in the world it is powerless to do so as long as the competitive element remains and the trade rests in private hands. "As things stand, the Trade cannot abolish competition without abolishing itself, and with rare exceptions the Trade does not really want to return to the prewar position. Large profits have undoubtedly been made during the war but the future is full of uncertainty and taxation is not likely to be reduced. Improvements requiring a heavy outlay are demanded by the public and if the Trade is unable to reach the new standard of public taste, the consequent outcry will add heavily to the forces in favour of prohibition. A fair scheme of State Purchase would be best for the community and best for the trader". A letter to the Times (22. 9. 1919) from the Secretary of the Brewers' Society, P.C. Morgan, reinforced the opinion that, "A return to the old conditions was out of the question and nobody was more anxious than the brewers to bring about improvement, but improvement of the public house environment was practically impossible to carry out at the present time. The licensed trade itself had therefore formulated proposals for amending the existing licensing law and its administration, and since the Government was preparing a Bill for the setting up of a Commission to carry on certain of the duties of the Control Board it was regrettable that the requests of the licensed trade to be included in the consultation process had been refused".

Owing to the war situation which had extended over the past four years there had been a general lack of knowledge nationally of the true importance of the work of the C.C.B. in Carlisle and district which had served as a testing ground for the totally new concept of the state working in direct competition with private enterprise. Once the government had purchased the public houses and the breweries, a unique economic unit had been formed which was responsible for brewing its own beer as well as supplying it, and when the war was over the government had to decide whether this unusual wartime measure was capable of being extended into peacetime conditions - and if not, how it was to be unscrambled. There was a strong case being made from many quarters that the future of the trade should be regularised and brought under Parliamentary control and for statutory law to take the place of the arbitrary system of administrative orders as existing. . . that whatever restrictions might be imposed in the future they ought to be embodied in an Act of Parliament. On 13 December, 1919, Lord D'Abernon, chairman of the Central Control Board tended his resignation to the Prime Minister. His letter ran as follows: "Since the termination of active hostilities I have been anxious to see the work of the Central Control Board brought to a close and a new authority established to take up the work of Liquor Control. The Central Control Board was essentially a war-time body, but I have found myself in full agreement with the view which you impressed upon the House of Commons in 1915, that the Board and its regulations could not wisely be done away with until Parliament had had an adequate opportunity of considering the question of the peace-time regulation of the liquor trade. I have, therefore, while urging on general grounds that there should be no avoidable delay in settling this question continued my work as Chairman of the Board. It is now clear, however, that no Bill setting up a new Authority can be introduced before February or March, and none will probably be passed before July. After some four and a half years service in the front line, I do not see my way to carry on for so long a period. Under present conditions the Board is compelled, if I may say so, merely to tread water, an unsatisfactory task, which offers no scope for initiative and which is essentially different from the war emergency control which I undertook. I am anxious to assist His Majesty's Government in this matter to the utmost, but it may well be that any help I can give in the vital task of establishing a satisfactory basis for future progress will be more effective if I am in a position of complete freedom and detachment. I shall therefore be glad if I can be relieved of my present responsibility at an early moment". (PRO HO185/231). Lord D'Abernon was not replaced and this would seem to have indicated the eventual demise of the Control Board after it had lingered on for another two years.

As time went by critics of the Board were striving to spread disenchantment with the scheme. Even North Cumberland's own M.P., Major Christopher Lowther, told the House of Commons that the great majority of his constituents with whom he had spoken regarded the experiment as exceedingly vexatious, unnecessary and tyrannical. One clear objection which he voiced was that it was a case of State trading, added to which, whatever rules, orders, or legislation may be adopted they should be the same for Carlisle and North Cumberland as for the rest of the country. Replying for the government the President of the Board of Education, H.A.L. Fisher said it would be unwise and improper to terminate the Board's existence suddenly and without due consideration before a measure had been introduced embodying the experience already gained. In August, 1920, the Times carried a thoughtful article under the heading, "Future legislations critical period". The general purport was that a licensing bill was long overdue and no-one wished to return wholly to prewar conditions, but the abolition of the Central Control Board would presuppose a return to prewar conditions. There must therefore be an act to make permanent those wartime regulations which could be applicable in normal times to the advantage of all. The article continued by declaring that such proposals as local veto and prohibition were alien to the principles of a liberty-loving people and that supporters of prohibition fully realised that the country would not knowingly accept it and did not intend to put it to the test. The general manager, Edgar Sanders, in his report of March, 1919, had already indicated that, "Although the trend of local opinion cannot be diagnosed with complete accuracy, it appears incontrovertible that any proposal to hand back the licensed trade to private interests would be received with dismay by the great majority of the inhabitants. There have been put into operation most of the generally accepted temperance proposals made during the last half-century and this has been done without any sacrifice of the reasonable rights and privileges of the community and without undue interference with the liberty, tastes and preferences of the majority of the adult population. It has been done too, not only without financial loss, but with a very substantial margin of profit". An invitation had been extended to Sir Edgar Sanders to speak to members of the House of Commons on Wednesday, 25 February, 1920, on the results of State Management of the Liquor Traffic in the Carlisle area - an invitation which was readily accepted but which carried a request that no press be present.

This was followed later, on 17 March, by a letter from Sir Edgar to the Rt. Hon. Neville Chamberlain, M.P., hoping that he could enlist the M.P's influence in the direction of a prompt extension of the State Purchase experiment. The letter stated that: "It appears to me that among reasonable people the feeling is growing that State Purchase offers the most equitable and promising solution of the licensing problem. There are however four strong parties opposing it today: those who believe that the State in its present financial position cannot face the pledging of the country's credit to the extent which State purchasers a policy for the whole country would involve: brewers and licensed victuallers: a portion of the Liberal party who would impose such restrictions coupled with local veto as would alienate the sympathy of large sections of the public as being unjust: and that section of the Temperance party for whom prohibition is the only goal in sight. . . The Carlisle experiment while not being a large enough scheme on which to base a national policy, does demonstrate the desirability of having one or two additional and large areas, with say about 3,000 licences in each in order to form a sounder judgement. . . the government should, in their licensing Bill, definitely legislate for this and schedule one or two such areas. This may be considered an unnecessary complication but knowing as I do the bitter controversies which are engendered whenever any licensing proposals are brought up, it seems to me that it would be more satisfactory to have one severe fight and not invite further controversy if and when areas should be selected at a later date. . . Profits of the brewing trade reached high water mark last autumn but owing to the retail price being fixed and the continuous rise in wages and materials, profits are steadily falling. If the fall continues for much longer the postwar profits will soon be on a par with those earned before the war. Brewers already know this - licensed victuallers hardly recognise it at present. . . Carlisle has been fortunate in sharing in the three years of great trade prosperity which it is obvious is now passing away. . . I view with considerable uneasiness the latest battle cry of the trade against a continuation of the Carlisle experiment. After endeavouring to discount its success by so

SMS Rum. This liquor could not be bought on Saturdays for a period after the First World War. (Courtesy Tullie House Museum)

many arguments which have been falsified they now say that it is degrading for Carlisle to be singled out for exceptional treatment when the war is over. If Parliament would say definitely that it is sufficiently satisfied with the results at Carlisle to try similar and extended experiments elsewhere, it would help our position here very much". (PRO HO 190/865).

It is interesting to note that three months later an experiment in a reformed public house, somewhat on the lines of a fusion between the Carlisle system and the Birmingham "surrender" plan, was authorised by the Hull magistrates. The Hull Brewery Company agreed to surrender four licences in the central part of the city and build a new inn known as the Polar Bear, Springbank, with a large cafe capable of accommodating a light orchestra and selling coffee and light refreshments as well as liquor. If successful, it was deemed possible that an extension of the principle might be considered.

A letter to the Times in November, 1919, from the chairman of the Brewers' Society, W. Sykes, and the chairman of the National Trade Defence Association, K.P. Whitbread, stated clearly that: "While the Trade is prepared to cooperate in measures which will promote temperance it is not prepared to accept without the most strenuous opposition conditions which, without promoting temperance will continue arbitrary restrictions which for so long have prevented the public house supplying the varied needs of the public". At the same time twenty-six London and provincial journalists were paying a visit to Carlisle to assess the situation for themselves and their verdict was that: "Carlisle is no longer a city of dreadful Saturday nights. Customers, although some of them were frankly antagonistic at the outset, have learned by experience the benefits of direct control and are now generally in favour of the new order of things. The undoubted success of the Carlisle experiment gives food for thought It may be that the time is not yet ripe for an extension of the principle throughout the country, but if it should ever be a case of choosing between outright prohibition and direct control, no-one who has been to Carlisle and seen things for himself could make any mistake as to the course to be adopted". An editorial in the Scotsman of November, 1919, was tenaciously upholding the principal of accountability: " Much of the criticism of the Central Control Board has been due, not so much to its policy as to the fact that the House of Commons has had practically no opportunity of expressing an opinion. The licensed trade will lend their assistance to any scheme for providing better public houses but they will resist the perpetuation of the system of giving bureaucratic powers to an irresponsible body. There is a general dislike of the system of placing administration in the hands of bodies which are responsible neither to Parliament nor to local authorities".

Chairman of the Local Advisory Committee, F.W. Chance, considered that the system of a large monopoly out of which the state could draw a substantial revenue was much too dangerous to continue, and speakers on behalf of the United Kingdom Alliance were everywhere meeting with the cry that the Government and the Board refused to give the figures of the sales at Carlisle. Sir Edgar Sanders, in a letter to Arthur Sherwell, M.P., admitted that, "It is obvious that I am precluded from supplying information which the Cabinet have already refused to give in the House of Commons. The main objection to publishing any figures relative to the sale of intoxicants in Carlisle is that there are no reliable comparative figures for other towns where the conditions are similar". A revealing letter from Sherwell to Sanders followed a month later saying: "The Trade mean to make a desperate fight against the Bill and in the present temper of the House they may succeed. If they press the fight obstinately, I entirely agree that the PM should withdraw the Bill; throw the responsibility upon the Trade; and leave things as they are pending permanent legislation. Unfortunately the position with regard to such a policy has been much weakened by the failure of the Government to appoint a successor to Lord D'Abernon. The situation has been mis-handled all through and the Government's difficulties are of its own creation". (PRO HO 190/864).

At a monthly meeting of the Local Advisory Committee in June, 1921, its chairman, Sir Frederick Chance, took the opportunity to review the position to date in the light of how best to adapt to times of peace the experience gained during the period of the war. "Under the ideal chairmanship of Lord D'Abernon the Board had a very difficult task to carry through which had involved a great deal of work-all unpaid as far as members were concerned and some of the criticism, and even abuse they have had to endure has been most unfair. One of the difficulties in connection with the Carlisle experiment has been that we have had to contend against extremists on both sides, one taking the line 'touch not the unclean thing', and the other 'touch not this anointed trade'. The Carlisle experiment has been neither a miracle nor a failure but a success both financially and socially. After making allowances for capital expenditure there has been a very handsome return indeed and I think in a few years the whole of the capital will have been repaid. The Advisory Committee, having no executive power, has had a difficult part to play but has maintained a significant role throughout in keeping the Board in touch with public opinion". Following this review the Mayor of Carlisle, Mr. H.K. Campbell submitted to the Local Advisory Committee in September, 1921, a scheme for the local acquisition of the Board's undertaking in Carlisle and District which would place it under the control of a body of trustees composed of representatives of the local authorities and government departments which would carry the "experiment" a step further.

Thus the controversies continued to sway this way and that, both inside Whitehall and outside. Dr. Thomas Jones, C.H., who had joined the Cabinet Secretariat on its formation in 1916 and remained as Principal Assistant Secretary of the Cabinet Office until 1930, admitted to Andrew Bonar Law, Lord Privy Seal and Leader of the Commons, that there were few ways in which statesmen could increase the happiness of mankind so much as by taking away the profit-making motive of the sellers of strong drink. Similar opinions were also being made on a local level in favour of prohibition by local option. The Carlisle Temperance League and the Carlisle Railway Temperance Union were particularly vocal. The British Womens' Temperance Association held a rally in the grounds of Homeacres, Stanwix, which was chaired by Sir R.A. Allison. Thirty-two clergy and ministers of religion in Carlisle sent a letter to the Cumberland News to declare their approval of the work of the Control Board . They suggested that a majority of the members of the Local Advisory Committee should be appointed by popularly elected bodies such as town and county councils.

A Labour campaign for the public ownership and control of the liquor trade was launched under the chairmanship of the Rt. Hon. J.H. Thomas to confirm that the Labour Party saw the key to temperance reform in taking the entire manufacture and retailing of alcoholic drink out of the hands of those who found profit in promoting the utmost possible consumption. It was essentially a case in which the people as a whole must assert its right to full and unfettered power for dealing with the licensing question in accordance with local option. At the Labour Party Conference held in Scarborough, the drink resolutions for public ownership were lost. "Apparently the Scottish miners threw their weight against public ownership and the nonconformist element in the Miners' Federation followed this lead. . . It is very unfortunate that the miners went against us, especially as they represent the biggest single block in the conference. . . We cannot disguise the fact that the vote at the conference is a serious setback to our work". (Letter from Arthur Greenwood to Sir Edgar Sanders. PRO HO 190/495).

In July, 1919, a pamphlet written from the standpoint of the local publicans and entitled "A Last Word from Carlisle", was produced by the Carlisle and District Licensed Victuallers' and Managers' Association. It was sent to the Prime Minister for the consideration of all members of Parliament. The Association's president was the well-known Carlisle "character" John H. Minns, who, until December, 1915, had held a number of licences in the city and possessed a significant knowledge of the old prewar inns. The pamphlet lost no time in stating its case: "The war is over. . . DORA is dying; and the Control Board (as such) is moribund. . . Why has Carlisle only, and not Newcastle, Liverpool, Cardiff, and other large towns been subjected to special restrictions and impositions and selected for the exercise of the Board's most unreasonable and confiscatory powers? Why should Carlisle be the only town where they not only lay down the conditions under which the trade shall be carried on - it is the trade! This is more, much more than control - it is considered unfair and iniquitous localised state monopoly by confiscation. The imposition of no sale of spirits (wholesale or retail) on Saturdays was a terrible imposition. . . as were the special and ridiculous conditions imposed on their managers (which remember means ALL the publicans in Carlisle). . . No-one will deny that during the war the efforts of the Control Board in some respects were laudable and effective but it is equally apparent to those who live in and around Carlisle and have observed more closely than outsiders ALL that the Board has done, and the way they have done it, that they have on occasions exceeded their powers, and have not justified their selection of Carlisle for their specially autocratic regulations. . . . There never was any real reason for selecting and so treating Carlisle. . . Why should the Board punish Carlisle for Gretna's sins? The Board had no reasonable right to sacrifice Carlisle and its sober and law-abiding citizens for their sake. No! This reason for mounting their high horse in Carlisle was thin, very thin". The pamphlet then concluded by reminding the Prime Minister that tenants and licensees in Carlisle who had been called to the colours found on return that, not only had their nameplates gone from the premises, but their wives had been installed as managers. Prior to this pamphlet John Minns had already sent a telegram to the Prime Minister in 1917 requesting a public and impartial inquiry to be held in Carlisle to give the citizens an opportunity of vindicating the city's honour against what he termed the slanderous and vindictive statements by the Control Board and their advisors.

In August, 1915, Minns had made an application to the Ministry of Munitions for work as an Inspector of Canteens, but, as a result of enquiries, it was thought prudent to have nothing whatever to do with him. He had the reputation in Carlisle of being a very heavy drinker, a typical "mine host" of Victorian times, and a great showman in public life. Before the advent of the Control Board he had been one of Carlisle's leading licensed victuallers. He had owned the Apple Tree, the Carlisle Arms popularly known as the Gaol Tap), the Golden Lion, the Linton Holme Hotel and the Wellington Hotel in English Street with its unusual and magnificent Baronial Hall. The flamboyant style of the pamphlet would seem to endorse the life-style of the man himself. By the beginning of 1916 he had been gradually forced, through financial difficulties, into giving up the last of his licences. Eventually, the Carlisle breweries stopped his credit and would only accept cash payments. Notwithstanding this episode in his public life, Minns went on to become chairman of the highways and streets committee; a member of the general purposes and water and baths committees; and a representative of the city council on the king's roll committee for finding employment for disabled ex-servicemen; and in 1925 he was elected alderman. Always a man of ideas, he had himself anticipated the Board's policy by introducing sausage and mash at the Gaol Tap, had formed the "Beautiful Carlisle

Society" in 1920; had suggested the use of the slogan "Stop at Carlisle" to bring in tourists; and had consistently advocated the development of leisure activities including a municipal golf course, swimming pool, and boating lake beside the River Eden. When he died in 1942 his obituary in the local newspapers regretted that his undoubted gifts were never fully recognised and that, had his lot fallen in a wider sphere, his talents would doubtless have found greater scope.

After the various facts and opinions had been voiced, a solution to the question of the future of the Carlisle experiment could no longer be delayed and in November, 1920, a bill was introduced in the House of Commons to continue temporarily the Defence of the Realm (Liquor Control) Regulation 1915 and to substitute a new authority for the Central Control Board. As a consequence, the powers previously held by the Board were transferred to the Home Secretary and the Secretary of State for Scotland. In June, 1921, the government appointed a conference of M.P's to consider how best to adapt the experience gained in wartime to times of peace. A bill had been promised in the King's speech at the opening of Parliament and the government's hand was being forced by Colonel Gretton's private bill. This had been introduced in April and was only withdrawn on the promise that an agreed measure would be passed before the end of the session. Colonel Gretton's bill called for the repeal of DORA and all regulations made by the Control Board. Since it said nothing explicitly about Carlisle, the consequence would have been to tacitly abolish direct control in Carlisle along with the rest of the country. Arthur Sherwell was alarmed at this and was anxious to warn Parliament and the country of the financial loss that would result, and of the folly of surrendering a valuable revenue-producing asset. (PRO HO 190/864). The conference resulted in the introduction of a ministerial bill in July which passed with some amendments in August, and came into force at the beginning of September, 1921. This Licensing Act of 1921 abolished the Central Control Board and restored to the Home and Scottish Offices powers relating to liquor licensing. At the same time it firmly entrenched the continuance of the Carlisle experiment by providing that the power to acquire premises compulsorily would apply only in the Carlisle district. Prior to the regulations which the Central Control Board had introduced, the sale of intoxicating liquor had been permitted continuously each day for 19½ hours in London; 17 hours in other towns; 16 ½ hours in country districts; and 11-13 hours in Scotland. The CCB reduced these at a stroke and when it was dissolved under the Licensing Act of 1921 the shortened opening hours which it had imposed on the scheduled areas were extended to the whole country. Meanwhile the temperance campaign remained strong in Carlisle throughout the 1920s. Although it was not as strong as it had been in the early years of the war yet the city remained a kind of cockpit of the trade and temperance controversy. The temperance movement played a part in persuading the government to take a look at the chaotic state of the licensing laws in the country at large, and to uphold the restrictions introduced in wartime. This issue was examined by the Royal Commission on Licensing 1929/32 set up by Ramsey MacDonald's second Labour government during the years of depression. The Commission was carefully constituted to take account of the views of both the trade and the temperance movement and it recommended a more rapid extinction of licences; the furtherance of public house improvement, more experiments in state ownership; and greater control of clubs. However, no action was taken by the National Government of 1931-5 on the reports of the Royal Commission and any attempt to extend the system of state management proved abortive.

The statutory responsibility of the Home Office was discharged by the Aliens Division from 1922 to 1931, H Division (which was set up mainly to deal with liquor licensing) from 1931 to 1959, and after that by E Division. Management was carried on through an advisory committee and the State Management Council appointed by the Home Secretary and the Secretary of State for Scotland. A State Management Districts Central Office in London was made responsible to the Council for the overall direction of the English and Scottish districts and their administrative offices in Carlisle and Glasgow. The nine members of this Council for the State Management Scheme (SMS) acting as a policy advisory body for the Home Office met quarterly in Carlisle and Scotland and half yearly in London (until 1949) and comprised, as well as the Permanent Under Secretary of State for Home Affairs and his assistant; the Secretary to the Scottish Office; two representatives of the brewing industry; two members of the Local Advisory Committee; and two other members. The General Manager had overall responsibility for the Scheme at local level and an annual report was presented to Parliament as to the procedure in connection with the management of the districts, while the system of a local advisory committee which was initiated by the CCB was continued by section 16(3) of the 1921 Licensing Act.

This committee in Carlisle appointed by the Secretary of State was composed of representatives of the municipal and county authorities; the Trades Council and other interests in the city and county. Meetings were attended by the general manager and in this way the Secretary of State was kept in touch with local opinion. Their services were offered on a voluntary basis and over the years proved to have been an important factor in the successful conduct of the experiment. Harry Redfern, FRIBA, continued in his position as chief architect with Joseph Seddon, ARIBA, as his assistant. The schemes were later reorganised in 1949 and given separate headquarters in Carlisle and Edinburgh when the central office in London was dissolved. It was in this year that the chief architect, Harry Redfern, retired at the age of 88 after 33 years service.

From 1949 to 1952 plans were developing to extend state management into the new towns. Due in part to the financial situation in the country and the devaluation of the pound in 1949 these plans proved abortive and the licensing of premises in the new towns was left to their individual development corporations. The State Management District at Carlisle and the remaining Scottish districts of Gretna, Cromarty, Dingwall and Invergordon were abolished in 1971 by the Licensing (Abolition of State Management) Act and the property held by the Secretary of State in connection with the Scheme was sold off by 1973. The properties of the small Enfield scheme had already been sold by auction in December 1922.

Central to any attempt to justify the schemes of state management is the question of convictions for drunkenness. Before the war the level of drunkenness on which the police would apprehend, and the justices would convict, varied from town to town. Consequently, any comparison between towns in this respect is unfortunately of little value. In addition, the number of convictions fluctuated for different reasons in different places. Sir Leonard Dunning, Chief Inspector of Police in England, declared in 1920 that: "The returns of prosecutions for drunkenness are often taken as a measure of the vice of intemperance whereas they are more nearly a measure of the action of the police and of the standard of public decorum adopted in the particular locality". (PRO HO 190/864). It follows from this that there may be an appreciable amount of public drunkenness in the country which is not reflected in the statistics of convictions. Prior to the advent of the Central Control Board, legal control of the traffic in drink had not been based on any definite principle. The legal control of the habitual drunkard had been introduced mainly on scientific/medical grounds and was based on the theory that inebriety was a disease and not simply an offence against public order. In judging the actual effects on public sobriety of the Carlisle scheme the only statistical evidence to work on are the records of the convictions for drunkenness. It is in some ways an unsatisfactory guide but the Carlisle undertaking treated the problem of public drunkenness as essentially a problem of management and sought to make the state responsible for methods as well as results. It was not so much a question of drink or no drink, but of good or bad management.

The first step was to bring the state and the public house manager into a relationship of master and servant in lieu of the previously existing relationship of lawgiver and subject, and this involved a complete break with the old theory of licensing regulation. No-one employed in the scheme was to have any financial interest in the quantity of liquor sold. It followed that the manager stood to lose nothing by enforcing strict sobriety in his house. In this way the establishment of an identity between the state and the licence holder lay at the root of the state's attempt to defeat drunkenness by direct management. It meant that the battle for sobriety ceased to be primarily a disciplinary matter for the police, but became a system of collaboration and advice which carried no suggestion of hostility or clash of interests. The Central Control Board was however aware that a certain amount of drunkenness was inevitable under any system, but it set out to show that drunkenness above a residual minimum was preventable, and its prevention was mainly a matter of rational regulation and management of licensed premises.

Female drunkenness was an issue which confronted the Board in its early years. In October, 1915, a committee of women under the chairmanship of Mrs Creighton was appointed to inquire into the alleged excessive drinking among women and advise the Board on the subject. The committee reported an increase of excessive drinking, but added that it was mainly confined to those women who had habitually drunk to excess before the war. There was no evidence to support the notion that women and girls who had not indulged in liquor before the war were now doing so to excess because of the war. In its conclusion the committee expressly deprecated any restrictions dealing specifically with women "both on account of the inherent injustice and because the evil of excessive drinking must be combated as a whole".

Up to the outbreak of the war in 1914 there had been little ground for optimism with regard to national sobriety. The amount of alcohol consumed and the consequent convictions for drunkenness throughout the country showed an upward trend but then the military regulations and restrictive orders by the licensing justices, together with certain voluntary arrangements with the trade for earlier closing hours and the non-serving of women in the morning, brought about a considerable measure of improvement. Convictions from 1915 to 1918 in England and Wales dropped from 33,211 to 7,222. This represented a decrease of 78 per cent. In Carlisle they fell from 277 to 80, a decrease of 71 per cent

The three main changes brought about by the Control Board during these years were the curtailment of drinking hours; the closure of public houses for several hours in the afternoon directed against irregular drinking between meals and the habit of soaking (the continuous drinking for many hours at a time); and the treatment of clubs on the same footing as public houses (which was an innovation). The influx of thousands of navvies and their propensity for drinking chasers heightened the need for firm action. An order prohibiting the sale of spirits on Saturdays was first applied in the Gretna districts from February, 1917. The price of spirits was also increased, and the CCB introduced a new order prohibiting the sale of whisky, brandy. rum. or gin for sale on or off premises unless it had been reduced to 30 degrees under proof. These measures resulted in a remarkable decrease in convictions on Saturdays. They fell from 112 to 26 . The same kind of decrease was obtained in Carlisle where the streets became much quieter and more orderly. The general manager, E.C. Sanders, noted in his annual report that the drinking of spirits was the most potent cause of drunkenness and the prohibition of spirits on Saturdays in Carlisle and Longtown had been justified by results.

The Chief Constable reported that the year 1916 had been one of exceptional difficulty. Apart from the shortage of regular members in his force, the influx of thousands of workmen and the great increase in drunkenness had thrown an enormous amount of extra work onto the police. This work had involved dealing with Defence of the Realm regulations, special work for the Central Control Board, and work connected with the registration of aliens - often complicated by language difficulties. The following year had also seen its burdens with the ever increasing duties placed on the police by the Home Office, the military authorities, the Ministry of National Service, and the Ministry of Food. All this was making it impossible to give the necessary supervision to the streets and many complaints had had to go unattended. The shortage of police and the excessive number of drinking men in the city made it difficult for the force to apprehend anything like the number that should have been apprehended. As a consequence we know statistically the numbers that were apprehended, but we do not know the numbers that were not apprehended. In June, 1916, the Carlisle City Council's Watch Committee received a report from the Chief Constable stressing the depletion by enlistment which had left his force totally inadequate to meet the existing requirements of the City having regard to the large influx of workers at the Gretna munition works. He urged that steps be taken for the release from military service of all married police constables who had been permitted to join the colours but who were subsequently found to be unfit for general service. The Town Clerk communicated with the Home Secretary and three months later was able to report that the Army Council had given instructions for two of the men to be transferred to Class "W" of the Army Reserve so that they could return to police duties immediately, and this was followed during the rest of the war period by the return of eight more men. Finally during 1919 the Carlisle Force saw the return of 21 of its servicemen.

The number of navvies in the area reached its maximum in June, 1916, and remained constant for the remainder of that year. By July the Board had commenced their operations and private interest in the sale of intoxicants was being rapidly eliminated. The licensees, as they became salaried managers under the Board's control, had been exhorted to make the sobriety of the workers their first consideration and were being educated into a new mode of carrying on their trade. The great drop in convictions from 953 in 1916 to 320 in 1917 was certainly due in part to the changing character of the male population, and in part to the "spiritless Saturdays" which had been introduced in the February of that year. Editorial material in the local press was stressing the opinion that the improvement was not a consequence of the action of the Board but of "The passing from our midst of the excessive drinkers whom the State itself had brought into the vicinity, and this must be clearly borne in mind when we come to appraise the lessons of the Carlisle experiment. The great decrease in convictions for drunkenness will not in itself prove the experiment".

When the number of convictions for drunkenness in Carlisle during the year 1918 dropped to just 80 it was the lowest on record since statistics began. The Chief Constable was able to report that the beneficial effects of this increased sobriety were far reaching and fundamental. He put the result down to three main causes: fewer public houses with less temptation to drink; better supervision of the houses with a total of 653 surprise visits by the police; and a general scarcity of intoxicants due to the Food Controller's regulations. Because of this shortage of liquor, other parts of the country were experiencing short rushes of heavy drinking followed by long periods of closure. In Carlisle the Control Board had rationed supplies to all houses so that a reasonable amount of liquor was available during licensing hours. The conduct of the trade in Carlisle during the year had worked with remarkable smoothness. The number of convictions remained low for 1919 in spite of the augmentation of the police force, the extended hours of sale, the increase in the supply of liquor, and the return of large numbers of men from the army. Other significant factors affecting the figures for the next two years were the removal of the restriction of output in June, 1919; the raising of the gravity to 1044 degrees; and the removal, by November 1919, of all restrictions on the clearance of spirits from bond. However, a good deal of criticism was directed to the increased number of convictions. They had risen to 136 in 1920 and to 154 in 1921. Tthe inference was drawn that, in this respect, Carlisle was no better, and in many cases, worse than other towns. Of the 143 convictions for drunkenness in 1920, 7 were discharged, 88 were residents of Carlisle and the remaining 55 were strangers to the city. A number of these had been arrested by the Railway Police at the station indicating that they had obtained their drink prior to arriving. The general manager, Sir E.C. Sanders, had been moved to reveal in a letter to Arthur Sherwell, M.P., that, "The Carlisle police are certainly much more inclined to take a strict view about drunkenness now than they were before the war". (PRO HO 190/864). and over the next ten years it is gratifying to record that the number of convictions dropped steadily (with one or two small hiccoughs) until by 1931 there were only 60 proceedings in a city of 61 public houses (58 full licences and three off) with the proportion of population to each licence standing at 936. Of the 13 registered clubs in the city with a total membership of 7,000, three were open to public inspection.

The bare statement of numbers of convictions needs to be seen as a record, but not necessarily as an interpretation of the overall situation with regard to public drunkenness, as distinct from private drunkenness. The average yearly pre-war number of proceedings over the six year period prior to the advent of the Central Control Board was 244. In 1916 this rose alarmingly to 964 (953 convictions) but by 1931 had dropped to 73 (60 convictions) representing a quarter of the pre-war average. The breakdown of the statistics for these two sample years is as follows: 1916: proceedings 964; simple drunkenness 540 (516 male 24 female) 7 discharged; drunkenness with aggravation 387 (340 male, 47 female) 4 discharged; drunkenness other offences (employment of children) 37. The number of times the same person had been convicted during the year: 78 (twice); 17 (three times); 5 (four times); 1 (five times); 1 (six times). As far as can be ascertained, of the 964 proceeded against: 788 worked at Gretna; 47 were strangers passing through Carlisle; and the remaining 129 were residents. Taking account of the 136 multiple arrests during the year the proportion of non-residents facing proceedings for drunkenness was 84 per cent of the total.

In 1931 there were 73 proceedings: simple drunkenness 25 (20 male,5 female); drunkenness with aggravation 42 (all male); drunkenness with other offences 6 (all male). Of these 73, convictions were passed on 60 (50 male, 3 female) while 13 (11 male, 2 female) were discharged. Those discharged were practically all tramps or persons with no means or fixed abode who were allowed to go after they had given an undertaking to leave the city immediately. 24 males and one female had previously been convicted for drunkenness and of the persons charged in 1931, 43 per cent were non-residents of Carlisle. When the number of proceedings dropped even further the following year, the Chief Constable, in his report, issued a warning not to overlook certain factors so evident in the city: the large amount of unemployment, the high cost of all intoxicating liquors, and the general decrease in wages. He added that he was "firmly convinced that the low figures of this year cannot be expected to be maintained when conditions again become normal".

The depression hit Carlisle more seriously and earlier than London or some of the other towns, and life there in the 1920s and 30s was tough. There was an urgent need for dwellings to be erected at the earliest possible date. With the limited amount of labour available in the building trades, the city council had to request the Board in June, 1920, not to undertake any alterations or reconstructions of their premises that would interfere with the housing programme and the Board agreed to postpone any such work for six months. It was crucial at this stage, however, that if the regulations and advances introduced by the CCB were to be maintained, the projected programme of improved public houses under the SMS should commence as soon as it was possible and practical.

The main thrust of Redfern's contribution to this programme occurred therefore between the period of the 1921 Licensing Act and his retirement in 1949. He built 15 "model inns" in 13 years: Apple Tree, 1927; Malt Shovel, 1928; Coach & Horses, 1929; Horse & Farrier, 1929; Black Lion, 1929; Spinners Arms, 1930; Rose & Crown, 1930; Cumberland Inn, 1930; Crescent, 1932; Magpie, 1933; Earl Grey, 1935; Wheatsheaf, Abbeytown 1935; Crown, Stanwix, 1937; Cumberland Wrestlers, 1938; and the Redfern, Etterby 1940.

While awaiting the launch of this comprehensive building project it is apposite to mention the Intoxicating Liquor (Sale to Young Persons under 18) Act 1923 presented by Viscountess Astor. The act made it illegal to sell, purchase, or consume intoxicating liquor on the premises for 18 year olds, nor for any adult to purchase drink on their behalf. Beer, porter, cider and perry could however be sold to persons aged 16 and over for consumption with a meal partaken in a part of the building which was not a bar. This Act consolidated a view expressed two years earlier in a letter to the Observer (17 April, 1921) from the High Master of Manchester Grammar School, J.L. Paton, in which he wrote: "By the Education Act of 1918 the State took over the educational supervision of young people from fourteen to eighteen - the 'unguarded years'. Teachers on whom this new responsibility falls cannot undertake the burden laid upon them unless the young people entrusted to them are definitely excluded from the atmosphere of the public house. Adolescence is the great epoch for formation of habit. This season of accelerated growth is characterised by the love of excitement. It craves strong feelings and new sensations. Is the exhilaration of alcohol the fitting and wholesome satisfaction of these cravings? The atmosphere of the drinking fraternity is incompatible with the influences of education. The fourteenth year is a critical one especially for those who enter the industrial world. Boys and girls are up against all manner of new temptations. The senior people with whom they are thrown for the most part take no pains to protect them; many of them take a low pleasure in initiating them into what is called 'life' or 'the way to spend your money like a man'. The art of statesmanship in dealing with the young is the art of wise defences".

CHAPTER SIX
HARRY REDFERN

Harry Redfern was born on the 5 April, 1861, in Loke Street, Berwick St John, Wiltshire, the son of George and Mary (nee Hayward) Redfern, and was baptised in the village church on the 2 October. The church was being almost entirely rebuilt by the architect Henry Woodyer with Harry's father as the clerk of building works. This was a time when the Victorian urge to restore and in some cases to rebuild old churches which were falling into disrepair was reaching its peak, and Wiltshire with its small villages and large parishes witnessed many comings and goings of the well-known architects of the day. Thomas Henry Wyatt(1807-1880) who was consultant architect to the Diocese of Salisbury undertook the restoration or rebuild of about fifty churches in Wiltshire as well as being responsible for the building of several new ones. In the thirty-three years between 1850 and 1883 William Butterfield completed at least twenty church commissions for restoration work or rebuilds and added at least two new buildings, one at Landford in 1858 and one at Foxham in 1880.

Such was the spirit of the times into which Harry was born - a time of mounting confidence. Albeit the burgeoning industrialisation in the cities brought in its wake the spectre of flaunted wealth alongside abject poverty, disease and the

The Church, Berwick St John, Wiltshire.

unparalleled destitution of the manufacturing districts. But it was also a period of well-intentioned and sincere moves by liberals, evangelicals and the temperance movement to solve some of the difficult moral, religious and political issues of the day so that there emerged an overall movement towards reform for the more desperate areas of society.

Although by virtue of his father's employment Harry happened to have been born in Wiltshire, his roots were very firmly in Derbyshire and the Derbyshire/Staffordshire border. He came from a long line of stonemasons, all born in Longnor. His father, uncle and grandfather were all stonemasons and all had lived in Back Street, Longnor. Twenty-four years before Harry was born, another line of the Redfern family had culminated in the birth of James Frank Redfern in Hartington in 1837. His father, uncle and cousin were also all stonemasons and the uncle had also lived in Back Street, Longnor. Harry's great, great grandfather, Matthew, had married Lydia Needham of Milldale in 1758 and had four children by her from whom Harry was directly descended. They were born in 1758 (Elizabeth), 1760 (Joseph), 1766 (Lydia) and 1769 (Hannah), but in 1768 he had a son (Matthew) by a lady called Margaret from Grindon. All these children were registered in Alstonefield. Margaret bore three more children, from whom James Frank is directly descended. They were born in 1773 (Francis) 1776 (Dorothy) 1781 (Margaret) and they were all registered in Grindon. Harry Redfern, architect, and James Frank Redfern, sculptor/mason, were both descended from the same ancestor.

James Frank was born on the estate of Alexander James Beresford-Hope on the 22nd January, 1837, the son of William Redfern, stonemason of Longnor, Staffs and Mary, nee Todd from Hartington, Derbyshire. Beresford-Hope, stepson of Viscount Beresford and son-in-law of the Marquis of Salisbury had been born in 1820 and educated at Harrow and Trinity College, Cambridge. He assumed the name Beresford by Royal licence in 1854. He was rich; he was an Anglo-Catholic; and he was a Liberal-Conservative favouring the Established Church as both a divine institution and an estate of the realm. He sat as M.P. for Maidstone in Kent from 1841 until 1852, and again from 1857 until 1859. After that he sat for Stoke from 1865 until 1868 and then for Cambridge University until his death in 1887. He had been President of the RIBA in 1865; a Trustee of the British Museum; and patron of two livings. He embraced the tenets of the Cambridge Camden Society and the Ecclesiologists which had been founded by two other Trinity undergraduates in 1839 - John Mason Neale and Benjamin Webb. Ecclesiology was held to be a liturgical science insofar as it indicated how a church should be built or re-furbished to make it fit for its purpose regarding the rituals and rubrics of the Anglican church. Like Pugin and his adherents they paid tribute to the spirit of Gothic architecture. At the same time in Oxford the Society for the Promotion and Study of Gothic Architecture was being set up which closely identified itself with the Tractarian Movement, or, as it became known, The Oxford Movement. While the High Anglicanism of Oxford concentrated on the theological aspects of their faith and work and stayed firmly within the Anglican fold, the romantic toryism of the Cambridge Movement led them, like Pugin, to nurture the aesthetic side of their faith and work. But Pugin was a Catholic and these were not comfortable days in which to use the term Catholic and so the Cambridge Camden Society decided that it would be wise to separate out the Ecclesiologists from their Society. From that time onward when they removed themselves to London, the name was changed to The Ecclesiological Society.

James Frank Redfern was patronised from an early age by Beresford-Hope and Lady Mildred, who, on seeing some of the figures he had been fashioning in marble and idleback, quickly recognised his talent and placed him under the care of the incumbent of St. Luke's Church, Sheen, the Reverend Benjamin Webb. He attended the school at Sheen for three years and, when he was 19 years old, Beresford-Hope sent him to London to study with a well-known firm of stained glass designers and illustrators, and then sent him to Paris for six month's study. This all prepared him initially for what was to become an eminent career. He first exhibited work at the Royal Academy in 1859 with figures of Cain and Abel. These were to attract the attention of the sculptor J.H. Foley whose seated bronze figure of Prince Albert was finally installed in the Albert Memorial in Hyde Park in 1876 and as a consequence James F. Redfern himself contributed figures to the spire of the monument depicting moral and Christian virtues. Other exhibits followed at the Royal Academy, almost annually until 1876: a Holy Family in 1861; the Good Samaritan in 1863; Diana and Cupid in 1864; Sir W H. Cope, Bart. in 1865; a marble relief of the young son of his patron Beresford-Hope (posthumous) in 1866; George Wingfield Digby in 1867 followed by the Entombment of Our Lord to be executed in marble for the Digby Mortuary Chapel at Sherborne. Then in 1869, he exhibited Fortitude, which was one of a series of eight statues designed to represent the four Christian and the four cardinal virtues for the Prince Consort Memorial in Hyde Park. Bas-reliefs of the Annunciation, Baptism, Entombment, and the Walk to Emmaeus followed in 1873; a panel in the reredos of St. Stephen's Church, Lewisham; and a marble relief of Mrs Pim were exhibited in 1873 and 1874. In the year of his death he was showing a Crucifixion of St Andrew - one of a series of subjects to be executed in marble for Kirby Church in Yorkshire together with a Crucifixion of St. Peter. Most of Redfern's work was of a religious nature. It is to be found in such famous buildings as Windsor Castle; the Chapter House, Westminster Abbey (Our Lord in Majesty); Ely Cathedral (The Apostles); Lichfield Cathedral (Angels in the Lonsdale Monument); Bristol Cathedral (Adoration of the Magi in the south porch); Gloucester Cathedral (figures and groups: south porch, north transept reredos; and presbytery/sanctuary reredos); and Salisbury Cathedral (over sixty life-size figures on the West Front). One of Redfern's most interesting assignments had been for the reredos in St. Andrew's Church, Wells Street, Marylebone, London. The church was built by S. W. Daukes & J. Hamilton in 1845 and consecrated in 1847. It was not a particularly interesting looking church from the outside, but, inside, it was a veritable treasure-house of artistic talent and design. Beresford-Hope became its churchwarden in 1853 and Benjamin Webb was its vicar from 1862-1885. The congregation was rich and fashionable and an excellent musical tradition was rapidly established. The church had a resident choir school and professional lay clerks who sang the psalms twice daily while each Sunday they sang masses, by Cherubini; Haydn; Mozart; Schubert; Hummel; or Beethoven. Charles Gounod was a frequent attender and his motets were adapted from the Latin for the choir by Benjamin Webb. It was at St. Andrew's

Church that Gounod's sacred music was first heard in this country. His Petite Messe Solemnelle was adapted to the English Eucharist and performed there on St Andrew's Day, 1863. The high altar was designed by Pugin, but, unfortunately, the stained glass of the original East Window, designed by Pugin and made by Hardman, was destroyed in the Second World War. Butterfield designed a handsome two-sided brass lectern and Burges designed a litany desk in walnut inlaid with maple which is now in the Victoria and Albert Museum. Burges also designed a silver chalice and a full set of altar plate. Alongside all this prestigious work, G. E. Street designed a sumptuous reredos which Redfern executed between 1865 and 1872. It was a virtuoso statement of Victorian religious art stretching right across the East wall of the chancel and flanking the east window to the height of its tracery. The band of five bas-reliefs were sculpted in alabaster and were contained within richly carved tabernacle work. The centre group of the Crucifixion was the first to be erected and was given in memory of the vicar's brother, George Webb, while the group of the Resurrection was given in memory of Benjamin Webb who had died in 1870. Other figures which were included in the group of Our Lord in Majesty were of the patron saints of the Ecclessiological Society, John the Evangelist, Luke, Etheldreda, and George. Sadly it was the changing social conditions of Wells Street after the end of World War I that hastened the decline of St Andrew's, and with the choral tradition abandoned, the church was closed in 1932; dismantled in 1933; and then transported completely to Kingsbury in Middlesex where it was re-erected and re-consecrated in 1934. Almost all the treasures have survived.

In a letter written on April 22nd, 1874, from his home in Queen Anne Street, Cavendish Square, London to an old friend from his Hartington days who was living in America, we learn that James F. Redfern was married with two children, a girl aged 4 and a boy aged 18 months, and he was expecting a third child. In an update of his activities for his friend he wrote: "I still keep chipping away. . . . one of the very last blocks I knocked into shape was sent to New York and is to be found in St. Bartholomew's Church in that city - East 15th Street. It is a sculptured angel, over life-size, holding a shell as a font and is worked in marble. . . . I had previously worked one for Inverness Cathedral.

"I exhibited and gained an award in the Great Exhibition of '62 and soon after began work earnestly on my own account and from that day to this I have been chiefly employed on works for public buildings, chiefly for cathedrals. My first important work was for Salisbury Cathedral - the Dean and Chapter giving me a commission for forty statues at once - and I have now executed over sixty, all over life-size for the West front of that cathedral. My next commission was for the large gilt statues at the top of the Albert Memorial in Hyde Park and so on over the subsequent years I have done sculpture for the Cathedrals of Gloucester, Ely, Lichfield, Limerick, and Inverness besides important works for the Chapter House, Westminster Abbey and for numerous churches. The figures for Gloucester Cathedral are almost as numerous as those for Salisbury besides a large reredos containing sculptured groups of figures.

"There is in America now one of our most notable men - the Rev. Charles Kingsley who is starring it by a lecturing tour. In his church at Eversley - to which

Harry Redfern as a boy
at Abingdon Grammar School.

place quite a stream of intellect-worshipping Americans make pilgrimages every year - one of my earliest works is to be found: a recumbent effigy of Lady Cope, wife of Sir William Cope, Bart. carved in alabaster. . . . the Americans have, I find a more thorough appreciation for sculpture than the English. . . . You will see I have done enough to reap honour if nothing else. "

Two years and two months after writing this letter James Frank Redfern died in Hampstead, London, on 13th June, 1876, aged only 39.

It was in the Spring of this same year that Harry Redfern left his grammar school in Abingdon, Berkshire, at the age of 15. The town of Abingdon in the Thames valley had grown prosperous in the 18th century by manufacturing malt and sending it by barge down to Billingsgate in London which, until the mid-19th century was an important coal port as well as a fish market. A proportion of the coal Billingsgate received would have been sent on to towns like Henley, Abingdon or Reading in exchange for corn or malt to be used by the London brewers. Christ's Hospital, Abingdon, was originally a body set up in the sixteenth century when the Fraternity of the Holy Cross attached to the Church of St. Helen's was dissolved, and it was they who owned the only wharf in Abingdon and prospered accordingly. Later in the 19th century the Charity Commissioners were able to release funds and land for several new enterprises which included a site for a cottage hospital, a free library, a town park with its own Albert Memorial and a new site for the grammar school. This became Abingdon's select area. The church of St. Helen's was closed from June 1871 until July 1873 while Woodyer with George Redfern (Harry's father) as clerk of works carried out restoration work. Harry was admitted as a day pupil to Abingdon Grammar School in September, 1871, at the age of ten, leaving, in 1876 at the age of 15, to enter the office of Henry Woodyer at Grafmam, near Cranleigh, Surrey. In his own words, in an article written in retrospect in April, 1944, for the Architect and Building News, he recollects that he found Woodyer a distinguished-looking man. "Tall, rather spare; always attired in an easy-fitting blue serge suit loose shirt collar and crimson silk tie. His soft black hat,rather wide in the brim, bore a small steel brooch in front. During inclement weather a long dark inverness cloak was worn. (It had become greenish with age!). A most picturesque figure, often smoking an extremely fragrant cigar. I envied him! Into these most pleasant surroundings I came as a pupil and passed a very happy apprenticeship there, lodging in the village of Bramley, three miles away and traversing the distance to and from the office across the geese-haunted Surrey commons in all sorts of weather. I say 'traversed' advisedly for I became the possessor of a bicycle with wooden wheels and iron tyres - a veritable 'bone-shaker'. On reflection I am disposed to think that, all things considered, walking would have been preferable. . . . Many new churches came from Woodyer's hand and there were innumerable restorations of ancient churches up and down the country. All these were sympathetically handled; but it must be confessed that some amount of conjectural restoration, as opposed to mere repairs - did in fact take place. This was in accordance with the thought of the time, and no harm was intended or indeed conceived of. We take a different standpoint nowadays and have become extremely virtuous on the subject. Nothing was done which could be construed as vandalism. His was a varied and very pleasant practice with a small staff of elderly and well-trained assistants brought up in his own ways. Henry Woodyer's outlook on architecture was entirely different from that of his friend and master, Butterfield, but they had in common an intense dislike to anything that savoured of professionalism or of publicity and would not permit their designs to be published. Neither of these men was a member of any professional society. . . Henry Woodyer was, in my long-considered view, a fine architect. As a pupil I venerated his work".

Redfern was his pupil for about eighteen months. At the end of 1877, Woodyer recommended him to William Butterfield and he had the good fortune to be taken onto Butterfield's staff at 4 Adam Street, the Adelphi, London, first as an 'improver' and then as an assistant. An 'improver' was a young person who worked to improve his position within the profession but would receive little or sometimes no payment if he was working in the office of a successful practitioner. Life in the metropolis and in Butterfield's office was a complete change of atmosphere for Redfern and, as he related himself, "It made a deep impression on me and the memory of that period never left my mind. . . . The office atmosphere was of a solemn - not to say serious cast, with lengthy periods when 'the wind was from the East'. The staff worked hard and kept long hours. Each member, if he happened to be lucky, had an alternative Saturday afternoon off duty. There was no break for lunch and in those remote days the notion of having tea in an office - still less of smoking there - had not entered one's mind. I was living at Windsor and leaving home by an early train and returning by a late one found the experience exhausting. The fog-bound winter train sendee was a factor which did not make for one's happiness. Butterfield took no holidays and allowed few to his staff. However we were permitted to absent ourselves on Christmas Day, Good Friday and Ascension Day, and in spite of these and other difficulties and restrictions the office routine worked smoothly and well. At least we revered our master and sought to do him service. . . A certain number of jobs was allocated to each assistant whose business and responsibilty it was to work out the scheme from start to finish, but not to visit the site or the building during its progress. Butterfield attended to all that himself. We found it difficult in these circumstances to acquire and maintain that interest in the problem so desirable in matters of this kind - or indeed of any kind. (Years of experience in a procedure diametrically opposed to the above has convinced me that this method was a mistaken one)".

Redfern judged Butterfield to have been eminently practical in his building method and all that he did in this connection to have been ruled and guided by his acceptance of the conditions of the problem in hand and its solution in terms of suitability and strong common sense. He was truly a Master Builder with an original outlook uncoloured by sentiment and Redfern stood to gain valuable experience from his connection with Butterfield. Redfern then moved on to work in several offices: namely those of Alfred Javers; Alfred Y. Nutt; Peter Dollar; Frederick J. Robinson; and William Young. Frederick J. Robinson of Derby was a local architect producing a prolific amount of work, many churches and much restoration. Alfred Y. Nutt had entered H.M. Office of Works, Windsor Castle, and as surveyor to the Dean and Canons in 1874 had carried out exterior restoration work at St George's Chapel.

Redfern's talent for, and enjoyment of restoration work was being nurtured as he travelled over a great part of England and Wales sketching and measuring old buildings. On January 8th, 1889, he married Edith Gore at St Matthew's Church, St. Pancras, London, having first moved back to the parish of St. Peter's, Derby, for a short period. He was now a mature man of 27 and his wife was 25. Edith was the daughter of Thomas Gore, a jeweller of 13 Harrington Square, London. They had two daughters by the marriage: Dorothy who was born on the 14th October, 1889 at Parkfield Villas, Stafford Street, Derby; and Phillis who was born on the 27th May, 1895, at Birkbeck Road, Acton, Middlesex. Both girls remained spinsters throughout their lives and, after Edith Redfern died of heart disease in 1937, Dorothy continued to live in the family home during the next thirteen years of Harry's widowerhood until his death of pulmonary thrombosis and heart degeneration in April, 1950, at the age of 88.

In 1896 Redfern moved to London and into private practice in partnership with John James Stevenson, MA; FSA; FRIBA; at No. 4 Porchester Gardens, a partnership which lasted twelve years until Stevenson's death in 1908. From the time that Stevenson took into partnership Harry Redfern all his work was carried out in conjunction with his junior partner and these were rewarding years for Redfern professionally. Many of the assignments he had jointly undertaken faced him with aspects of architectural design and planning which would surface again later in his career when dealing with such practical items as ventilation or the adequacy and placement of sanitary arrangements in public-houses. Stevenson had been born in Glasgow in 1831, educated at his local Grammar School and progressed to Glasgow University where he gained his M.A degree before continuing his studies at the Theological College, Edinburgh. His original desire to become a Presbyterian minister began to fade after a visit to Italy when an equally strong desire to become an architect took precedence. He therefore became a pupil of David Bryce, RSA of Edinburgh in 1856 and two years later continued his further training in London in the office of Sir George Gilbert Scott. On leaving Scott's office he undertook the usual sketching tour in France after which he settled down to practice, taking up a partnership with Campbell Douglas in Glasgow which lasted nine years. His office was known among Scottish draughtsmen as "the stepping-stone to London" and he moved to London himself in 1869 to join the architect E.R. Robson who had just been appointed architect to the then newly formed School Board. The 1870 Education Act had required the building of many new schools, particularly by the London School Board and it was E.R. Robson and J.J. Stevenson who were the first architects to be successful in the competition for the design of these buildings. They selected and adapted for these schools a type of hybrid brick architecture which afterwards became known as "Queen Anne", a name which Stevenson, a keen publicist, readily adopted. Like other architects of the time who were intent upon advancing their London reputations, Stevenson built for himself The Red House, Bayswater, a very early example of this Queen Anne style of brick architecture. In his publication, House Architecture of 1880, he recalls that it was his practical experience in the building of this house that made him realise how adaptable the style was to every modern necessity and convenience. Stevenson was convinced that it embraced a mode of building which had the merit of truthfulness for the British workman who had been apprenticed in the common vernacular style. Stevenson was seeking an architecture which might happily penetrate all levels of society. The Queen Anne detailing of gabled dormers and projecting bay windows altered the character of street architecture in London for a generation. For many years his home on Bayswater Hill was a centre of contemporary literary and artistic life. It was through his personal friendship with William Morris that Stevenson became associated with the Society for the Protection of Ancient Buildings and a member of the original committee of that Society. "He never ceased to take an active interest in its work, for he held strong views on matters connected with old buildings and detested all attempts to tamper with their history under the guise of restoration". (Obituary; Journal of the RIBA 6 June 1908 by F. W. Troup (F) and Harry Redfern (F)). A long list of works stands to his credit prior to 1896 which includes churches, country houses, and London houses in Prince's Gate; Lowther Gardens; Melbury Road; Kensington Court; a group of seventeen houses in Buckingham Palace Road on the Grosvenor Estate; a group of five houses in South Street, Mayfair; and others in Hampstead, Belgravia, and Kensington Palace Gardens. When Stevenson died in 1908 Redfern completed any outstanding business.

The principal architectural works during the period of Redfern's partnership with Stevenson included laboratories for chemistry, metallurgy, physics, biology and parasitology at Cambridge University in 1889 with additions in 1908; laboratories for morphology and bio-chemistry at Oxford University in 1899; repairs at St John's College (1889) and Oriel College (1899) Oxford University; a block of sets and lecture rooms at Christ's College, Cambridge (1886) with additions in 1906. There were also designs made for additions to Sidney Sussex; Trinity; and Clare Colleges; and for the Sedgewick Geological Museum at Cambridge.

Many new houses were built in different parts of the country: at Haywards Heath (Lindfield) East Sussex; Camberley and Weybridge in Surrey; High Wycombe, Bucks; Westerham, Kent; Hampstead in London; together with some business premises in Windsor. Structural repair of Abingdon Abbey in Berkshire was carried out for the Corporation and two blocks of Board School buildings at Abingdon were built to accommodate 500 children. The schools were in red brick with Doulting stone dressings and slate roofs. They were placed on the north side of

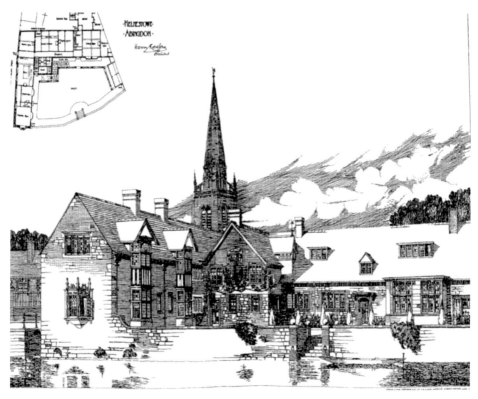

Redfern's drawing of Helnestowe in Abingdon

the site to give extensive playground space which was open to the sun. Then in 1897 Redfern designed a small house for his old school in Abingdon as a Masters' Lodging to accommodate under one roof a residence for the porter and lodging for two masters. It was designed in a modest Queen Anne style. Writing to me in January, 1994, the Headmaster of Abingdon School, M. St. John Parker, M.A., informed me that, "The Lodge which Redfern designed for the school remains a thoroughly useful building which has been comparatively little changed over the years. Initially constructed as lodgings for bachelor masters it was subsequently used as a small junior boarding house, and then as a sanatorium before being converted about 15 years ago for use as the offices of the school bursary. Apart from a little trouble with damp - hardly surprising since Redfern inadvertently constructed it on the line of an underground water course - it has lasted well and sits very happily beside the main school entrance".

In 1901 Redfern made alterations and additions to the house Helnestowe in Abingdon. Writing in the Builder of August 24th, 1901, Redfern himself tells us that, "This house stands on the site of the nunnery of Helnestowe, a medieval foundation from which it takes its name. At the time of the alterations the ground was occupied by a malthouse and cottages with sheds abutting upon the river. The sheds were taken down and the malthouse and cottages were gutted; the excellent timber roof of these last forming a feature in what is now the hall. Various pieces of old work were brought to light, including some oak panelling re-used in the hall; and the traceried head of a fourteenth-century window which has been completed and now helps to light the drawing-room. The old buildings supplied much of the required material. The owner was his own builder, engaging and superintending local workmen, with very frequent visits from the architect. This arrangement has answered admirably and the work has been extremely well done".

The partnership with Stevenson was responsible for the British Hospital at Port Said and, in 1902, for the design and fittings of the saloons and drawing room on the P&O steamship Orontes. Stevenson had been the first architect invited to design the fittings and interior decoration of the principal rooms in a large steamship and had done this for the Pacific and Orient Company's mail ship, Orient, in 1879. The Orient was the first ship on the Australian run to be electrified and able to boast the use of refrigeration. Several other ships followed: the Royal Mail steamer: Ormuz (1887), in which he designed the dining room, drawing room, and library; the Austral; Ophir; and Omrah. When the Orontes was built in 1902 at Fairfield's shipyard on the Clyde, it was the tenth in the London to Australia line and was built for the mail and passenger trade, which meant that both speed and comfort were critical. Of necessity the architecture and design of such ships had to be functional. Everything had to

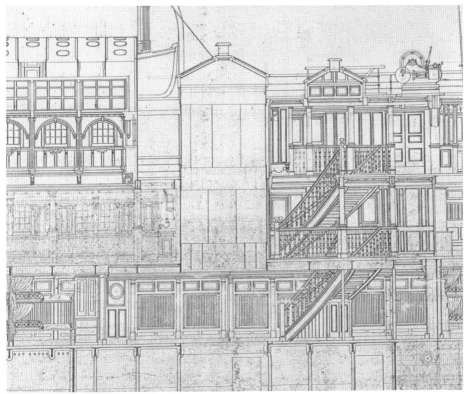

Detail from a drawing of Redfern's design for the liner Orontes.
The panelled style in which the interior was fitted out bears comparison to the smoking rooms of the Scheme's pubs.

stand up to wear and tear and take account of the effect of salt air on the materials used. Fitments had to be bolted down; furnishings and decoration had to avoid what is called the "squeak and chatter" element; and surfaces which would entail extensive upkeep or cleaning needed to be avoided. An article in the Illustrated London News of October, 1902, praised the work saying: "The new vessel is magnificently decorated. The first-class dining-saloon which is surmounted by a dome with panels of stained glass is fitted in mahogany. . . the smoking-room is in grey fumigated oak and the seats and settles are upholstered in green Russian leather. The drawing-room has been carried out in bleached Italian walnut below and in satin-wood above, and the sofas and chairs are covered with art cretonnes". The Sphere of September 27th,1902, also mentions in its article on the Orontes that: "The lavatory and bath arrangements were on the liberal side and great attention was given to ventilation throughout the steamer using noiseless electric beeswing fans to keep the air in motion".

Following Stevenson's death, Redfern set up his own practice at 5 Bedford Row, London in 1909. In the same year he became Chairman of the Art Workers' Guild and a committee member of the Society for the Protection of Ancient Buildings; and a member of the Ecclesiological Society and the Georgian Group. He gad been admitted a Fellow of the Royal Institute of British Architects in 1903 at the age of 42 and subsequently became a member of their Council from 1914 -1917 and during the same period of the Finance and House Committee and of the Fellowship Drawings Committee. He was sometime member of the Art Standing Committee and served as an Honorary Examiner (Architecture) from 1920-21.

From 1909 there followed a body of work for him in Cambridge with commissions for several houses for the dons. He built these in a wonderfully sympathetic Arts and Crafts manner. The first of these houses was Conduit Head at 36 Conduit Head Road, which was built as a wedding present from Francis Darwin (Charles Darwin's son) for Francis M. Cornford, Trinity Professor of Ancient Philosophy, and Frances Darwin, the granddaughter of Charles, whose mother, Ellen (nee Crofts), had been Fellow and Lecturer in English literature at Newnham College. Originally the plan of Conduit Head was similar to the Red House built for William Morris by Philip Webb. lt was L-shaped with a staircase tower and lift in the angle. Entrance to the house was by a porch on the west side which led on to a corridor with access to the sixteen foot square study. Above this study on the first floor was the drawing room with bay window. This corner of the property was subsequently demolished because of foundation settlement. The front door of solid oak was then relocated within a new projecting porch facing south west and leading directly into the living room. This room, with its pitch pine block flooring, overhead beams and tiled hearth, had an exit at the far end onto the stoep or verandah. This had been paved with red Staffordshire tiles as a suitable area for eating out of doors. The owner's bedroom and dressing room, both with a tiled hearth, were on the first floor above the living room and had access to an open sleeping balcony above the stoep for summer use. Beyond the corridor on the ground floor, lay the sixteen foot square kitchen with its red Staffordshire tile paving and cement hearth. Beyond this was the scullery with its cement floor, and doors leading to the knives and boots compartment; the fuel store;

and the well house. This latter feature provided Conduit Head with drinking water direct from the Trinity College Conduit since the College owned the freehold of a large area around the house and the original water supply to the College came from the land immediately adjoining the grounds of Conduit Head. A spare bedroom and two bedrooms for the servants lay above the kitchen and scullery on the first floor facing south east. The house was constructed with plenty of plumbing and a 50 volt electricity circuit. The walls of the lower storey were of brick thirteen-and-a-half inches thick, lime-whited externally and plastered internally, while the brick of the upper storey was rendered externally with lime plastering and plastered internally. The walls lay on foundations of cement concrete with a similar concrete six inches thick over the ground floor area upon which could be laid woodblock floors. The roofs were covered with grey hand-made tiles and Redfern, true to his Arts and Crafts principles, had ensured that the garden area also maintained his aesthetic vision by himself drawing some of the plantings into his plan. Conduit Head, 'the house that Redfern built', was the venue for some of the most exhilarating gatherings in the Cambridge social life of the day. Gwen Raverat (nee Darwin). a cousin of Frances Cornford, in her book Period Piece says: "I admired Frances tremendously; she seemed to live in an up-to-date sophisticated world where Art and Literature were taken seriously". Gwen Raverat's husband Jacques was one of Eric Gill's most sympathetic friends and it was Gill who carved the cornice plaque at Conduit Head: "Francis Darwin Built This House For Francis & Frances Cornford - 1910", and it was Gill's brother, Macdonald, who designed the beautiful tiled fireplace in the living room.

Eric Gill had been born in Brighton in 1882, the second of thirteen children. He was apprenticed to the architect Caroe of the Ecclesiastical Commissioners in 1900, but left three years later when the architect Edward Prior offered him a job in

Conduit Head

Longfield

Cambridge. Prior was building the new School of Medicine in Downing Street and invited the young Gill to cut some inscriptions for the building. This offer changed the course of Gill's career. He abandoned the idea of becoming an architect and opted instead to become a letter-cutter and later a monumental mason, always insisting on being recognised as both artist and craftsman. He enjoyed staying in Cambridge with the Cornfords where the talk would flow freely, frequently encompassing arguments of philosophy and religion.

Redfern built several more houses for dons before the outbreak of the First World War in 1914. The next house was Longfield, built in 1912 for Professor G.H. F. Nuttall, FRS - a most attractive house set in a long, narrow field, as its name suggests, in an acre of land on the south side of Madingley Road beyond Trinity Hall Cricket Ground. The rooms in this house were considerably higher than those in Conduit Head, probably at the request of Professor Nuttall himself. The vaulted entrance corridor off the hall led to the dining room, study and drawing room. The oak panelled study and drawing room were linked by large folding doors while the drawing room led into a small 'den'. Once again Redfern provided generous space on the ground floor for the domestic working requirements with his usual kitchen, scullery, pantry, store houses, wine cellar and, this time, a dark room. There were four bedrooms on the first floor, three of which had their own dressing rooms and the owner's daughter was provided with her own private sitting room leading off her bedroom. There were two rooms for the maids in the attic. The garden with its central axis had compartments set out with yew hedges and two formal rose gardens which were cut into the turf beyond the terrace.

Of the four further impressive houses which were built by Redfern and completed by January, 1915, three are now in multiple occupation, namely Conduit Rise built for Harold D. Hazeltine in Conduit Head Road (1913); The Elms built for Dr. S. Ruhemann at 6 Adams Road (1913); and No. 70 Storey's Way built for V. S. Vernon-Jones (1914). Bredon House built for Professor J. Stanley Gardiner in

Selwyn Gardens (1914) became Wolfson College in the late 1960s for the use of post-graduates in educational studies . All these Cambridge houses reveal Redfern's flair for interpreting the tenets of the Arts and Crafts Movement; understanding the aesthetic requirements of his clients; and at the same time making a markedly positive move in catering for the working conditions and comfort of the domestic staff. (With hindsight we know that this attitude to his architectural designing was carried forward in his work for the State Management Scheme in Carlisle and District in furtherance of the improved public house movement. The managers of the new public houses were given generous living quarters - sometimes with three bedrooms, while the requirements of the bar staff and domestics were fully considered in his drawing up of the plans).

Conduit Rise was a multi-gabled brick building with roughcast rendering painted white and three large chimney stacks also rendered and painted white. The front elevation had a centrally placed brick-paved hall with an arched entrance doorway above which was a double-hipped dormer. On either side of the entrance was the dining room (16 foot by 20 foot) and the drawing room (16 foot by 24 foot) with a lead off to a retreat (6 foot by 6 foot). The garden elevation had two smaller, boarded gables and the roof on the west side swept down to ground floor level to form a verandah, a feature we see Redfern repeating in some of the public house buildings later in his career. The fenestration of Conduit Rise was asymmetrical and the casement windows were set in wooden frames with leaded lights. On the ground floor the maids were favoured with their own sitting room away from the kitchen, while on the first floor the maids were provided with three bedrooms and a bathroom. The first floor also comprised the owner's bedroom and dressing room; a boudoir; and a study (16 foot by 16 foot) together with two spare bedrooms. The three houses were all in rural settings, but, when Redfern came to build The Elms in Adams Road, he was faced with an urban setting and was subject to a building line 20 feet back from the road. The elevation therefore was more vertical and the massing symmetrical. The fenestration however in reflecting the uses of the rooms behind was asymmetrical since the drawing room and dining room on the south side with their bay windows were separated from the kitchen by the pantry. The kitchen was therefore also given a bay window, but it was made blind and contained store cupboards. This was another impressive house with its six bedrooms; two dressing rooms; two bathrooms and a boudoir at first floor level.

Bredon House, Selwyn Gardens and 70 Storey's Way were the last two of Redfern's distinctive houses to be completed before the onset of the First World War. They were built in January and April, 1915, respectively. Bredon House in its original setting had a very large fruit orchard which extended to Barton Road; a long avenue of pink horse chestnut trees; and an attractive sunken rockery. The ground floor of the house consisted of the usual dining room, drawing room, and study all beautifully panelled; together with a day nursery and loggia; while at first floor level, as well as the owner's bedroom and dressing room containing a strong room, there was a night nursery with its own bathroom. There were two spare bedrooms on this floor and three bedrooms for the domestic staff with their own bathroom. The attic floor comprised another bedroom; a children's room and a play gallery.

Bredon House, built by Redfern for Professor J. Stanley Gardiner, which in 1965 became Wolfson College, Cambridge. The design shares many of the features of the Coach and Horses before its brick work was rendered.

70 Storey's Way, Cambridge; Redfern's last work before the onset of the First World War. Many features were later adopted in the Scheme's pubs including the roof swept down to ground floor level.

The last in this series of houses, 70 Storey's Way, off Madingley Road, again bears witness to the rare talent of Redfern who deserves to be better known as an architect using a free-play interpretation of the Arts and Crafts style. The ground floor comprised the same selection of rooms as the other houses, but here the open planning between the drawing room and dining room had gone and, unlike 6 Adams Road, the pantry did not come between the dining room and the kitchen. The bonus on this plan, however, was the inclusion of a garage or "motor room" as it was called in 1915. It measured 12 foot by 16 foot. There were seven bedrooms on the first floor, including the owner's bedroom and dressing room together with two spare bedrooms; two child's' bedrooms; and two maid's bedrooms. There was also a gallery and a balcony, while on the attic floor Redfern provided a store room (8 foot by 12 foot); a box room (20 foot by foot); and a fruit room (22 foot by 8 foot). In all these houses we cannot help but notice Redfern's progressive attitude to the domestic staff giving them generously proportioned rooms for the times; providing them with bathroom facilities; and housing them under the one all-embracing roof. All these houses have weathered well over the intervening years.

Although the onset of the First World War interrupted the building of domestic houses for private clients, Redfern maintained his connection with Cambridge University. He was responsible for all the restoration work in Magdalene College throughout the 1920s and 30s. It was probably as a result of his association with Professor Nuttall of Longfield that Redfern went to Magdalene in 1911 to work for A.C. Benson, Fellow, and, from 1915, Master, of Magdalene College. The Old Lodge, which Professor Alfred Newton had occupied in the later part of the nineteenth century and from where he had founded the British Ornithologists' Union in 1859, had become unoccupied at his death. In 1911/12 Benson decided to move in. With Redfern as his architect, he undertook a radical reconstruction and unification of buildings on the site. He added a worthy dining room (now Benson Hall) complete with minstrels' gallery. There was a butler's observation window at the north end, and a Venetian window at the south end. Once again Redfern utilised materials salvaged from demolished outhouses in a way he had done earlier at Abingdon when working on Helnestowe. We shall also see when looking later at some of his public houses in Carlisle how partial he was to using a minstrels' gallery and a Venetian window when it was fit for his purpose.

Opposite the College, on the west side of Magdalene Street, there evolved an open-plan campus over a period of 45 years between 1925 and 1970, which was the work of three successive architects, namely Harry Redfern; Sir Edwin Lutyens; and David Roberts. It was Redfern who prepared the original plans for Benson Court. The initial nucleus of this development was the Mallory Court complex, which owes more to Redfern than anyone else. It began with the conversion, into a hostel providing a dozen sets for undergraduates, of an early nineteenth-century vinegar factory in Ekins Yard. The conversion was funded by Benson in memory of one of his favourite pupils, George Mallory, who had died on Everest the previous year (1924). A plaque to this effect was placed above the entrance door of the conversion. The brewery was a very odd, tall, tower-like building with a large factory chimney, but in Redfern's hands it was pleasantly set off by a new lower wing and the conversion of some of the early nineteenth-century cottages nearby for College use. It all added up to what Pevsner referred to as "felicitous informality".

Redfern undertook his own shopping forays to suitable furniture for the hostel's communal room and found two tables and twelve chairs at William Morris & Company's shop at 17 George Street, Hanover Square, London. One of the tables had been designed in oak by Philip Webb for Lord Leconfield but when the question of rugs was raised the College found Redfern's suggestion of a Ramadan and a Ferahand too expensive and he had to settle for an Axminster carpet of Morris design. There were other financial queries along the way as is not altogether unusual when final figures begin to vary from initial estimates. Redfern intimated to Benson that nothing would have distressed him more than that he might have given a false impression of the probable cost of the work or led him to undertake it unwillingly. He consequently submitted two schemes which involved a variation in accommodation and costs. After careful consideration Benson decided that the total price was not too high for the good value they were going to get from the outlay. He was magnanimous in his praise of Redfern in a letter dated 22nd April, 1925:"You are most good in accepting and working out criticisms". In June of this same year Benson unexpectedly died. Redfern subsequently built a handsome annexe to the College's Old Library in his memory. Even so, it was not without the need for some pleading on Redfern's part for the College to grit its teeth and decide to proceed with the addition, explaining that in an undertaking like this more has to be done than can be shown on any drawing.

Some years later, in 1934, the Steward of Christ's College, Cambridge, T. C. Wyatt, sought from the Bursar of Magdalene College, T. Peel, the name of the architect who had recently carried out work at Magdalene. The architect being referred to had in fact been Sir Edwin Lutyens, but Peel suggested that they might care to consider Redfern with whom they had had the most helpful dealings. They had found that Redfern was especially good at catching the spirit of a building and made no effort to draw attention to himself. Some two years later in February, 1936, Peel volunteered the information to the bursar of Christ's College, S.G. Campbell, that Redfern was not expensive; that his estimates were most accurate; and that he always considered the College. At the same time, in a letter to T.C. Wyatt, Steward of Christ's College, he showed how well Redfern was regarded by the College: "He has been architect to the College for twenty years and is a most attractive person to deal with. . . his great forte is altering old buildings". Other assignments in the 1930s included further work on cottages in Mallory Court; a new undergraduate Reading Room; the re-modelling of the kitchen and buttery; and a new lantern in the gatehouse of First Court. In 1937, the College had wanted to remove the tapestries on the walls of the College Chapel as they interfered with the acoustics for the choir. Redfern had cherished the hope that in replacing the hangings behind the altar a reredos might be considered which he, with his family background, would certainly have enjoyed designing. But this was not to be. The walls were eventually panelled in French walnut and posterity has been denied the intriguing prospect of a Harry Redfern reredos in a Cambridge chapel.

During this same period, at a time when he was already fully committed to his assignment for the State Management Scheme in Carlisle and District, Redfern was also building a new bio-chemistry laboratory for Oxford University in 1924 with additions and alterations in 1936. Bio-chemistry was an expanding faculty in the 1920s and 30s which placed specific requirements upon the architect (as indeed did the building of the public houses in Carlisle). The first floor of the laboratory comprised two large classrooms, the upper part of which were carried to the mezzanine above as was the lecture room. There was also a staff research room, a preparation room; two balance rooms and five fume chambers. On the mezzanine above the lecture theatre, there were two animal rooms - one for physiology and one for bio-chemistry purposes from which the library and common room could be reached by means of an open bridge. A research room for gas analysis and a constant temperature room were also located on the mezzanine. The original plans for the second floor ,drawn up in 1924, comprised an animal washing room; an experimental bathroom; a professor's room; and an assistant professor's room. These were all interconnecting. There were separate rooms of varying dimensions for operations; sterilization; bacteriology; two staff rooms; a balance room and a research room together with an aquarium and an all-important fan room. Preliminary plans for additions and alterations to the second floor were made in February, 1936, the final plans being adopted in August, 1936. A roof extension was made and internal additions comprised two rooms for dogs; a mortuary; a sterilising room; and three separate laboratories - for the professor; for his lab assistant and for the assistant professor. A dark room was also added. The original two staff rooms were turned into a research room and a micro-analysis room, and the 1924 space allocated to bacteriology, operations and sterilization was re-arranged to give separate spaces for anaesthetising and bath room.

At the onset of the First World War, Redfern moved from his home address in Birkbeck Avenue, Acton, London to a newly built semi-detached house at No. 1 St. Dunstan's Gardens, East Acton. The property was built on land belonging to the Goldsmith's Company, who had decided, through its surveyor, Burnett Brown, to ask Leonard Hammond, a foreman who had built other property in the area, to develop the site. Initially a pair of buildings were commissioned, 1 & 2 St. Dunstan's Gardens. The company's surveyor signed the completion certificate on the 14th August, 1914, and undertook to build a further six houses, in three pairs. (Goldsmith Company Archives B. III. 4. 49). Redfern's wife, Edith Ashulet Redfern, signed an agreement to purchase the property at No. 1 from Leonard Hammond on the 8th August, 1914, (Goldsmith Company Archives B. III. 4. 24) which was witnessed by Harry Redfern. A draft lease of 99 years dated the 30th September, 1914, states that the cost of the house due to Leonard Hammond was £650 with a yearly ground rent of £7. 10s. 0. payable quarterly due to the Goldsmith's Company. (Goldsmith Company Archives B. III. 2. 54). Harry was to live in this house for the next 36 years until his death there in 1950. His wife pre-deceased him and, after her death on the 4th May, 1937, an assignment was completed on the 27th September, 1937, between their two daughters, Dorothy and Phillis as vendors and Harry (then aged 76) as purchaser. Harry, in his own last will, made on the 19th March, 1948, at the age of 87, then assigned his estate to his two daughters: two-thirds to Dorothy and one-third to Phillis. Following his death on the 6th March, 1950, the house was subsequently sold on the 14th February, 1951.

It was not long after having settled into the new house with his family around him, that, in 1915, Redfern was appointed the Assistant Director of the Survey of Greater London. It had been in 1870 that the London School Board, which was the first democratically elected metropolitan local government body, was beginning to wrestle with the task of educating London's untaught population. By 1889, when the London County Council superseded the Metropolitan Board of Works, it was given increased powers to expand its work in the fields of slum clearance; street improvements, provision of working-class housing and other social amenities. In pursuance of these admirable objectives, there arose however a growing anxiety concerning the destruction and demolition, sometimes unwittingly, of a number of the capital's historic buildings and monuments. An Ancient Monuments Act had been passed in 1882, but the government's awareness and commitment in preserving its historic buildings at this time was inadequate. The Act, for all that it established the principle of the protection of a national heritage, seemed only to cover monuments such as Stonehenge that were uninhabitable. Consequently a more positive action was taken by dedicated individuals and a Committee for the Survey of the Memorials of Greater London, (later to be known as the London Survey Committee) was formed in 1894 by the Arts and Crafts architect C.R. Ashbee. Working with a group of like-minded colleagues, their first task was to compile a register, parish by parish, of important buildings that were under threat and then to alert Londoners of the situation. Some of the work was done by volunteers and the committee was ever mindful of the additional need for professional expertise and supervision by an architect.

1 & 2 St. Dunstan's Gardens, Harry Redfern's very ordinary home.

Clear objectives were set out by way of a form to be completed augmented by sketches, photographs, and occasionally a measured drawing. A Conference of Learned Societies held on 4 December, 1896, which was attended by Ashbee and representatives from both the Society for the Protection of Ancient Buildings and the newly formed National Trust resulted in the London County Council's commitment to the preservation of buildings and monuments in its area with a request that the work should be extended to cover the whole of the L.C.C. area. From this date the L.C.C. obtained the powers to spend money from the rates to safeguard its historic buildings and monuments. It was unfortunate that the work had to be suspended to a large extent owing to the outbreak of the First World War which had resulted in the mobilisation of so many of the staff. The L.C.C. then sought both to use, and give employment to, men who were not eligible for the armed forces and it was decided that these men should serve in the Ministry of Munitions. The 54-year-old Harry Redfern had become Assistant Director of the Survey of Greater London in 1915 and it was on the 30th of June of that same year that David Lloyd George as Minister of Munitions had set up the Central Control Board (Liquor Traffic) under Regulation 1 of the Defence of the Realm (Liquor Control) Regulations 1915. By 1916, Harry Redfern had been appointed Chief Architect to the Central Control Board, (later to become The State Management Scheme), a post which he held for the next 33 years.

CHAPTER SEVEN
THE SCHEME: REDFERN'S MODEL INNS

"Inn design is subtle and difficult". These are Harry Redfern's own words in the Journal of the RIBA of 3 April, 1939, when coming towards the end of his extraordinary assignment for the Carlisle and District State Management Scheme. If philosophies and movements have an effect upon history, then Redfern can be said to have completed his work in an isolated part of the country with the back-up of his belief in, and adherence to, the tenets of the Arts & Crafts movement. His remit had been to build improved public houses, to give as much air, space, and light as possible; to provide for proper supervision of both the customer and the staff by the manager; to encourage sit-down drinking instead of stand-up drinking; and above all to try to overcome the notion that the new type of public house was to be a place for drinking only, and to achieve this by providing positively for the sale of food together with the provision of facilities for games, music, and other forms of recreation.

Redfern would never have seen his work as seminal in evolving a new style, for he looked upon himself, along with so many of his contemporaries in the Art Workers' Guild, as craftsmen rather than celebrities, and that it was the building that mattered, not the builder. He was uncomfortable with self-advertisement preferring that his work should speak for itself, and along with fellow members of the Guild, he was content to keep the flame of aesthetics and craftsmanship burning for the following generation.

Redfern's article in the RIBA Journal of 1939 went on to say that the work carried out in Carlisle was of special interest to architects in that new standards in public house design were set which brewers had not been slow to follow. "To younger architects accustomed to fairly high standards of design in the newer inns about the country, the State Management designs will possibly not appear exceptional, but comparison should really be made with inns built by brewers immediately before the Great War when the immense general improvement brought about by the example of the State Management inns will become obvious. Even now many brewers could learn much from the recent work, particularly as regards interiors. No two houses present identical conditions; locality, patronage, and trade are peculiar to each case. Beyond these conditions the architect must create an exterior that is welcoming and an interior that is comfortable. Inn patrons are conservative and they like or dislike inns by instinct rather than by reasoned analysis. The interiors must be such as to become as unchangingly familiar as are the homes of the patrons. In this respect inn design differs somewhat from hotel design where the population is a changing one. The aim of the inn designer should be to attract the same people day after day.

"The elements of this quality of familiar comfort cannot be found on the drawing board alone. They lie partly in the arrangement, sizes, and shapes of interiors but also very much in the careful use of enduring materials that will improve with age and cleaning. In design the exceptional or unfamiliar must be avoided since patrons tend to be conservative. Design must not be in advance of current local ideas. In consequence, traditional and familiar forms will be found repeated in the new buildings. It is possible that different methods and more advanced design might be desirable in areas where the population is less conservatively minded than in northern Britain. Certainly they would need to be different in, for instance a south-country seaside resort. Consequently the Carlisle inns must be judged only in the light of their own peculiar requirements. Mere imitation of their design - as has often been done - would not necessarily be successful elsewhere. It should moreover be pointed out that no photographs or plans can portray at all faithfully the quality and atmosphere of these inns. They need to be studied on the spot. For architects it is much more than a unique social experiment, since it calls for a careful study of human desires and needs - impossible to express in words - and a feeling for sensitive design in the highest degree. It is, in fact the essence of architecture".

Before studying in some detail many of Redfern's inns built during his consistently productive period post-war from 1927 to 1940, it would be rewarding to consider just what are the many factors that an architect has to encompass as he sits at his drawing board with the notion of designing a model inn. Whether the building is to be an inn selling food in addition to liquor, as were Redfern's, or the usual type of public house, it is still a house for the public - for everyman - requiring an atmosphere of a certain specialised kind. Of course that atmosphere can change with the times as evidenced by James F. Redfern's nostalgic comment on revisiting his hometown of Longnor at the end of the nineteenth century that, "There was no longer the "snuggery with its stuffiness and hub-bub, churchwardens and mugs", which can be set alongside a contemporary comment a hundred years later that, "You go in stone sober and come out stone deaf". But for all that, the interior of the public house is still one of the trickiest architectural problems of any age.

The importance of the Carlisle Scheme was that it was permitted to make unhampered experiments in many directions and especially in the evolution of the improved public house. Keeping the national interest in view at all times, the Central Control Board, followed by the State Management Scheme, consistently tried to make each decision undertaken serve the future as well as solve a present problem. Few types of buildings are so circumscribed with restrictions and regulations as the English public house. The architect, in designing his project, has to unify the formal elements with social needs, countless measurements and a liberal degree of common-sense. Redfern, given his unique commission, kept his head and sought always the utilitarian qualities of strength and fitness for purpose to obtain beauty by honesty. He produced a body of work, using local labour whenever possible, which offered variety within an overall unity. In each case a sanitary, substantial, and comfortable public house was produced with a controlled use of both old and new materials in a quiet and dignified way. Each design had its revolutionary aspect which had been made possible in a conservative community such as Carlisle because of the State's monopoly and unique system of management His influence was subtle rather than overt, but he left his architectural fingerprints on the buildings and many of the model inns carry features which are easily discernible as Redfern's. He worked to create a feeling of homeliness - the house image as distinct from the shop image which had preceded it. Cosy inglenooks and wood panelling were a special delight for him and he enjoyed incorporating a minstrels' gallery or a Queen Anne revival window wherever and whenever it was deemed suitable. Other features included weather vanes, decorated water downspouts, deep and delicate gutter brackets, dormer windows, bowling greens, loggias, pergolas, and garden beds. In 1927, as Redfern was embarking on his allotted task of building model inns, Thomas Mawson, the plantsman and landscape gardener had just published his autobiography, The Life and Work of an English Landscape Architect, for which the title page bore the motto, "I look backward that I may better press forward". It would seem that Redfern could well have assumed the same guiding principle for which he was so eminently qualified.

For a long time past, the local alehouse or small inn had looked much the same as its surrounding dwellings and shops and was slow to acquire an appearance of its own. Eventually the shop-front image was abandoned to be replaced by the house image and with skilful planning it could not have been mistaken for anything other than an inn or public house. Using a freeplay of the Arts and Crafts principles, Redfern effected a return to simplicity, sincerity, good materials, and sound workmanship. He made an eclectic choice of traditional forms to create a pleasing aesthetic, and while disliking any form of rigid historicism per se, he nurtured a sincere respect for the past and a willingness to judiciously mix elements of past styles in order to update tradition in his own way. British Arts and Crafts thinking did not seek to produce a definitive style but assumed that an appropriate form would emerge from the proper regard for materials and function.

Redfern was not alone in this thought process at the time. What was unique in his case was that he used these tenets consistently on a whole series of public houses in one area in the country. The State Management Scheme afforded him great scope for planning and relieved him of much of the usual procedure concerning the licensing justices. Nevertheless he always submitted a set of plans to Carlisle City Council purely as a matter of courtesy. In a few instances he was constrained in his design and had to concede certain details in deference to local byelaws, as with the original beautiful hanging sign for the Apple Tree and the proposed hanging sign for the Cumberland Inn. He naturally co-operated with the council, but as his letter concerning the latter revealed, he was not well-pleased. These were examples of the architect on occasion having to allow his tolerance and common sense to prevail over his aesthetic. The weariness and national inertia following the experience of the First World War and then followed by the years of depression, left the public and a number of the architectural profession itself with a feeling of indifference in the 1930s. It was the State Management Scheme's architectural commission with its social implications which directed interest towards future possibilities and set a new standard in public house design in which one architect was speaking for the overall concept.

Because of the State's monopoly in Carlisle and its system of disinterested management, it was deemed unnecessary, for commercial considerations, that the proposed public houses should occupy the best sites. The ideal site is rare anyway, but all sites fall mainly into one of four categories: open, corner, closed, or island.

A dormer window at the Horse & Farrier.

Interlocking rooflines with a stench pipe woven into the brick and through the rooflines. Rose & Crown, Upperby.

Elegant bracketry on a window shutter at the Rose & Crown, Upperby

Stained glass rebus in recognition of Redfern's collaborators: Ernest A. Streatfield, clerk of works, and J. Bell, the builder, from the Cumberland Inn, 1930.

Dormer and chimneys at the Magpie

Ornate guttering and bracketry at the Magpie.

Moulded leadwork and leaded window, the Crown, Stanwix

The Apple Tree soon after its completion in 1927, but before permission to hang its
striking inn sign was withdrawn in October of that year.
The sign can be seen in the Tullie House Collection, Carlisle.
(Courtesy of Journal of the Royal Institute of British Architects)

The architect has to be thoroughly conversant with the nature of the site and the purpose and nature of the business for which he is designing. He will want to know the site's history, its orientation, the nature of the sub-soil, the water table and any liability to flooding, the site in relation to its environment including the rights of any adjoining neighbours with regard to light and air, drainage, party walls, and rights of way. The architect will also want to check on the weathering and exposure hazards of a particular site and will want to assess whether its size and shape is going to be adequate for the proposed accommodation required both initially, and for any future increase in the number of customers or class of trade. Open sites and corner sites offer the architect greater freedom to plan a building which is more open to light and air and does not get cluttered up with long passages. This is especially important as the plan has to facilitate the complete circulation of the premises by the police on their routine inspections. When an entirely open site is available the architect will invariably choose to place his building more or less in the centre of it. The closed site, however, presents far more difficulties, especially where it abuts other buildings on either or both sides, as for instance with the Crescent Inn and Cumberland Inn. When this is the case, the planning is dependent upon installing larger windows to the front and rear and sometimes to make use of roof or area lighting. Another signif-icant problem which can arise with a closed site is the possibility of expanding the drinking space should the custom increase at some future date. A study of the plan for the Apple Tree reveals that Redfern allowed for this by enabling the ground floor bar to be opened out at weekends or other busy times. The existence of an island site is a rare phenomenon and does not arise in the case of Carlisle now under discussion. Regulations dictate that the proposed licensed premises must be self-contained with no communicating access to adjoining property, and that any off-sales departments must communicate directly with the street, are not permitted to have any seating, and are subject to direct supervision from the street by the police. A good example of planning for off-sales is the Rose & Crown at Upperby. However, as the State Management had already provided several separate off-sales facilities in well-distributed areas of the city to take the place of the extinguished grocers' licences, by 1930 it considered the outdoor department was unnecessary in several of its houses. No off-sales departments were included in the plans for the Malt Shovel, Apple Tree, Cumberland Inn, and Crescent. No windows or hatches were permissible between passages and the servery and no liquor was to be consumed in any passage. In planning a public house it is best that passages are kept straight and that they are wide enough to take traffic in both directions but not so generous as to invite customers to consume their liquor in them. Public stairs need to have easy and direct access with no windows and with ample crush space at the top and bottom of the flight. Good lighting is essential and it is best that the bottom stair is wider than the rest of the flight

No public house can function efficiently without a good cellar and its situation in relation to the servery is of vital concern. Basement cellars which are directly beneath the servery are preferable as they curtail the length of piping required between storage and pumps. The cellar must be planned on generous lines as it is not always easy to enlarge it at a later date if the volume of trade increases. There should be no direct sunlight and no contact with any form of heating apparatus, and the floors need to be of impervious material best able to resist the disintegrating effects of beer spillage. Internal access to the cellar should be available directly from the servery, but on no account should it be in such a position as to be accessible to the public, and the servery itself must be so planned as to enable the manager to supervise the whole of the drinking area. Efficient planning of the servery helps the manager in his duty to give direct service to all public rooms and garden areas, and in addition needs to take account of what duties go on behind the counter, on top of it, and in front of it. It also needs to allow bar staff to pass each other with ease between the back fitting and the counter without having to take any unnecessary steps.

The fireplace was an important feature in the days before the benefits of central heating and it offered both a warming welcome and the advantage, by means of an updraught, of helping to clear the room of tobacco smoke and vitiated air, but it called for careful planning. In size it needed to be compatible with the dimensions of the room yet generous enough to accommodate all who wanted to sit nearby. Most patrons seem to dislike open windows so that the ventilation flues in the chimney breasts and stacks and the warmth of the adjacent smoke flues helped in creating the necessary updraughts. Public houses, like other buildings where numbers of people

The main upper floor room of the Apple Tree; the Mixed First Class as it appeared in 1935. There is ample natural light. Each window is decorated with a stained glass apple tree motif. (Courtesy of Tassell Carlisle Ltd.)

gather internally, benefit from thorough but inconspicuous ventilation in order to be comfortable. Patrons had most likely walked some distance, often in the wind and the rain and entered the public house in wet clothing which would then partially dry out. In addition, Carlisle being an agricultural town, farmers would bring their cattle to market and then resort to the public house to transact business. Redfern understood this and chose a system of ventilation which trunked the stale air to a large extractor fan housed on an upper floor where, as in the case of the Crescent Inn, it was concealed and disguised as a minstrel's gallery. The choice of fan was crucial so that the system worked well under all conditions and Redfern's previous experience on the laboratories in Oxford and Cambridge possibly contributed to his success in this matter.

The most important of all the planning requirements in designing a public house, especially a model inn where food is to be served, is the close attention paid to the sanitary arrangements as this affects, and is affected by, all the other accommodation. Correct positioning is essential, but is full of difficulties because it is often, of necessity, dictated by the site. Ideally, access to toilets should be within easy reach of the patrons of every bar according to their sex without the necessity of passing through another room or bar used by a different category of patron. All entrances to toilets should be planned for peak trade and offer quick and easy access without stairs. They should not be so secluded that they are not easily found nor should they be unavailable to the manager to supervise them. By way of effecting a compromise between supervision and privacy. Redfern, for instance in the Crescent Inn, glazed the panels in the top portion of the door leading into the bar in a pattern of clear glass and then used the same patterning, but with mirror glass, for an identical door leading to the toilets. This benefitted both the patrons sitting in the bar and those seeking the services of the toilet. The grouping of the rooms is another feature which calls for care.

Public bars are usually the noisiest so that any billiards room is best situated near to the men's smoking room with access to the servery and with a space of six foot allowed on all sides of the table for cueing. A Victorian billiards room had been viewed in its time as a kind of "rakish retreat or club" and had on occasion been decorated in a Moorish or Turkish style. (This point will be further investigated when describing Redfern's vision for the Crescent Inn).

Historically the smoking room was generally the superior room and reserved for men at a time when it was not deemed desirable for women to be seen on licensed premises. At the outset the State Management Scheme encountered a strong tradition against unescorted women mixing with men in the public houses and a resentment by the men of their presence. The administration decided that, in order to rectify the situation and prevent the women from having to resort to the corridors or the old jug and bottle area, it would provide separate rooms in certain houses. Steps were gradually taken in connection with the reconstruction scheme to provide rooms open to both men and unescorted women as well as for men only. Gradually mixed drinking began to alter the requirements within the plan so that all rooms were available to both sexes, and as this required a larger floor area it often involved the use of the first floor. Publicans knew well enough that the volume of their trade was done on the ground floor where customers could walk in straight off the street, and they would never have contemplated asking drinkers to mount a flight of stairs for their liquor. However, once again, because the State Management Scheme operated a policy of disinterested management in which the manager was not asked to push sales, Redfern was able to adopt a quite revolutionary attitude to the planning of his model inns.

A bowling green with access to toilets and services placed on the less frequented side of the house and laid with Cumberland sea-washed turf became a pleasing feature of many of the model inns, as were the tea rooms and verandahs.

Redfern also recognised that much value can also be gained from a good inn sign which is interesting to look at as well as being a good advertisement. It needs to be of a useful size and easily visible from a reasonable distance both during daylight hours and to conform to local byelaws. It needs to be well constructed and securely fixed. Free-standing signs are usually positioned near to the boundary of a site which is set back from the road and they rely on a standard of brick, stone, wood, or occasionally wrought iron and, if wood is used, it needs to have a strong base of a less perishable material. Alternatively, a sign can be fixed flat to a wall or swung on gallows suspended from a wall or fixed on brackets securely attached to a wall. The height of signs above and projecting over a public thoroughfare are subject to the local byelaws. The architect in planning the inn sign is dependent upon the skills of a good artist and the prevailing weather conditions of the site. Too much wind around a swinging sign can cause it to creak annoyingly. Redfern will have known all about creaking from his work on the liner Orontes during his partnership with J..J. Stevenson.

These are just a selection of the many functions the architect has to allow for when designing his model inn, but over and above these is the evidence of the architect's own attitude to work and the conception of his role in society. Perusing the organisations to which Redfern belonged, it is clear that, through the unity of the arts, especially in building, he strove to satisfy needs and at the same time to refine tastes. Some of the forms found in English Arts and Crafts architecture are realised in Redfern's model inns: dipping gables, dormer windows, wide eaves and delicate gutter brackets, tall chimneys, stone mullioned windows, expressed drain pipes, moulded leadwork, diamond motifs, and the use of stained glass. In essence several of the elevations of the model inns are a re-invention of his earlier domestic style in Cambridge which, with its consciously elegant simplicity, was a joy to both the architect and the client. Professionally, Redfern was intensely jealous of his aesthetic convictions and stood guard over them until his retirement. It is encumbent upon us to understand and evaluate his buildings for what they were in their original state and historical context, and not to be diverted from this by what has happened later.

Needless to say, functional considerations are the touchstone for any building project, but a pragmatic arrangement of data and facts alone, important as they are, will not of themselves generate a pleasing and satisfying form. Without idealism the results will be sterile. Redfern's talent lay in absorbing the multifarious aspects of his remit and then by skilful planning and a fresh eye, incorporating a measure of idealism into the functional requirements of his model inns in pursuance of an improved public house.

He delivered a sound, unostentatious service to the community, and Carlisle became a place of pilgrimage for aspiring public house architects. He was always happy in his dealings with builders and their workmen, which surely is confirmed by the fact that fifteen major undertakings were completed in thirteen years, but he declined invitations to be present at the opening of his buildings by making it known that he disliked such events.

The model inns now stand as the only visible monument to a uniquely promising enterprise.

The first of these model inns in the period under discussion was the Apple Tree in Lowther Street. This was a complete rebuilding of a small Victorian drinking shop. This large three-storey brick and slated public house, four times the size of the old building, was built with local labour by Messrs. John Laing & Son of Carlisle with joinery work in the hands of J.H. Reed of Carlisle, and was opened in May, 1927. The overall frontage to Lowther Street was 63 feet. To achieve this, two shops in Lowther Street and three cottages in Kings Arms Lane had to be acquired. There was no off-sales department in the new building and the entrance was straight off the street. The special feature of this public house was the addition of a bar upstairs and the adaptability of the rooms for additional space at weekends, as well as for the separation of the sexes if this was required. As will be seen from the plans there were bars for counter service on the first floor as well as on the ground floor. At the time this was unusual and experimental but remembering the State Management Scheme's

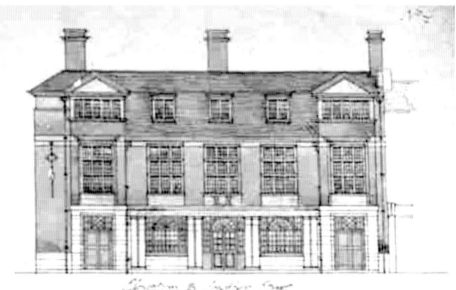

Top: Front and
side elevations of
the properties
demolished to
build The Apple
Tree.
Middle: Apple
Tree: front eleva-
tion from
Redfern's plan.
Below: The
Apple Tree in the
sixties.

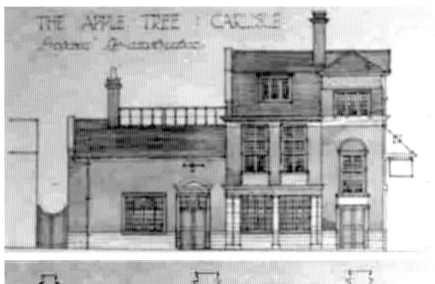

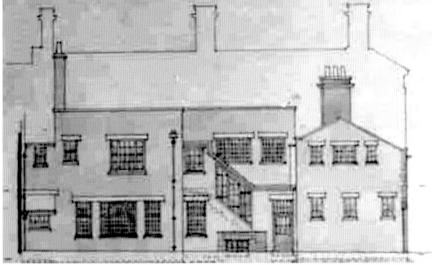

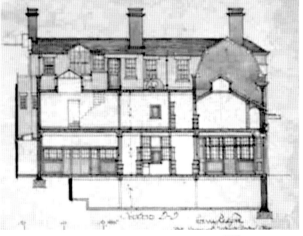

The Apple Tree: side, rear and exposed elevations from Redfern's plans.

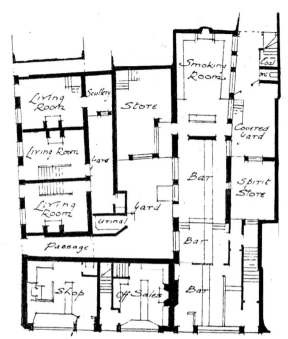

*Left: Ground flloor plan of
the original Apple Tree.
The old plan incorporated living
quarters with a shop and off-
sales to the street and the public
areas consisted of a series of
small bars and smoking room.
The toilets were across the court-
yard.*

*Below: The ground floor plan
for te new Apple Tree. Redfern's
design offered a week-end room,
men's, mixed and women's
"second class" rooms.*

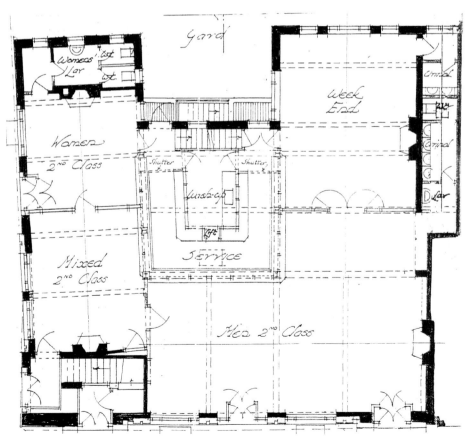

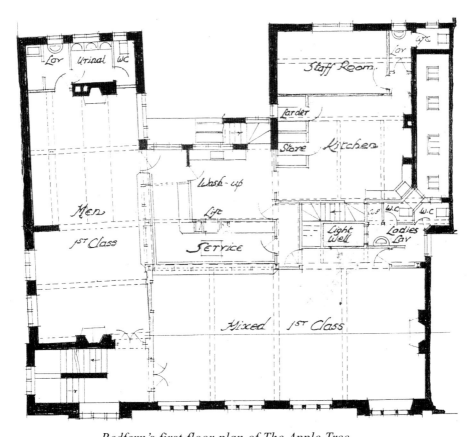

Redfern's first floor plan of The Apple Tree.
On this floor there were men's and mixed "first class" rooms and indoor toilets for women as well as men, and adequate staff areas, including a kitchen.

monopoly and lack of competition in Carlisle, bolder deviations from the orthodox could be undertaken in the knowledge that it was immaterial which houses the public patronized. Elsewhere in the country it was unlikely that a brewer would ask his "short-quick-one" customer to mount a flight of stairs to the upper bar, and so we see that Redfern catered for the second class customers on the ground floor while inviting the first class customers upstairs. A service staircase led from behind the bar on the ground floor to the first floor only, while the main staircase (on the left of the plan) led further up to the manager's quarters which had three bedrooms, a sitting room, a bathroom and a wash house on the top floor. The service area was central on both floors, giving adequate supervision to all rooms with a generous amount of space being allotted to the wash-up and kitchen area on the first floor. This was done in order to provide for the servicing of food, with or without liquor, in every room on both floors, but since there was a smaller demand for food on the ground floor, it was adequately met by the use of a lift service. Ample and convenient lavatory accommodation was provided for both sexes, although at this stage the entrances still led off the public rooms. It was not until later ,when such houses as the Magpie were built, that the improved planning of lavatories placed them off lobbies or porches.

Above: The newspaper caption ran: "Pupils of Carlisle Art School at work on the mural paintings of classical history in The Apple Tree, a Carlisle State-controlled public house".
Below: the serving hatch and some of the interior decoration in The Apple Tree.

The three bars on the ground floor comprised a men's second class with optional extension, a women's second class with access to their own lavatory of two wcs and a washbasin (which was decidedly revolutionary at the time, especially in Cumberland) and a mixed second class with access to lavatories for each sex. The two bars on the first floor comprised a mens first class and a mixed first class with access to lavatories again leading directly from the bar. For the women there was a passage to cross. The first floor plan also indicates the generous proportions of the kitchen and staff room with direct access to their own lavatory. In addition this plan indicates the position of the ventilation trunks either side of the lift shaft. Redfern's remit had included the request for more light and air in the new houses and this is clearly demonstrated on the elevation plans where the first floor windows to Lowther Street have been heightened, and where extra windows have been introduced in Kings Arms Lane. A symbol of an apple tree in stained glass was introduced into the top centre pane of the five clerestory windows on the first floor facing Lowther Street. Using Carrara-ware facings with York stone plinth and thresholds, the entire building was symmetrical in design with a recognisable axis giving a feeling of satisfaction.

Unfortunately on the 14 October, 1927, the Highways and Streets Committee resolved that "the permission given to the State Management Scheme to erect a projecting inn sign be withdrawn and they be requested to erect the sign flat against the wall". And so the beautiful hanging sign, designed by H. Sexton, ARCA, showing an apple tree in blossom on one side, and the same tree in fruit on the reverse, was taken down in deference to the local byelaw governing the projection of hanging signs over public thoroughfares. Redfern had no authority to make any formal application himself to the City Council.

The Farmer's Bar on the first floor was furnished with writing materials and periodicals - Punch, The Field, and the Illustrated London News, - and a refectory table at which the farmers could transact business after visits to the auction marts. A decision was made to add, as an experiment, painted murals which was quite an innovation at the time. The classical fable of the Golden Apples of the Hesperides was chosen and depicted in six separate scenes using flat oil paint. The fable runs as follows: Hercules was the son of Jupiter and Alcmena but Juno, the wife of Jupiter was always hostile to the offspring of her husband by mortal mothers and so she prevailed upon Eurystheus to set Hercules a succession of desperate adventures, the Labours of Hercules. By far the most difficult task was that of recovering the Golden Apples of the Hesperides. These were the apples given as a wedding present to Juno by the goddess of the earth, and their safe keeping had been entrusted to the daughters of the evening, the Hesperides, whose father was Atlas. But Atlas had warred against the gods and was condemned to take the weight of the world upon his shoulders. Hercules temporarily took over that task so that Atlas could seek out the golden apples, killing the fearsome dragon Ladon on the way. The apples were found, given to Hercules, and Atlas resumed his burden. The murals were painted by artists of the Carlisle School of Art, Miss Helena W. Brown and Mr. C.H. Lawrence, and the frieze of apples intertwined with leaves was painted by Miss G. Anderson Brown.

At the same time as the Apple Tree was being built, the Southborough Committee's Report on Disinterested Management was being published as a White

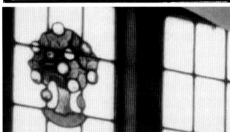

The Apple Tree
Above: The painted sign
Left: Detail from a window.
Below: A settle in front of panelling.

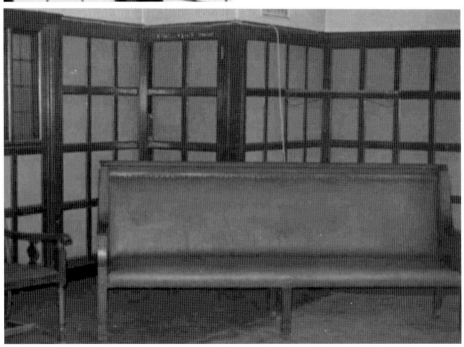

Paper and one aspect which has relevance to the Carlisle Scheme was the statement that: "The evidence which we have heard indicates that in England the closing of structurally undesirable houses is hindered by the ease with which a new club can be registered in or near the same premises". This may well be a clue as to why Redfern and the SMS chose to make the new town houses as "clubby" as possible in the light of eleven new clubs having been opened in Carlisle between 1921 and 1926 with an additional two by 1928 bringing the total membership to approximately 8,700. The clubs were: Border (1920), Ex-Servicemen's (1921), Conservative (1922), 203rd Battery RFA (1922), 4th Border Regiment (1922), Carlisle Locomen's (1925), Southend Constitutional (1927), and Carlisle Labour (1928). From 1926 some of these clubs were made subject to inspection by the police and officers of the State Management Scheme. The Chief Constable in his report of 1926 said: "This is the first time a registered club has been put on the same footing as a public house and in this respect it should prove a very interesting departure from ordinary practice". Concomitant with this, the State Management Scheme found when it took over in 1921 that there was a strong local custom in which the men objected to the presence of women in their public bars. The women were accustomed to congregating around the doors or in the passages. The State Management however did not share the view that it was undesirable for women to enter a bar, and maintained that it was perfectly possible for them to do so without feeling any loss of their respectability. As a consequence they were catered for at the Apple Tree but even so, were still not allowed in the main bar.

It is appropriate now before moving on to discuss other buildings, to put on record the sterling work done by two of Redfern's assistants. Joseph Seddon, FRIBA was born in 1882 and articled to a Bournemouth firm in 1897. He remained as assistant until 1902 when he moved to become assistant to his father, J.P. Seddon, FRIBA until 1906 when his father died. (C.F.A. Voysey had worked as a pupil in J.P. Seddon's office from 1874 to 1880). Seddon was then principal assistant to a London firm of architects and took his ARIBA by examination in 1909 and practiced in Buckingham Street, the Strand, in 1912 taking over the practice of W.H. Hillyer who had been killed in the war. He joined the Army in 1915 and was subsequently declared unfit for military service in 1916. It was then that he was appointed principal assistant to Harry Redfern and the Central Control Board. Once a new public house was in the offing Redfern would make a freehand sketch of what he envisaged, indicating proportions and all relevant details and Seddon would then draw up the plans for Redfern to sign. These plans were a thing of beauty in themselves and they all carried an easily recognisable quality of artistry.

Ernest A. Streatfield was the architect's assistant and clerk of works from 1919. Born in 1895 he had been articled to Harry Redfern in 1909 and joined the RNAF in 1914. He returned to work with Redfern after the war in 1919. His duties as clerk of works were to see that the detailed drawings were correctly interpreted, that the contractor's work was up to standard, to bring forward points for consideration as operations advanced, and to note any variations between the contract and the work as executed.

The old Malt Shovel

The MALT SHOVEL. (Builders: J. & R. Bell. Inn sign: E. M. Dinkel ARCA)
An article in the Carlisle Journal, 14 March, 1919, had drawn attention to the decreasing amount of stabling in the city. "In the old coaching days every public house with any pretensions possessed stabling for the horses. Of late years there has been a steady decline in the number of inns providing stabling for the country people attending Carlisle market. Among the recent closures were: the Malt Shovel, Bluebell, Scotch Arms, Wheatsheaf, Three Crowns, George & Dragon, Durham Ox,

The new Malt Shovel

Lion & Lamb, Grapes Inn, Spread Eagle, and King's Head. Their extinction excited no regrets apart from sentimental associations so long as the farmer could stable his nag somewhere. With the advent of the motor car several mews have been converted to garages, but the majority of farmers still jog along in the old fashion".

In earlier times any Scotsman arriving at Carlisle after dark would not be allowed to enter the city and so inns were established outside the city walls to accommodate travellers. The most famous of these inns was the Malt Shovel and the most famous traveller was Robert Burns who stayed there in 1787. He had arrived on horseback and turned his horse out to grass, but the unfortunate animal had wandered into an adjoining field belonging to the Corporation and the Mayor had promptly impounded it. Burns response was in verse, naturally:

> Was e'er puir poet sae befitted,
> The maister's drunk - the horse committed,
> Purr harmless beast, Tak thee ne care,
> Thou'lt be a horse when he's nae Mair.

The old Malt Shovel was closed for reconstruction at 10 p.m. on Sunday, 27 February, 1927, and by October it had been levelled to the ground so that Redfern could build his first entirely new model inn on the site. But what an awkward site it was, with the soil at the bottom of Rickergate appearing to be all sand, and the river Eden flowing gaily about in a random kind of way through it all, making it prone to flooding. Redfern was advised by the general manager of a previous experience which they had encountered at the Fox & Hounds nearby, when they had been forced to lay an all-concrete cellar, "working day and night so as to avoid anything resembling a joint in the concrete. This worked excellently and has proved to be the only dry cellar in Rickergate that I have ever heard of. It is perhaps worth considering the same method for the Malt Shovel". (PRO HO 190/96).

As a preliminary step Redfern had sent plans to the city council providing for the setting back of the premises in Rickergate and an alternative proposal for the improvement of the corner of Rickergate and Corporation Road. This was suggested in order to meet the requirements of the covenant contained in the conveyance of 12 May, 1894, from the Corporation to the Workington Brewery Co. Ltd. This alternative proposal was approved by the council, but the Corporation reserved the right to affix and maintain on the outer walls of the Malt Shovel a notice board containing the list of tolls.

A memorandum was sent for the attention of the State Management Council in August,1926, stating various requirements which the Malt Shovel and the Fox & Hounds ought to meet between them. It was suggested that, as Carlisle was a great place for cattle dealing, the owners and buyers would need smoking room accommodation while the drovers needed bar accommodation, but bar prices were to operate throughout the Malt Shovel while smoking room prices were to operate throughout the Fox & Hounds. It was also noted that Rickergate was the main thoroughfare for country lads seeking farm engagements on the four hiring days and special arrangements needed to be made to accommodate the crowds on these days. It was felt that the neighbourhood was not one where much service in hot meals was anticipated especially as the Blue Bell restaurant was close to hand, but an off sales department would be needed which should include a jug trade as well as bottled goods. (This did not materialise at the Malt Shovel). Redfern was requested to work out a plan for the new Malt Shovel and consequential alterations to the Fox & Hounds. Seats were to be provided for all customers under normal conditions with no stand-up drinking except on the four hiring days. An effort was to be made at the Malt Shovel to combine sit-down drinking with self-service as a consequence of which the service fronts could be very short. No kitchen or dining room would be required in the new building, but pies and sandwiches would be available. There was to be one large room for men only and another large room, which Redfern referred to as the parlour, for recreational purposes - draughts, dominoes and possibly a wireless. The memorandum suggested that this room should fall into two sections by means of an arch or similar dividing structure so that one section could be used by men and their wives and the other by women only. The idea was that customers would divide themselves naturally and not by rules fixed by the management.

On 10 September, 1926, Redfern sent his proposed plans to the general manager, J.S. Eagles with the covering message: "It seems to me that simplicity is the keynote here, and I have endeavoured to embody it in this scheme. The plans speak for themselves and I hope you will not think it necessary to suggest any radical changes therein. Some editing on your part is doubtless desirable, but I hope not much". (PRO HO 190/96). The general manager considered that, apart from minor details the general idea of the plan so far as permanent accommodation was concerned, was on the proper lines. Redfern had reckoned on an estimate of £11,500 for the work and the council had sanctioned this figure with a further £1,000 provided for furniture. Tenders were received from John Laing and Sons of Dalston Road for £12,927 and from J & R Bell of Nelson Street for £12,399. The council accepted the lower tender. This drew a somewhat sharp rebuke from Redfern. "I hope

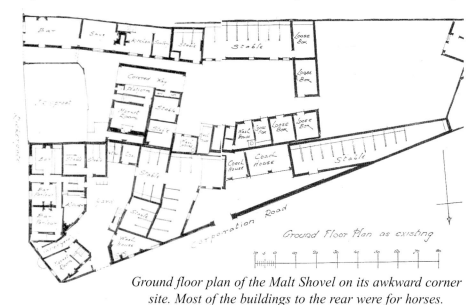

Ground floor plan of the Malt Shovel on its awkward corner site. Most of the buildings to the rear were for horses.

138

you will not ask me to water down the scheme for the sake of trying to save £899. 1 have assumed that everything in the building would be as good as at the Apple Tree, and I am sure we ought not in any new public house do less well than that - expensive though it may be". (PRO HO 190/96). Within a month the council had rescinded its decision, and covering authority was given for acceptance of an estimated excess expenditure of £900. Vacant possession was the last hurdle to jump before work could begin. In October, 1926, the general manager, John S. Eagles interviewed the current tenant, Mrs Mathews, to inform her that the long discussed plans for the Malt Shovel had now been settled and work would begin at an early date. This would necessitate the closing of the house for business together with the evacuation by Mrs Mathews of the domestic part of the premises. Consequently one month's notice was given demanding possession. The family of Mr and Mrs Mathews comprised one girl aged 23; two boys aged 21 and 19 ; another girl aged 8; and a baby of 3. The husband was on a short working week of three days, and the elder son who had served his time as a fitter and was employed at Carlisle crane makers, Cowan & Sheldon, was now completely laid off. Mrs Mathews was told that, in the circumstances, if the SMS had any suitable work for her or the grown-up daughter, or either of the sons, they would let her know. Three months later the family had still failed to find accommodation for themselves, but they were finally able to move into the Currock Hotel cottage in February, 1927, so that work could begin. When the new premises was ready to be opened in August, 1928, Mrs. Mathews applied for the its managership. As it transpired the SMS had already decided to make Mr. and Mrs. Mathews the first offer as it was their intention to have a joint man and wife managership. This was to be on the condition that her husband gave up his current employment to give full-time sendee to the SMS and for the managership to be in his name. The Mathews family agreed to the terms and conditions which gave them a wage of £3:10:0 per week and barmaid work for their 23-year-old daughter at £2:0:0 per week.

Built on a prominent corner site the new brick and slated construction comprised a public bar, parlour, winter garden with glass roof, and a billiards room at ground floor level with the manager's quarters of three bedrooms, sitting room, kitchen, bathroom and wc on the first floor. The basement comprised the draught beer cellar, bottled beer store, and boiler house. Outside was a large yard and garage space for five cars, stabling with stalls for eight horses, and a midden. The market room which had previously occupied a position at the front of the old building was moved to the rear to be close to the stalls and garages. The servery area, with its wash-up included in it, was compact and ingeniously arranged to permit supervision of all four rooms. There was ample lavatory accommodation for both sexes, but it was still, at this stage, leading off the public rooms.

Ten rectangular tables were provided - nine in the public bar, one in the billiards room, and four with glass tops in the parlour - and a dozen circular tables - eight in the winter garden, two in the billiards room, and two with glass tops in the parlour. The wood for the furniture was, in all cases, of African mahogany stained with "Stainax", the floor covering was "Ruboleum", and the draperies were scarlet. The 17 armchairs supplied by Messrs Pollock of Beith, and the 32 tub chairs supplied by Messrs. North of City Road, London, were all finished in black with red Rexine seats. Several fixed seats with moveable arms were also included in the plans in preference to the completely tip-up style used in the Apple Tree which Redfern considered out of place in a public house. Beautifully coloured top windows in stained glass depicting the malting process from the sowing of the seed to the final sweeping of the floor were featured all around the ground floor rooms. Colour was everywhere and visualising the hard times of the 1920s and '30s it must have gladdened many hearts. When Redfern sent his plans to Carlisle, setting out the general arrangement of the seating and tables in the public rooms, he added: "I think this cannot be improved upon and I also think that set out in this way you would get the best public bar interior I have ever seen; so I hope you will not think it necessary to make any serious changes in the suggested arrangement". (PRO HO 190/96).

Two final problems needed to be resolved. The inclusion of a billiards room had been at the suggestion of the general manager as there was already a table sitting in the store. Redfern found the legs on this table to have been "an unpleasant shape". He requested that they be returned, stained and polished to harmonise with the rest of the joinery in the room and that, when this had been done, Messrs. C. Mitchell & Co. of Morecambe should replenish the cushion rails and level and re-cover the table. The other problem, however, had elicited what was an unambiguous response from Redfern and it concerned an old fountain which stood on the site. "I think it would be a pity if we spoil the corner of a nice new building with such an ugly stone. The general manager thought local sentiment might be offended if it was scrapped. He thought the Local Advisory Committee should be consulted. It appears to me that if there is any body of local opinion that attaches any sentimental importance to the preservation of the fountain it is for them to find it a new site. But rather than let it deface the new building it would be preferable to glue it on to the Fox & Hounds or the Golden Fleece".

There was plenty of other work in progress during these years. The Prince of Wales in Denton Street had space added at the rear for the supply of food both on and off the premises. Improvements were carried out at the Board Inn, Castle Street, the Sportsman Inn, Heads Lane, the Caledonian Inn, Botchergate, and the Fox & Hounds, Rickergate. An attractive villa in Botchergate, St. Nicholas View, was converted to a public house keeping its original character, and in 1927 the Near Boot at Tarraby was reconstructed with a bowling green. Then 1929 proved a most productive year with the building of the new Black Lion at Durdar, opened 6 May, the Coach & Horses at Kingstown, opened 10 August, and the Horse & Farrier at Raffles ,opened 16 September. All were built by J & R. Bell of Carlisle.

BLACK LION INN, DURDAR, a fine new detached public house with a deeply sloping hipped roof, was built on a prominent site at a road junction three miles south of Carlisle to replace the existing inn opposite. Its first manager was Henry F. Long who had served for 21 years with the Second Battalion of the Border Regiment. He submitted five references when applying for the post, one of which stated that he was leaving the Colours "with an exemplary character and should be a useful man in a capacity of trust". His appointment was approved by the Chief Constable of the Cumberland & Westmorland Constabulary and the terms of his employment stated that he would be paid for his services, including assistance

The Black Lion, Durdar

rendered to him by his wife, a salary of £1.10.0. per week with an increase of two shillings and sixpence per week commencing week ending 14.9.1930. When he died in July, 1946, the managership passed to his widow, Mrs Elizabeth Long, at a basic wage of £2.7.6 per week plus a war wage award of 15 shillings per week. She resigned in December, 1947. Two years later an agreement was reached with the Civil Service Union that the gross wage for the manager at the Black Lion should stand at £5.0.0. per week (with 15 shillings deductible for free meals) and a gross payment of £1.0.0. per week for the wife as assistant.

The final statement from J. & R. Bell for the erection of the inn amounted to £2265. 2. 6. This included certain items not included in the original estimate. These were: the building of all external walls in stock bricks instead of ordinary bricks; the waterproofing of all exterior walls; the building of an attached wash house; gas services and fittings; electric light tubing; the painting and erection of an inn sign and post, and installing posts and chains to the front boundary. On the exterior, all the walls and chimney stacks were limed white with tarred plinths. All the woodwork was white including the gates and posts while the chains, rainwater pipes and gutters were black. All the doors were in middle Brunswick green - a popular colour of the period but Redfern left a specific instruction that the elm weatherboarding should not be touched or treated in any way. Five months after the premises had been opened for business, Redfern felt the need to make an observation to the general manager, A. E. Mitchell that it was "high time the accounts for this building were squared up" and that it was due to the "extreme reasonableness of Bell's contract "that there existed a difference between the £2400 which the City Council had sanctioned and the final cost of only £2265. By 1934 electricity had become available in the Durdar district and the SMS considered installing it at the Black Lion since the tubes for electric wiring were already in place. At the time the premises were built and gas was installed, they had given an undertaking not to change over to electricity for the next five years. By 1934 this promise had expired. By April, 1930, another matter was calling for the architect's attention: "The scum from our drainage effluent". Redfern's solution was to introduce a filter bed on the outfall side of the cesspool. Trenches would be filled with fine coke and the effluent passing through this should leave the scum behind and be clear from that point. This kind of incident demonstrates how the architect is involved in the mundane practicalities and functions as well as in the pursuit of aesthetics.

At the time that the SMS acquired the site, the Treasury were informed that they were buying enough land to provide a bowling green when the development of the locality warranted it. The public house was susceptible of some enlargement with a verandah and some outdoor drinking on the terrace, according to Joseph Seddon in March, 1947. However, even after a year had elapsed, no decision could be reached on the suggestion as "No work of this nature would be put in hand under present conditions".

COACH & HORSES INN, Kingstown opened on 10 August, 1929. The existing Coach & Horses Inn together with two adjoining cottages were demolished in order to make room for an entirely new and larger premises. These were required because of the rapidly increasing domestic housing programme extending Carlisle's suburban growth to the north. The new inn was built by J. & R. Bell at a cost of £4523 of which £1273 was written off leaving £3250 to be added to capital. J.& R. Bell kept about 200 men on their books and owned their own brickworks at Kingmoor. They were in full employment at this time and found it necessary in some circumstances to buy in bricks from elsewhere thus indicating the amount of work they had on hand.

The Coach & Horses was set back from the road with wide folding gates flanked by a low country-style garden wall and flower beds. The Spectator of 20 September, 1930, described it as, "A charming old brick inn with a small garden of stocks, gladiolas and roses ". Redfern had chosen to use multi-coloured bricks in an English bond of alternate stretchers and headers to give an authentic appearance to the whole elevation including the dormers and chimney stacks. An existing three-panelled painting of a coach and horses was affixed to the external wall above the smoking room and the inn sign painted by J.W.Temple, an employee of the Works Department, was erected on the grass forecourt. The asymmetrical elevation comprised two entrances and stone mullioned casement windows with leaded lights. One entrance led directly to the tea/club room which itself led internally to the smoking room which in turn led to the public bar, passing the ingeniously placed off-sales department on the way. It was a brilliant piece of economical planning by any standards. The servicing areas were divided into two parts, one for the bars and a separate one for the tearoom.

Once again the sanitary arrangements needed to be carefully considered for a public house of this small size. A two-stalled urinal was surreptitiously tucked away between the tearoom and the smoking room with access from both. In addition a lavatory approached by a little passageway was provided for the tea/club room customers at the rear of the building, close by the tea service area. But there still remained the problem of how to provide for the public bar customers who, because

The Coach and Horses after rendering and (below) as it appears today.

of their numbers, would be requiring more spacious lavatory accommodation. The solution was to provide them with a separate outbuilding at the rear, reached under-cover from a lobby at the back of the bar. A small coal store was built on the opposite side of the yard to balance the plan.

This was a small and simple public house with a touch of country charm but it had a problem, albeit a delayed-action problem. It concerned damp in the external walls of the building which had begun to show itself in the mid 1930s and had been treated with Silexine, a waterglass remedy of the time. It appeared to be successful

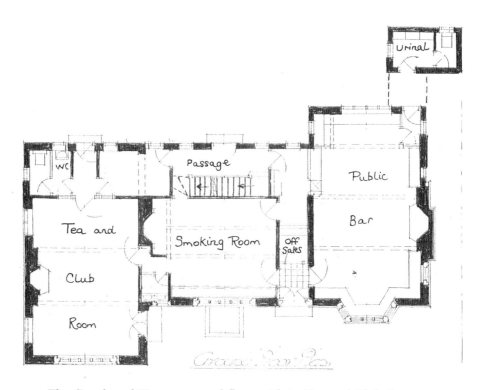

The Coach and Horses ground floor with its Tea and Club Room,
in addition to the Public Bar and Smoking Room.

but the same walls needed to be re-treated in the mid 1940s. The only portions not treated were the shawk stone window frames, mullions and stone copings to the gables. It then transpired that the stone dressings were also porous. In June, 1945, the assistant secretary of the Managers' Union, at a meeting of the Joint Consultative Committee, was extremely sweeping in his condemnation of the building. The architect had to be consulted on the issue and at the advanced age of 84, Redfern sent the general manager of the SMS a most detailed and helpful reply in which he acknowledged that for some reason there had been trouble of this kind ever since the inn was built and that it was one of those obstinate cases which are "as difficult for an architect to cure as is a cold in the head for a doctor". His reply went on to state that: "The insuperable difficulty here is that the bricks appear to be defective, but I know of a house in the suburbs of London, built at the same date and with some of the very same bricks (with walls not so thick), which has given no trouble whatever in this regard". He continued to say that he found it a mystery that water had penetrated the stone dressings. "I have never known such a thing to happen. It is local shawk stone used in countless buildings in Carlisle and the neighbourhood and never a hint of this trouble has reached me until now". He then recalled the treatments that had been applied in the past, but because one of the essential ingredients of Silexine came from Malaya the makers were unable to supply it at the present time. Redfern then offered an old-fashioned remedy for trying in the interim. "Two coats of limewash made of stone lime slaked with boiling water to which a generous quantity of

Russian tallow has been stirred in". He explained that Silexine, whose active ingredient was sodium silicate, was the scientific treatment in which the remedial effect took the form of filling up the minute interstices in the brick or stone with a substance which combined to fuse them together. But it must be understood, he added, "that no known external coating is permanent. It must be renewed periodically as required and that this should be done during dry weather". Taking into account the exposed position of the inn and knowing the heavy rains and winds it had to withstand, in due course the whole elevation was rendered white which is how most Carlisle citizens remember it.

One final addition in 1948 to the original building, which merits a mention in the light of previous successes elsewhere, was the petition for the amelioration of tobacco smoke. The varying height of the ceilings in the public bar and smoking room and especially the presence of one cross beam meant that the use of horizontal air trunks was out of the question. A plan was drawn up to install a vertical trunk starting at the same point in the ceiling of each room as near the centre as possible. The trunk then terminated in an extractor fan and the offending smoke was emitted to the open air through the roof.

THE HORSE AND FARRIER, Raffles opened 16 September, 1929. When Redfern built this large and attractive public house on a prominent corner site on the west side of the junction of Wigton Road and Orton Road in an area of expanding private and council housing estates, he was replacing an old Horse & Farrier which had stood on the east side of the junction. This old public house had occupied the end of a range of buildings which had included a joiner's shop and a smithy, which no doubt accounted for the name. In 1889/90 the city council gave planning permission for a new

The Horse and Farrier on Wigton Road

The Horse and Farrier seen from the side with the bowling green in the bottom left of the picture.

building to replace it and for it still to be known as the Horse & Farrier but its fate as a public house was short lived once the State Management Scheme came along with its plans for something better. It was, however, retained after 1929 as a private dwelling.

As a consequence of the Corporation of Carlisle's proposal in the autumn of 1927 to widen the Wigton Road opposite the site of the proposed new building, Redfern needed to re-locate his new Horse & Farrier by setting it back about 12 feet behind the original position shown on the contract drawings. This delayed commencement of building operations. After considerable excavation work had been carried out for the provision of enlarged cellars according to revised plans, the foundations were finally laid in May, 1928. The L-shaped building on an open, triangular corner site was given a NW/SE axis enabling the splendid bowling green bordered by rhododendrons and roses in season, to enjoy the warmer south-west aspect. So popular did the bowling greens at the public houses become that the SMS Bowling League president, E. Mitchell, at the annual dinner in 1938, was calling for more, saying that the League was playing 480 matches in 14 weeks on their present six greens. All the elevations to this country house style of public house were most attractive and it is rewarding to take a second look. The deeply pitched roofs topped by a weather vane were of grey/brown tiles enhanced by tall chimney stacks. Identical bay windows on two storeys beneath tile-hung dormers

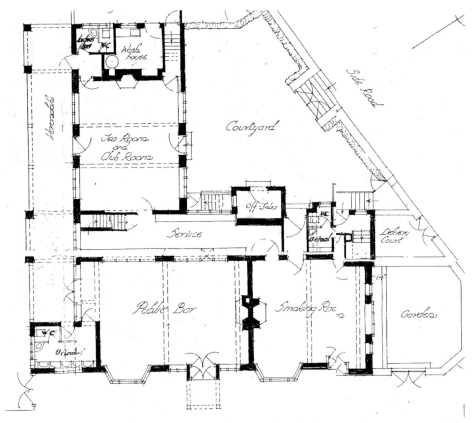

Ground floor plan of the Horse and Farrier. On the left is a lengthy verandah overlooking the bowling green.

carried distinctive fenestration of unaffected charm. A decorative wrought iron arch at the top of a small flight of semi-circular stone steps led the way to the two separate entrances of the public bar and smoking room while a similar arch on the NE side led to a flagged delivery court.

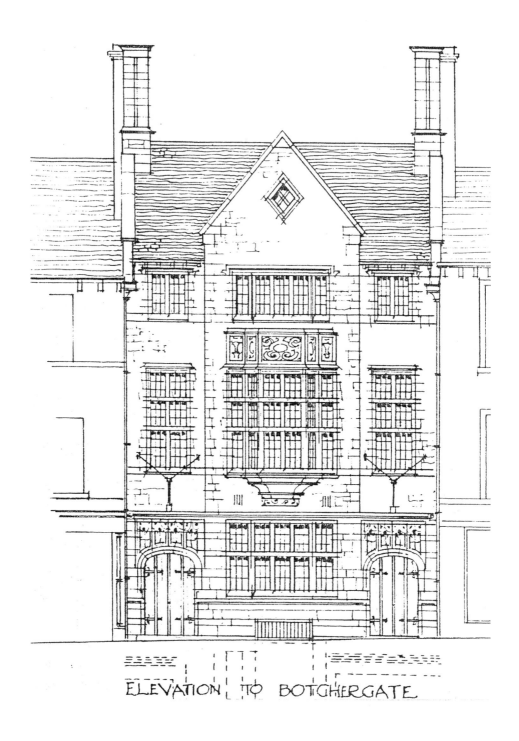

ELEVATION TO BOTCHERGATE

The Cumberland Inn: elevation to Botchergate

CHAPTER EIGHT

MODEL INNS FROM THE 1930s

The CUMBERLAND INN, Botchergate was opened on 29 September, 1930. It was built by J. &. R. Bell at a cost of £13678 of which £2678 was written off. It was an urban public house reconstructed on a very cramped, closed site with the street frontage faced with local stone and the roof covered with Westmorland slates and was in a style reminiscent of English domestic architecture of the late sixteenth century. Redfern himself said that great pains had been taken to make the new place a credit to Carlisle. He paid due homage to those people chiefly concerned in its erection by inserting a stained glass rebus in six of the windows in the mixed first class bar at first floor level. These comprised designs for Ernest A. Streatfield (clerk of works); a window each for Robert Bell and John Bell (builders); AEM for A. E. Mitchell, general manager; three fern leaves coloured red for Harry Redfern, architect; and JS for Joseph Seddon, assistant architect. The long narrow site stretched back from Botchergatc to Collier Lane with no space for an off sales department. A large skylight was needed for extra light. The ground floor comprised two entrances from the street; one leading along a corridor to the public bar straight ahead and the other to the right leading to a mixed second class bar with weekend extension. Two

The smoking room in The Cumberland. Note the art work.

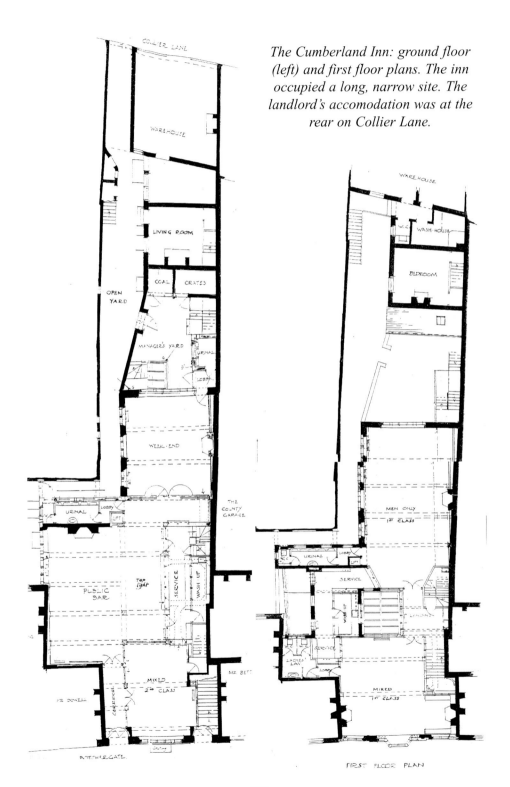

The Cumberland Inn: ground floor (left) and first floor plans. The inn occupied a long, narrow site. The landlord's accomodation was at the rear on Collier Lane.

gents' lavatories were provided, but the ladies had to go down to the basement for their lavatory. The manager was given a living room and yard behind the warehouse to the rear of the ground floor and one of his three bedrooms was placed on the first floor above this living room. As with other model inns, the manager's quarters comprised three bedrooms and two reception rooms in total. The first floor with its oriel window and open coal fires comprised a mixed first class bar overlooking the street with access to a ladies' lavatory via a lobby, and a men only first class bar to the rear with access to the gents' lavatory, also via a lobby.

Internally the walls of the public rooms were panelled to a height of about seven feet in Japanese oak (which, according to the clerk of works, tends not to crack internally) and this useful oak was finished with Stainax in a warm grey tint to harmonise with the slightly deeper grey tone of the Ruboleum flooring. The oak furniture in the public rooms was specially designed and upholstered in blue Rexine for the ground floor and haircloth for the first floor. Writing to the general manager, Redfern explained: "We must have something different from Rexine or we do not get a sufficient distinction between this and the seating on the ground floor. We cannot afford hide and I think haircloth would suit the purpose excellently. It wears like iron and looks well". The whole of the interior colour scheme exuded a soft and restful aura with a positively "clubby" atmosphere. The two splendid oak overmantles to the fireplaces, on opposite sides of the mixed first class bar on the first floor, carried five panels, each measuring 10 inches by 15 inches, which were beautifully decorated in gold leaf and alternatively presented a design of vine leaves and popular verses of the time:

> Go fetch to me a pint o' wine
> And fill it in a silver tassie -
> That I may drink before 1 go,
> A service to my bonnie lassie.
>
> (Robert Burns)

> St George he was for England
> And before he killed the dragon
> He drank a pint of English Ale
> Out of an English flagon.
>
> (G. K. Chesterton)

> Lo! some we loved the loveliest and the best
> That Time and Fate of all their Vintage prest,
> Have drunk their cup a Round or two before,
> And one by one crept silently to Rest.
>
> (Omar Khayyam).

> Ah, my Beloved fill the cup that clears
> To-day of past regrets and future Fears.
> Tomorrow? Why Tomorrow I may be Myself
> With Yesterday's Sev'n Thousand Years.
>
> (Omar Khayyam).

In August, 1930, Redfern had written to Mitchell, the general manager, saying that he wanted to add the last finishing touches to the scheme in the form of some colour decoration: "Not a great deal, but some - and very good. . . . and if we are going to have this colour emphasis (as we really must), do for goodness sake let it be done now. I can't always get the man I want when I want him". Mitchell procrastinated and didn't see why it was necessary to have the decoration executed immediately - he thought everything looked fine as it was, but Redfern knew that he had to procure the services of E.M. Dinkel, ARCA, and his wife when they were available. Work commenced without delay on 3 September, 1930, and was expected to take two to three weeks to complete. Redfern made the sensible suggestion to Mitchell that, "It would shorten the time and lessen the cost if it were possible to arrange for Temple (on the staff of the Works Department) to give a little assistance with the stencil repeats and so on, as he did when Sexton decorated the Citadel restaurant. Temple is keen to increase his knowledge of such matters and I am sure he will learn something to his advantage".

Each model inn in the Scheme presented its own distinctive potentialities and problems which it was not always possible to balance out completely in the circumstances, and the Cumberland Inn was no exception. The three main problems were: gaining possession of the entire site at one and the same time; frustration once again over the proposed hanging signs; and the actual naming of the new premises.

There were three cottages on one side of Collier Lane and one on the other side and the tenant of the cottage nearest to the existing premises was not rent protected, but the other two tenants were protected. Mitchell informed Redfern on 3 January, 1929, that, "All tenants had been given notice and so soon as we can get the tenant of the cottage furthest down the lane out by offering him a council house we shall move the unprotected tenant into this cottage". With regard to the other cottage which was let to the County Garage and sub-let by them, the tenant there was rent protected and refused the offer of a council house. Redfern sent a telegram immediately to Mitchell saying that the builder must be given possession of the entire site from the commencement of operations. He followed this up with a letter by return of post saying, "I am distressed to learn that the three cottages, the demolition of which is necessitated by the re-building scheme, are not yet available for handing over to the contractor, together with the rest of the premises. It was always understood that the scheme should be put in hand at the earliest possible moment, and I promised to have the necessary documents ready for a start to be made during the first week of January. Such a start means - and must mean - the possession of the entire site. For it must be remembered that this site is so restricted as to render it very difficult to build upon even under the most favourable conditions: there is so little space available for depositing materials required for the work. We shall clearly have to delay commencement until possession of the whole site can be given. . . please hurry up matters with this end in view. I can do nothing".

At the same time the manager of the existing Cumberland Hotel, William Hammil, was given notice that his appointment was to be terminated as from 20 January, 1929, and that he was required to deliver up possession of the whole of the premises, including the domestic portion, on or before that date. It was arranged that

Hammil would receive full wages up to and including 31 January, 1929, and that he could continue to run Harrison's auction mart with a remuneration of ten shillings per opening day. The SMS also agreed to meet his removal costs to a flat above the Board Inn in Castle Street and promised to make every endeavour to fit him into other employment if and when it could be found.

On 8 January, Redfern was again writing to Mitchell, saying that, "It will probably take at least three weeks to demolish the main building and if he is requested to do so, the contractor will probably be quite willing to leave the demolition of the cottages until after the main building is down, though, of course, this procedure may involve some risks of subsidence which may lead to trouble". On 11 January, Mitchell informed Redfern that he could proceed to make arrangements for the builders to start demolition work as from Monday, 28 January, 1929. This drew a response from Redfern warning that: "It would be altogether inadvisable for many reasons to begin the work of demolition if there were any likelihood that it would be brought to a standstill. . . if you can give me a definite undertaking that possession of the cottages will be obtained by that date and not later than three weeks from the commencement, I will stretch a point, if Bell agrees, and make a start. But I cannot do this in reliance on mere hopes or expectations". Redfern again pressed home the point in a letter to Mitchell on 28 January, 1929, saying that he couldn't make a start until the contract was signed nor did he like the notion of getting the contract signed until they could see their way clear to getting possession of the whole site. The management was also having difficulty in getting the tenant of Doughall's Court to move to accommodation owned by the SMS in Portland Place. Mitchell felt constrained to suggest to Redfern that, knowing Bells as they do, it would be possible for them to start the work and have the contract signed, even though they were not in full possession of the whole site. "If they commence demolishing, our recalcitrant tenant will no doubt find it very inconvenient and will do his best to clear out". On 31 January, 1929, Mitchell received a letter from Lt. Col. W.B. Vince, DSO, OBE, MC, secretary of the State Management Districts Central Office in London, saying that, having consulted with Sir John Pedder of the Home Office concerning the signing of the contract, it was thought that: "The contract ought not to be signed until there was an assurance of the actual date on which all three cottages would be vacant. It was felt that if Bell started work at once and was then held up at a later stage, the terms of the contract would have been broken and might delay the completion of the work to a greater extent than a postponement at the present stage". In the end the "recalcitrant" tenant gave up the possession of his cottage in Doughall's Court in consideration of a payment of £5 plus two guineas for solicitor's costs and an undertaking by the SMS to reimburse him for his removal costs to Mary Street. (All quotations are taken from PRO HO 190/72).

Rebuilding finally commenced on 11 February, 1929. Redfern was not working exclusively on these model inns but was executing many varied refurbishment assignments in the district for the SMS, as well as keeping his own private practice in businesses such as the restoration of an historic tithe barn at the Burford Bridge Hotel in Oxford for which he also engaged E.M. Dinkel to paint the murals.

Again there was an altercation over the issue of hanging signs. A year previously, in January, 1928, the city council's Highways & Streets committee had amended its regulations to include the clause that the approval of the Corporation must not be assumed in respect of any projecting signboard or signs even if they comply with the regulations, but each application would be considered on its merits. There happened to be two issues arising at the same time, namely the cellar flap and the projecting signs. Again, Mitchell contacted Lt. Col. Vince, secretary of the SMS central office in London, who in turn discussed the items with Sir John Pedder of the Home Office who agreed that, "We must avoid any quarrel with the Council but at the same time must maintain our position that as a Government Department we are exempt from the byelaws. The plans of our buildings are referred to the City Surveyor as a matter of courtesy only, and equally it is as an act of grace that we consider, and, if possible, conform to any suggestions he may have to make".

Pedder then reminded Vince of an earlier incident in which the Post Office had declined to enter into an agreement regarding their projecting lamp and the council had not taken any further action. Mitchell then wrote to the Town Clerk informing him that the erection of two projecting signs was being contemplated, giving dimensions and an acknowledgement that a rental of one shilling a year in respect of each of the two signboards and a pavement light would be paid to the Corporation. The boards would be illuminated during winter months from 5.30 p.m. to 10 p.m. and during the summer from sunset until 10 p.m. if necessary. The city surveyor thought the proposed signs appeared larger than his committee was likely to approve and, as they were not in favour of the multiplication of projecting signs, queried whether it was necessary to have two? Redfern's response in letters to Mitchell indicated that he was losing patience with the local council: "It is so disheartening that I think we had better drop the idea and do without them. Of course their absence will take away from the interest of the front of the building - if there is any; at all events it takes away my interest - if that matters". "If you can assure me that no objection will be raised by the Corporation to our putting up two projecting signs (remember there must be two signs) the projection being 3ft 6 inches, the height from pavement 10ft 3 inches and the area of each sign not exceeding 6 sq. ft. I will endeavour to produce something not too vulgar". "These regulations about the size of projecting signs is most exasperating none the less so because there is no mention of them in the byelaws (I have a copy to date) nor on the form which usually accompanies such applications. So how is one to know what they will or will not allow, unless by process of suggesting something and getting it turned down. In the circumstances I should hate that if the superficial area of 6 sq.ft. is to include the metalwork it reduces the size to absurdity and it prevents the introduction of any lettering visible to the naked eye at a distance of more than a few feet, which is absurd".

While waiting for the decision of the Corporation about the hanging signs Redfern was keen to start considering the design of the signs themselves, but he could not do that until a name had been decided. Hc asked Mitchell to settle the question. "You surely will not perpetuate the name now used, 'The Cumberland Hotel', (hotel ye gods!) nor can you say simply 'The Cumberland' so do let us get back to something sensible". Eventually the minutes of a council meeting held on 21 May, 1930, recorded that the name was to be "The Cumberland". Redfern's reply to

Mitchell (who seems always to have had to play the role of pig in the middle) was forthright and uncompromising: "Some people have a faculty of throwing away golden opportunities which amounts to a gift. You can hardly have a better instance of that than the decision arrived at last Wednesday afternoon to name these premises 'The Cumberland' instead of reverting to the earlier name (The Three Horseshoes) all because of a perfectly idiotic (I use the word advisedly) objection. Not only is the new name poor, meaningless and foolish, but it prevents us having any projecting sign for you cannot print the word "THE CUMBERLAND" in type large enough to be seen by passers by unless your sign projects farther into the street than the Corporation regulations permit. And thus what might have been an interesting piece of ironwork and an interesting and arresting piece of colour, is now impossible. All that is now possible is to put this silly wording in metal letters nailed over each entrance. So much for collected wisdom on matters of taste. It is really most disheart-ening". As his final coup de grace Redfern wrote to Mitchell: "By all means have a flare-up for the opening but of your charity forgive my not being present. As you know, I have always made it a rule to exempt myself on these dreadful occasions". (All quotations taken from PRO HO 190/72).

The CRESCENT INN, Warwick Road.

Whereas the Gretna Tavern had been a reconstruction of the old Post Office building in Lowther Street, Redfern was now able to erect a completely new public house adjoining the new General Post Office building in nearby Warwick Road. Once again, being an urban house the entrances were to lead directly off the street as with the Malt Shovel; Apple Tree; Earl Grey; and Cumberland Inn. The house was planned with care and precision to suit its rectangular but restricted site and perusal of the plans quickly reveals a marked economy in planning which gives the building a truly architectonic quality. Being on a closed site it could have windows only on the front and rear elevations but these windows were so designed as to play a signif-icant and elegant role in the overall symmetry of the building's facade. This model inn was faced with ivory-coloured pre-cast terracotta slabs from Art Pavements & Decoration of London. These slabs were of the faience style, that is fired twice - once without a glaze and once with a glaze. The roof was of distinctive green Spanish pantiles supplied by Adlard's of London and Newcastle, which were laid alternately concave and convex in courses, and, like the terracotta slabs, they washed themselves clean. The under-tile was the larger and there was a lap at both sides and at the head of each tile. They formed a beautiful roof which was flexible both in side-lap and end-lap. The amount of timber needed was considerable and the use of felting was also an important issue since any heat loss from the building would be dependent upon this underwork. The lead gutters were built up with timber and given a tile dressing in keeping with the symmetry of the facade. The Hispano-Moresque style of the Crescent was further enhanced by a recessed balcony approached by doors leading from each bar on the first floor and comprising three arches supported by marble pillars and fronted by three decorative wrought ironwork railings, the central one of which was gently bowed. The inner wall of this balcony had three windows enhanced by gold coloured curtains each carrying a semi-circle of gold mosaic work above and separated by engaged pilasters which were decorative but not structural.

The hispano-moresque Crescent Inn with its imaginative wrought ironwork

This loggia was illuminated at night by three orange coloured spherical electric lamp fitments, and sported three potted shrubs. In 1946, when the shrubs had died and the spherical lamp fittings had been blown down and smashed, the Superintendent, wanting to make the Crescent Inn and other places look a little less neglected at a time of shortages when it was difficult to get paint and painters, suggested using hanging baskets filled with flowers which were more readily available. But Redfern hastened to veto the notion declaring such things to be totally unsuitable for the most carefully designed Hispano-Moresque composition of the building. Redfern was 85 years old at the time and still keenly defending his aesthetic as a true professional.

The main central entrance leading off the street was a moulded door with label and had two flanking doorways carrying fanlights which led into each of

The Crescent Inn:
Above: interior. Below: Staircase with its arabesque ironwork.

the two ground floor bars. Fanlights were a favourite feature in many of Redfern's public houses. Between these doors, on either side of the central entrance, were two tall narrow windows with wooden balusters which indicated the existence of cosy inglenooks internally complete with carved wooden shutters. The inglenook was another favourite Redfern feature, it being a screened area

Lamp in The Crescent

with built-in seats which provided a popular retreat shielded from draughts.

The two ground floor rooms, each with a generously proportioned open fire grate, comprised a public bar with gents' lavatory accommodation leading directly off the bar, and a mixed second class bar with separate lavatory accommodation for ladies and gents, again leading directly from the bar. Like the Apple Tree this house also had bars upstairs, one of which was a first clas bar for men only. It had its own lavatory accommodation approached from the bar itself. The other was a mixed first

Railings in The Crescent

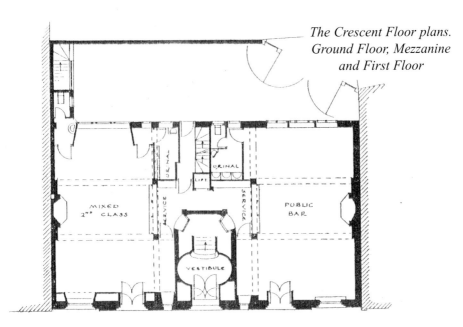

The Crescent Floor plans.
Ground Floor, Mezzanine
and First Floor

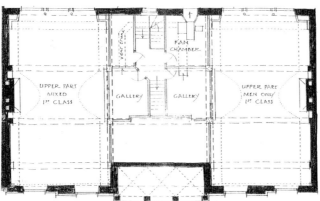

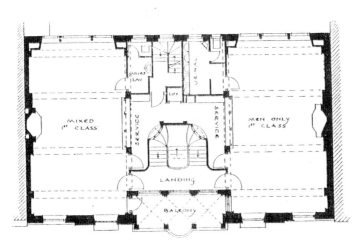

The Smoking Room in the Crescent Inn with its oriental ambience.

class bar with lavatory accommodation for women only, but also approached from the bar itself. Men from this bar could use the facilities provided for patrons of the men only first class accommodation by crossing the landing and making their way to the entrance at the rear of the bar.

A balanced ventilation system was installed which had fresh air inlets behind the radiators. The stale air was trunked up from the four corners of the service area and carried to a chamber above which housed a centrifugal fan. The teak vent trunks carrying the stale air were tongued, grooved and blocked in order to make them airtight and rigid. Redfern would have made all the necessary calculations to suit the type of fan of his choice and then designed the installation to suit the characteristics of the particular fan which had to be fixed with concrete eight inches thick with a bedding of anti-vibration cork two inches deep.

The mezzanine plan reveals Redfern's ingenuity in utilising the remaining space as a minstrel's gallery, which was another favourite feature which Redfern would use wherever the ambience of the situation was suitable. A good example of this was in the seventeenth century tithe barn from Abinger

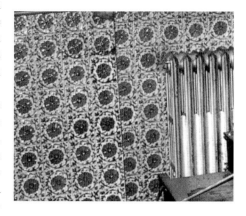

Some of the tiles in The Crescent

Manor, which Redfern restored and re-erected as an addition to the Burford Bridge Hotel at the foot of Box Hill in Surrey in 1935. In this instance he chose to amalgamate two of his favourite features by erecting a minstrels' gallery above an inglenook.

The influence of Islamic architecture in Europe had been limited to those regions once occupied by the Arabs, such as in the south of Spain where features of the mosques were modified and reduced in scale for use in secular buildings. The art of vaulting; correlated ceramic wall and floor tiles; and carved trellis work in wood all formed part of the influences imported into Europe. William Morris had greatly influenced the development of glazed wall tiles in the nineteenth century as had William de Morgan who found inspiration in the colours and beauty of Islamic ornamentation, especially the peacock blues and greens of Persian motifs. The Crescent's main entrance door of oak treated with silver nitrate bore a pattern of trellis-like design which was repeated on the internal doors, but this time in variation and with the description of the bar presented in lettering of inlaid mahogany. The glass in these doors was set in with chamois leather to obviate any cracking in use, a useful indication of forethought and craftsmanship. The decorative brass handles, although machine produced, were of good functional design and finish, and of an optimum size in relation to the measurement of the doors. The kidney-shaped vestibule had its curves accentuated by a line of tiles in green, white, and sienna at about head-height around the walls, while the grey marble stairs had their under-treads faced with the same patterned tiles, thus correlating floor and walls in the Islamic manner. The stairs leading to the first floor bars curved to left and to right enhanced by a beautiful, decorative balustrade surmounted by bronze handrails while a pair of mahogany bow-fronted glass corner cabinets hung on the wall on either side. An extensive use was made of Spanish sixteenth century styled tiles to cover the sides of the service area and the trunk pillars in the four corners. In the public bars these were four inches square and carried the motif of a flower in light sienna with a blue centre and green foliage within a green edging. In the bars on the first floor the tiles were ten inches square and coloured in a pattern of blue, light ochre and green. Because the ceilings in these rooms were gently vaulted, the tile decoration at either side of the fireplaces had to stop short at mantlepiece level, but, as a variant, they were used on the canopies. The open dog grates were set on brick. The fireplaces of Hopton Wood stone measured fifty inches across and were flanked by two pillars each fifteen inches in circumference standing on a nine inch square base. Originally the nine cast iron radiators were heated from a coke -fired boiler but when this was worn out, it was replaced by a new gas fired boiler (as had been done in the Malt Shovel) This was capable of heating the building without the use of fires. The windows on the south side of the first floor bars were models of excellent joinery. Glazed with panes measuring nine inches by twelve inches, the central arch was flanked by pillars nineteen inches in circumference standing on an eight inch base. Measurements quoted are intended to illustrate that Redfern's approach was generous, but not ostentatious, and that he achieved a fine balance of spaciousness and intimacy by virtue of his adherence throughout to principles of proportion.

Finally the question has to be posed as to whether the Crescent was too stylish and exotic for Carlisle? At that time. . . possibly, but not necessarily. Redfern was giving Carlisle a variety of public house buildings within an overall unity which adhered loyally to his remit. He was obviously familiar with the features of Islamic art and felt comfortable in using some of them in his own way to create an unusual and interesting building. Some of the local Cumbrian opinion felt that, like the Earl Grey which was to follow, the Crescent did not have the class of customer to suit the new image. At that time such exuberance was a visual innovation in Carlisle. The 1930s generally saw the increasing use of stainless steel, aluminium and chromed metal, particularly for restaurants and cinemas, which pointed the way to the future growing commitment to machine production. The Art Deco style of the Earl Grey was ambivalently "moderne" rather than ruthlessly "modernist" and consolidated Redfern's ability to handle the precepts of the old and the new in his profession by always providing an outcome which was good and honest.

THE EARL GREY, built by J. & R. Bell on a corner site in Botchergate/Union Street, was opened on 9 July, 1935. The Golden Fleece at St. Nicholas and the Queen Adelaide off sales department were closed at the same time. The advantage of the corner site meant that entrances to the public rooms could be well separated with the large public bar entered from Botchergate; and the smoking room, women's room, and off sales department could each be entered separately from Union Street.

The elevation was of yellow patterned brickwork with roofing of dark blue

The chrome front doors on the Earl Grey

glazed pantiles and metal window frames painted emerald green, while the external doors were chromium plated. Unfortunately the b r i c k w o r k discoloured over the ensuing years as the city was still, to a certain extent, in the age of steam trains and coal fires. The chromium plated doors also presented the authorities with a rather unusual problem in the years ahead. In 1941 the Chief Constable warned that the public bar front entrance doors reflected the light out into the street

162

The Earl Grey in 1935. A modernist design, its bold chromium doors to the street became a local landmark. (Courtesy of Tassell Carlisle Ltd.)

Interior of the Earl Grey in 1935 with its modern tubular steel chairs and tables. (Courtesy Royal Institute of British Architect)

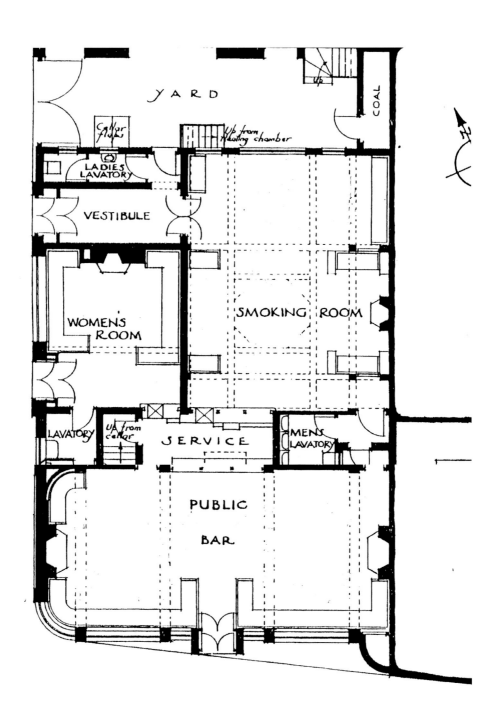

The Earl Grey plans. All three public rooms
could be entered directly from the street.

when the vestibule swing doors were opened. They thus contravened the wartime blackout regulations. A week later the general manager announced that they had succeeded in getting hold of a black paint that would not permanently damage the surfaceof the chrome and the doors were painted forthwith.

Internally, the Earl Grey was the first public house in Carlisle to have steel tubular chairs and tables in keeping with the Art Deco design of the building. The chairs were upholstered in green uncut moquette and were found to be extremely comfortable. The smoking room was surmounted by a large octagonal domed skylight for extra light and was lined with polished Australian walnut of a specially selected figuring. The artificial lighting in this room was provided by electrical fitments of clusters of white opaque cylinders while the skylight and large windows gave ample light during the day. As usual the manager's quarters were on a generous scale with the provision of three bedrooms (two on the first floor and one above accessed from a first floor bedroom), a sitting room, a kitchen with larder, a bathroom, and a wash-house. (How many domestic dwellings in Carlisle had bathrooms in the 1930s?). Once again heating for the public rooms was by a low pressure hot water system supplemented by open fires.

THE CUMBERLAND WRESTLERS, Currock Street, was opened on 3 October, 1938, to replace an old house of the same name which was ill-adapted for use as licensed premises in the light of the new requirements. As the Cumberland Wrestlers opened the Goliath Tavern in Crown Street and the London & North Western Railway Inn in James Street closed permanently for business as licensed premises. The building was situated on the corner of two streets and it was essential that there should be entrances from both streets but, at the same time, it was neces-sary that the ground floor should be at one level. The solution to this particular problem took the form of a terrace approached by a flight of shallow steps on the principal front enclosed by ornamental iron railings. A formal flower bed was planted at the rear of the building which could be viewed from the window of the mixed smoking room.

This new inn with its brick walls, stone dressings and green slated roof followed comfortably in the local eighteenth century tradition. The plan was straight-forward enough with a public bar, two smoking rooms (one for men only and one for mixed patrons) and an off sales department with a separate entrance all of which were supplied and supervised from one service area. The walls of the smoking rooms were panelled to a height of seven feet in either elm, or black bean, an unusual Australian wood of great beauty. The public bar was panelled in oak to the height of the chairs. The furniture was specially designed in the relevant wood to match the panelling and was upholstered in either rexine or hide. The name of the inn afforded Redfern a golden opportunity to have a good pictorial inn sign for which he called upon E.M. Dinkel, ARCA, once again. On one side was a full size portrait of the well-known Cumberland wrestler George Steadman and on the reverse was depicted a bout of Cumberland wrestling between George Steadman and Hexham Clark. A letter of appreciation was sent by George Steadman's son to the general manager saying, "How entirely pleased they were to see the pictorial sign with his late father's athletic Grasmere record so truly and attractively set forth".

The Cumberland Wrestlers frontage with a William Yournger's sign vying for attention with the Wrestlers inn sign by E.M. Dinkel, ARCA

The Cumberland Wrestlers Public Bar at time of its opening. Ladies in this bar would have to take the outside route to their lavatory through the side entrance to the smoking rooms. (RIBA Journal)

Other inns of equal merit and interest to this selection of urban model inns designed by Redfern, were built on the outskirts of the city and these were mainly in a country house style.

THE SPINNERS' ARMS at Cummersdale was built by J. & R. Bell in 1930. It was a small, but delightfully homely, public house of white-rendered brick and tiles with an asymmetrical elevation. As well as placing a dormer window in the sloping roof, Redfern added an oriel window above the public bar. Cantilevered off the main structure of the building and supported underneath by timber, an oriel window added extra light as well as functioning as a decorative feature. Such windows can be found in many buildings of the Arts & Crafts movement as, for example, the Red House designed by Philip Webb for William Morris or the Queen Anne Revival houses of Norman Shaw. A further decorative feature of the Spinners Arms was the east lead motif of yarn on the rainwater heads and the depiction of various animals on the gutters. These animals included a bull, a hare, a hound, a tortoise, a kangaroo, a

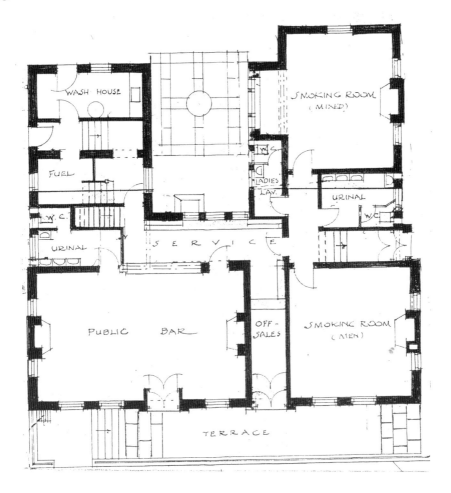

The ground floor plan of the Spinners' Arms

The new, delightfully homely Spinners Arms in Cummersdale

The old Spinners Arms, Cummersdale

The entrance and projecting gable of the Spinnners'Arms

crocodile and an elephant. The origin of the initial choice, and by whom, remains a conundrum.

The ground floor accommodation comprised an off sales department; a public bar; a men's smoking room; a mixed smoking room; a kitchen, fuel store and wash house while on the first floor there was the usual three bedrooms, sitting room and bathroom.

By June, 1930, an objection was being made that there was no provision of a bowling green. Redfern responded to the general manager that: "The planning of the new house gave no thought of the possibility of a bowling green in the rear. If a bowling green at the rear had been contemplated before the plans were made, it would have meant an entirely different arrangement of rooms. As it is we must make the best of it. For my own part I should not be sorry if the bowling green scheme fell through". (PRO HO 190/232). The issue surfaced again many years later in 1956 when the Cummersdale Parish council felt that there was an urgent need for bowling green facilities in the village and suggested utilising space behind the Spinners' Arms. The general manager explained, however, that the State Management did not own the land at the rear and that, much as they were in sympathy with the provision of such amenities in rural districts, the very high cost of providing a bowling green together with the purchase of the land ruled out such a proposition. The SMS at that time was being pressed at all levels to curb expenditure, particularly of a capital nature. They had found from experience that the upkeep of bowling greens was a very expensive matter and the income to all intents and purposes was negligible.

The ROSE & CROWN, Upperby was built by Laings and opened on 22 December, 1930. This public house which occupied a commanding site at the junction of the main road to Upperby and the new road leading to the Corporation's housing estates, pinpointed the changes in design which were taking place under the State Management Scheme.

The most striking features of the internal arrangements at the Rose & Crown were its extremely short counter length; its roomy off-sales department with its entrance quite apart from other entrances; and the complete separation of the public bar with low doors of counter height and shelf tops giving direct access to the other public rooms.

*The architect's drawing for the rear and side elevations
of the Rose and Crown in Upperby*

The external walls were built of hard Whitehaven bricks, treated with a damp resisting compound and finished in limewhite while the fawn rooftiles were accentuated by the emerald green doors and shutters. A swinging inn sign painted by E.M. Dinkel and mounted on an oak pillar stood in the paved forecourt. On the south side was a lawn and formal sunken herb garden with a sundial which said, "Time flies you say: ah no 'Tis time that stays: we go".

Redfern made allowances in his plans for a bowling green to be provided a little later on and the boundaries to be marked with posts and chains. It was found in time that the nature of this surround meant that the bowling green was too easily accessible to an active child and steps had to be taken to prevent children getting onto the green and damaging the turf. The

*The Rose and Crown,
Upperby.*

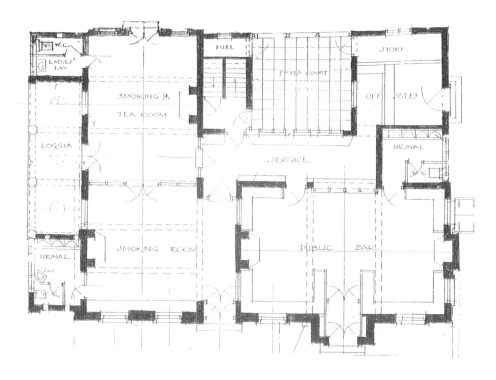

The ground floor plan of the Rose and Crown.
The service area was well positioned to serve all rooms.
The tea room opened onto the proposed bowling green.

The elegant, panelled tea room at the Rose and Crown.

The sign for the Rose and Crown

doors leading from the loggia to the bar service were placed centrally along the main garden axis. This made for ease in attending to customers seated in the loggia. The other pair of folding doors at the end of the tearoom led directly to the terrace overlooking the prospective bowling green. An inventory taken of the bowling equipment in 1951 once the green was operational listed: 42 pairs of bowling slippers; 12 bowling green mats; 48 pairs of bowls; nine jacks; 12 rink markers; two Minchin measures; 40 yards of chain guard; four pairs green steps; five garden seats; one bowls storage cabinet; one pair of shears and one notice board announcing the green fees. And all this after having laid 450 square yards of best Cumberland turf.

Lavatory accommodation at the Rose & Crown was still entered directly from the three public rooms

The bowling green at the Rose and Crown

but the two placed either end of the loggia overlooking the sunken garden had the added advantage that they acted as wind shields.

The interior of the premises was exceptionally bright and Redfern had encouraged the Carlisle workmen to excel in their various crafts. The settles, chairs and tables were of oak with black inlay work and the walls of pale fawn were decoratively stencilled with panelled lines of green and purple. Glazed Dutch blue/white tiles in the tearoom added an aura of cleanliness while a charming picture was hung over each fireplace - the Isle of Skye over one and parts of old York over the other. The clear glass windows were draped with a Morton Sundour chintz of small coloured flowers on a white background. The whole atmosphere was one of brightness and cleanliness and was a credit to Carlisle.

In 1941 the City Council had to make provision for a road block in case of invasion and pressed the SMS urgently for permission to store the cement blocks on the forecourt immediately behind the footpath. There was already a machine-gun post near to the Rose & Crown. Added to this the SMS was asked to make provision for feeding small parties of the Home Guard in the event of an invasion. Permission was granted for small parties of Home Guard not exceeding eight or ten in number to use the premises for cooking and eating their meals which they would provide from their own rations.

The MAGPIE INN, Botcherby, was built by Laings and opened 4 December, 1933. Two years previously the finance committee of the City Council had negotiated with the owner of Botcherby Hall to: "Throw part of his land into the highway for the widening and improving of the Warwick Road/Victoria Road area." The SMS was prepared to purchase approximately 4278 square yards of land fronting Victoria Road at an actual purchase price of £4333 and was also prepared to purchase and remove the Hall buildings and pay the Corporation £500 on that account. The new

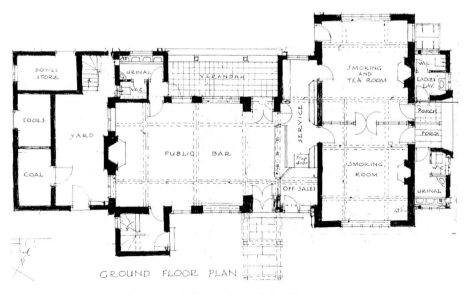

The ground floor plan of the Magpie Inn

173

A rear view of the Magpie Inn overlooking the bowling green

model inn on the outskirts of the city replaced the former Star Inn which had been a base for communal and sporting activities and had for many years been the only licensed premises in that part of the city.

The new inn was a black and white "magpie" house nestling in a hollow formed by two steep grass banks, and was built in a very English way making use of an uncluttered Arts & Crafts style with subtle asymmetry, half timbering, horizontal fenestration (as might be found in Baillie-Scott or Voysey), and a diamond-shaped window. Added to which was the deep pitch to the gable-ended roof, the hipped roof dormers, and the tall chimney stacks balancing the fenestration. A wide forecourt with car park was provided and a pergola porch was erected. At the rear, paved terraces and steps led to the bowling green fronted by flower beds for which Redfern had actually named the shrubs and plants that he wanted, and positioned them on his plan in the genuine Arts & Crafts manner in which the internal and external criteria are one entity. The nature of the sloping site made the changes in level necessary but they added greatly to the interest of the building. The overall site dimension was 140ft by 275ft and approximately half this space was taken up by the bowling green.

Internally a sense of restfulness prevailed by way of adopting a quiet colour scheme, the usual open coal fires, and the long low line of the windows the overall height of which had been planned to suit exactly the number of brick courses. The fireplaces were of white shawkstone brickettes with a selection of the blocks slightly veined in red. Reference to the plan indicates just how well-placed the lavatory accommodation was becoming by this time with its twin entrance porches for tearoom and smoking room customers while the public bar was served by a lavatory entered internally via a small lobby which also served the needs of the bowls players with an extra door from the verandah.

It is interesting to take a brief look here at some of the rules and regulations laid down by the State Management Scheme for work carried out for them in 1933 under contract which was, in this case for the installation of electric light wiring and fittings: "The whole of the work to be executed in accordance with the drawings to the entire satisfaction of the architect. Materials and workmanship to be the best of their kind and only skilled labour to be employed. A skilled foreman to be constantly employed during the execution of the work. Any defects which may occur during six months after completion of the work must be made good at the contractor's own expense. Payment will be made at the rate of 80 per cent of the value of the work from time to time as the work proceeds and the remainder will be paid at the rate of 10 per cent on completion and 10 per cent three months after completion. The contractor to commence the work immediately on receiving instructions from the architect and complete the whole of the work within six weeks from the date of commencement".

There are two items worth a mention before closing the file on the Magpie. A member of the Carlisle City Police Force reported in 1949 that he had noticed whilst passing the inn at 11a.m. a flock of about 25 sheep straying about the gardens and lawns of the premises. The manager stated that for the past fortnight these sheep had been in the habit of straying from the adjoining fields by way of a lane and causing considerable damage. The owner of the sheep said that although he kept the fences and hedges of his fields in as good repair as possible all his good work was undone by children and footballers taking a short cut through his fields and trampling down the hedges and fences. The SMS responded by erecting a post and wire fence dividing the car park from the adjoining lane.

In July 1949 Joseph Seddon submitted a detailed drawing showing a glazed enclosure to the verandah at the Magpie Inn arranged in such a way that during the bowls season a set of folding doors in the wide centre opening could be opened right back flat on the inner face. For the rest of the year with the folding doors closed the verandah could be used as a darts alley. It was suggested that the alley could be

The public bar in the Magpie Inn

heated by the installation of two 2-kilowatt heaters which at that time still carried a purchase tax of 66.6 per cent. Having discussed it with Redfern the plan was approved and the work was completed by 14 October, 1949, but the issue didn't rest there. The general manager pointed out that in view of the extreme difficulty of supervision during the busy nights at the weekend and of the very real danger of gambling, darts playing should not be permitted on Friday, Saturday, or Sunday nights. In most of the SMS houses where darts were played it would be too dangerous during crowded hours although that element of danger would not have arisen in the new alley at the Magpie. Nevertheless the danger of gambling would be ever present and the last thing the Management wanted was a prosecution for gambling. And so it transpired that darts were not to be played except under conditions where it was possible for the manager adequately to supervise the games, at least in so far as to prevent gambling.

The WHEATSHEAF INN in Abbeytown was built by Laings and opened on 16 December, 1935, to take the place of the Joiners' Arms and the Bush Inn, and the old Wheatsheaf Inn which had already been closed. It was a fine detached brick and tiled public house rendered white, with a low pitched roof, dormer windows, and a bowling green laid with turf from Millom. The green has since been covered over to make a car park. It was probably the best example of Redfern's country house style in the whole of the Scheme's area but like other inns it had presented some difficulties. The impermeable nature of the sub-soil on the site had occasioned a considerable amount of thought in devising some modification of the drainage scheme in November 1935, particularly as the authorities wanted the building to be ready for opening before Christmas.

Another aspect of drainage arose with regard to the bowling green. The

The Wheatsheaf sign

estimate given to the builders for laying the turf did not include any clinker bed, but Redfern was insistent that a lawn of Cumberland turf not adequately drained would be a waste of money. A year after opening it was suggested that the Wheatsheaf, had enough land for a greenhouse and putting green. Redfern was happy to fall in with the idea and set about making the greenhouse a little more presentable than the average structure which he thought was generally a hideous thing. As for the putting green was concerned, he saw no reason to object provided the formal path was retained. For him the formless greens beloved of the landscape gardeners - Repton and Capability Brown - were not for the SMS. A quotation for the supply and planting of shrubs and

The Wheatsheaf Inn in Abbeytown.
Probably the best example of Redfern's country-house style

The tea room in the Wheatsheaf Inn
(Courtesy Royal Institute of British Architects)

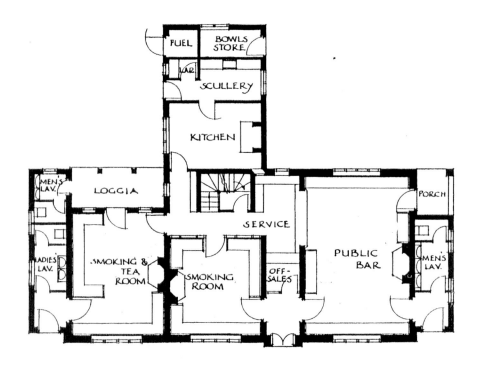

The ground floor plan of the Wheatsheaf

plants from Clark Brothers of Scotch Street, Carlisle, included the following comprehensive list: 2 flowering cherries, 4 almond trees, 4 standard roses in variety, 128 dwarf roses, 125 lavender, 4 rosemary, 230 violas, 28 thyme. 8 forsythia, 2 American Pillar roses, 4 white broom, 4 cotoneaster simmondii, 8 delphiniums in variety, 40 peonies, 48 dianthus deltoides, 100 London Pride, 36 gaillardia in variety, 100 veronica prostrata, and 100 nepeta mussone. The teak garden furniture was obtained from Castles' Shipbreaking Co. Ltd. of Millbank, London, and had become available in the 1930s when decommissioned battleships were being broken up. The advantage of this timber was that it could be left out in the garden the whole year round and the vagaries of the weather would not affect it. All it needed was an occasional scrubbing down with hot soda water corresponding to the holy stoning employed at sea. The furniture itself was solidly constructed, tenoned and morticed, and brass screwed.

The CROWN, Stanwix, completed in December, 1937, was a large town public house of brick and slate construction built in the Georgian style on a prominent corner site in a better class district of the city. The elevation was symmetrical with a generous forecourt and supported a weather vane. The public bar, refreshment room, smoking room, billiard room, and small off-sales department all had their separate entrances. The service area was as central as possible and was fitted with a sliding gate in order that the service could be closed off during non-licensing hours but a sizeable kitchen was provided so that food and teas could be served in the

The Crown on a busy corner in Stanwix.

Interior of the Crown at Stanwix with its drawing room feel.
(Courtesy Royal Institute of British Architects)

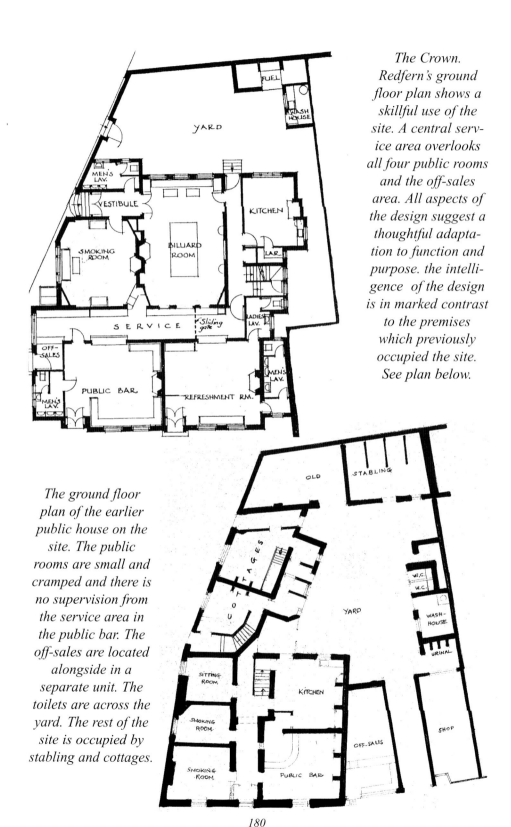

The Crown. Redfern's ground floor plan shows a skillful use of the site. A central service area overlooks all four public rooms and the off-sales area. All aspects of the design suggest a thoughtful adaptation to function and purpose. the intelligence of the design is in marked contrast to the premises which previously occupied the site. See plan below.

The ground floor plan of the earlier public house on the site. The public rooms are small and cramped and there is no supervision from the service area in the public bar. The off-sales are located alongside in a separate unit. The toilets are across the yard. The rest of the site is occupied by stabling and cottages.

The front elevation of Seddon's tribute to Redfern; the Redfern Inn photographed here in the 1970s illustrating the delicate guttering and windows almost identical to the ones in the Horse & Farrier

refreshment room. A men's lavatory led directly off the public bar while a ladies' lavatory led directly off the refreshment room, but the two remaining men's lavatories were positioned via a lobby. The walls in the smoking room were panelled in walnut and the fireplace was in a beautiful black and white marble.

Redfern suffered a heart attack in December, 1936, and spent a month in a nursing home, after which his doctors would not allow him to take any journeys into the country for some time. His wife, Edith, died in the following May, 1937. By this time, however, Redfern had bequeathed to the people of Carlisle and district and to the nation at large a fine body of work and he deserves to be better known. It was in this spirit of gratitude and homage that the REDFERN INN at Etterby was designed by his assistant architect, Joseph Seddon, FRIBA (with Redfern's collaboration) as a fitting tribute to a man who had dedicated his talents to the quest for an improved public house style.

The REDFERN was built by J. & R. Bell on an open site in residential surroundings and was opened on 1 October, 1940, at a time when the country was again at war. A one million pound RAF equipment depot at Kingstown was expected to bring about 3,000 workers to the area and temperance protesters were informed that fresh accommodation would be needed to obviate overcrowding in the bars. The scheme for this latest inn required the inclusion of a bowling green and this fact had

The rear view of the Redfern Inn, Etterby,
seen from the bowling green which was still in use in 2007

an influence in shaping the plan since there was only one available position for the green on this awkwardly shaped site. The plan took the form of an expanded "L" with the corner angle turned towards the green so that it could be overlooked from the windows of the principal public rooms. In addition, a single-storey timber verandah was formed on the re-entering angle for the use of the players and spectators of the game. In this case a strictly symmetrical layout of the plan did not naturally arise, nor was any attempt made to force the point. On the contrary the elevations were allowed to develop naturally from the plan with sufficient order in the grouping to make them pleasing when viewed from every angle. The treatment was somewhat reminiscent of a typical yeoman's house of the eighteenth century found in Kent or Sussex, hence the long lines of the roofing surmounted by a small cupola centrally placed and topped with a golden cockerel weather vane. Bricks in broken shades of russet brown were used at first floor level while the first floor was mostly hung with red tiles. The general horizontal lines of the building were punctuated by generously proportioned chimney stacks which served to stiffen the composition.

There was a small off sales department entered from a lobby while the public rooms which were all on the ground floor radiated from a circular hall. They comprised a large public bar; a smoking room for men only; and a combined tea/smoking room for men and women. Altogether there was an aura of charm and homely comfort. Seddon followed faithfully the principles laid down by Redfern for his previous houses even to drawing up a plan for the flower borders and ordering: 24 early flowering chrysanthemums, 24 bedding dahlias in variety, 200 antirrhinums, 250 calendula, 50 African marigolds and 50 French marigolds.

The erection of an inn sign was delayed because Dinkel's house at Chiswick had been bombed and some of his neighbours killed and a design which he had earlier submitted had been rejected in Carlisle. This rejection had drawn a rebuke from Redfern, as might be expected, for he had thought and hoped they would have

Harry Redfern

been captivated by the delicate fancy which had been brought to bear to this difficult task. Instead, it seemed they wished to take to, "The well-worn high road of the commonplace where there was no room for idealism". He did however mollify his attitude when praising Mitchell for his patience throughout the long months of delay which had "pierced the gloom like a bright morning star" and declared that he would always be grateful to him for that. The saga of the inn sign was eventually resolved after a memorandum to Mitchell from the assistant general manager suggested that he did not regard the sign as one of Dinkel's happiest efforts on account of it being pitched in too sombre a key. Rather than offend Redfern on a matter of this kind, particularly as his name was to be associated with the inn, "If he is satisfied with the design, I am prepared to accept it".

At a later date Redfern requested two sets of five photographs of the inn to be supplied by Messrs. Tassell (Carlisle) Ltd. which, when he received them, drew the following generous response: "I fell in love with the building when I saw it and should be proud to think I had designed it. But all the kudos for that goes to our good Seddon".

Following Redfern's death, Joseph Seddon contributed a fulgent obituary in the RIBA Journal, April, 1950, saying: "It was my privilege to be associated with Harry Redfern for more than thirty years principally in connection with the work of remodelling and rebuilding hotels and inns in the State Management Districts of Carlisle, Gretna, and Cromarty Firth. From the day in 1916 when he welcomed me to his office, until his retirement last September, I worked with him in happy harmony. He had the gift of making all members of his staff feel that they were his fellow workers, deeply interested in finding the best solutions to the problems that came along. When correspondence and official affairs were cleared off, he would be at the drawing board. He was happy when making all the drawings for such a job as a village inn; they would be beautifully drawn and designed in his characteristic, charming style. For others to work out, he made those scribbles (his word) which are an architect's shorthand. With a little practice in reading them, his scribbles conveyed much, or in a few words stimulate one's imagination and set one going often with a free hand on working out some scheme, with now and then a wise comment from the rich store of his experience. There was nothing of the aloof professional man about Harry Redfern, he was always happy in his dealings with builders and their workmen. He would talk over some bit of craftsmanship with a man, get him interested and say, 'That's the idea, just go on and enjoy yourself'. I am sure I speak for many in saying that we shall treasure the memory of the pleasure it gave to work for him".

CHAPTER NINE

ABOLITION OF THE SCHEME
TOM SEABURY

Despite many years of work on the manuscript for this book, Olive Seabury died in 2005 before completing the concluding chapter. This last chapter has been written by her son, Tom, mostly from her research material and notes in the hope it conveys historical detail of interest, and expresses sentiments shared with Olive.

The State Management Scheme was abolished by Act of Parliament in 1971 under the Conservative Government of Edward Heath, when Reginald Maudling was Home Secretary. By 1973 all the property had been sold off. Thus ended a unique working model of a a state enterprise operating as a monopoly.

M.P's who supported the abolition emphasised that the Scheme had been 'experimental' and had run for too long. Those M.P's who opposed it argued that there was no good reason to abolish it as it consistently made a contribution to the Exchequer.

On 14th December, 1970, Ron Lewis, M.P. for Carlisle, received a Parliamentary written answer from Mark Carlisle, M.P. confirming that no Home Office officials had had discussions with the chairmen of the Scheme's Local Advisory Committees, apart from routine matters. The Home Secretary did not wish to make a statement.

By 11th January, 1971, local managers had made representation to the Local Advisory Committee that sensational press reporting about the future of the Scheme was undermining morale. Soon after on 19th January, 1971, letters announcing the closure were sent to tenant managers from the Home Office. This coincided with written answers in Parliament from the Home Secretary[1]: [We] "have decided that there is no longer sufficient social or economic justification for the continuance of the State Management of the Liquor trade. Return on capital employed is low in the view of the restrictions under which the Scheme operates." There "would be a need for further substantial investment . . . if the present scheme were to continue".

The Carlisle and District Local Advisory Committee held a special meeting on 28th January, 1971, to consider the Government position. Ongoing correspondence with Home Office officials prompted the Committee to responded on April 15th noting "the apparent finality of the decision to proceed with outright disposal" and going on to propose that the Home Secretary make the continuing operation of the brewery a binding condition of sale.

Questions on winding up the Scheme had surfaced from time to time throughout its life. One instance, in 1952, was a proposal from Tory M.P. Gerald Nabarro, that it "should be no part of policy or purposes of the Conservative Party to own licensed premises or to promote the sale of large quantity of beer". In the same period, and by contrast, Rab Butler, Tory Home Secretary, said at a 1959 meeting of the Conservative Party Northern Council: "In practice I do not think [abolition] is going to operate to the advantage of the district. The monopoly seems to work".

After the Redfern era the Scheme added three new pubs in the 1960s: the Border Terrier (pictured here under construction) the Border Reiver and the Royal Scot.

There had been Parliamentary bills for the Scheme's abolition previously such as the State Management (Liquor Trade) Abolition Act 1925, introduced by Col. Sir Arthur Holbrook. This passed its first reading, but the Home Secretary of the time had it blocked by the whips. The bill was the same as the one brought by Holbrook but lost in 1922.

In the immediate lead up to the abolition bill, in February, 1969, Conservative M.P. Kenneth Baker asked why the profits [from the Scheme] had declined. He quoted a 52% drop between 1963/4 and 1967/8. Shortly following this, in April, 1969, a proposal was prepared by the Scheme's General Manager to dispose of some of the Scheme surplus properties, mainly Carlisle city centre shops and offices.

Around that time the Scheme's Carlisle and District Local Advisory Committee was discussing with the Home Office their desire to take on more executive powers as opposed to a merely advisory role. The Committee felt it exercised insufficient influence on the conduct of the Scheme. This approach was rejected by Home Office officials: "Within the present statutory framework there is relatively little scope for further delegation of functions". The Home Office was relying instead on support from the State Management District's Council.

This rejection was in addition to other rejections the Local Advisory Committee had had to their detailed policy proposals. One example was their proposed extension of the Scheme's area. Following their deputation to the Home Secretary in November, 1965, a note of 6th June, 1966, from the General Manager, J. N. Adams, restated the position that sales outside the existing geographic area, including supply of beer to the Workington area, were rejected by the Home Secretary as "without legal authority". A further piece of scene setting for the abolition bill was BBC2's Money Programme of 8th May, 1969. This carried an item on the Scheme which had a tone that was "largely derogatory" and the balance struck was one critical of the Scheme. The apparently disproportionate allocation of two full days of Commons time to the abolition bill was noted by M.P.'s. The political and legislative events contemporaneous with the first reading of the bill included a significant evolution of "the troubles" in Northern Ireland which led to the state's use of internment without trial in August, 1971. The strongly contested Industrial Relations Act was passing through Parliament. Unemployment was around 4%, and inflation was at its worst for twenty years. Around this time too the Concorde fleet was being built, and the membership of the EEC was being discussed. The privately owned Rolls Royce became insolvent developing the RB211 aero-engine. Willie Hamilton, Labour M.P. for Fife West, was at pains to contrast the attitude of the Heath government to the Scheme with their attitude to Rolls Royce: "A private enterprise that is going bankrupt . . . is taken over into public ownership".

The 1970 Parliament's privatisation agenda included far larger enterprises. There had been debates in the Commons between June, 1970, and April, 1971, on the Coal Industry Bill, on the sell-off of Thomas Cook, and of the publicly owned air routes. In the case of the Thomas Cook & Son sell-off, the Labour Party warned potential buyers that any future Labour government would buy the enterprise back at no more than the price that was paid.

Michael Cocks, M.P. for Bristol South, suggested the motives were "some sort of sop" for the forthcoming autumn Conservative Party Conference, a propaganda exercise to show that private enterprise was flourishing. Labour M.P. Neil Kinnock caricatured the criteria used by the Heath Government in selection of enterprises ready to return to the private sector ownership: "Profitable, risk free, and easy to transfer to private enterprise".

As well as engagement around the case for the sell off, the existence of any political mandate for it was strongly contested. The 1970 Scottish Conservative Party Manifesto had proposed to "Break the State Monopoly", but not explicitly to abolish the Scheme. There was no reference to the Scheme in the Conservative manifesto for England, "A Better Tomorrow". The nearest statement was to "stop further nationalisation", but it did say, "Specific projects approved by Parliament will continue to be given Government support".

The existence of a mandate for the denationalisation of the Scheme was strenuously challenged in the Cumberland constituencies. G.J. Coogan, a former member of the Carlisle and District Local Advisory Committee, stated that "no attempt at consultation . . . was entered into with the Committee by the Home Office'4. Conservative Councillor Jim Aspey, who was chair of the same committee, stated "Public opinion is opposed to the sale . . . they should have held a ballot". There certainly was controversy whether consultation by popular referendum was called for. The Home Secretary was adamant the sale was going ahead as determined by his office, subject only to the bill's passage through Parliament. The form of consultation was limited, relying mostly on M.P.'s to argue the case. Even so local M.P.'s had been affronted as the first they knew of the ministers' intent had been from an article in the Times. Differing views of public "interest" were aired. The Labour opposition not surprisingly held that the public interest and shareholders' interest were not the same. Similarly the Monopolies Commission report into licensed trade,

April,1969, concluded that the tied house system "operates against the public interest". The tied house system was not, however, challenged by the Heath government, and remained untouched for many years thereafter.

The principal argument the Government gave for selling off the Scheme was its low level of return on investment. This argument was however predicated on an accounting model in which the Scheme's capital assets must show a return as if they were a debt to the Treasury. This model was by no means universally accepted. The capital cost of setting up the Scheme had been repaid to the Treasury, so the assets were not costing the Treasury. Indeed, in 1941, when Herbert Morrison, Home Secretary, visited Carlisle, he noted that, "The whole of the original capital put into the scheme by the state had been paid off and new capital expenditure was now met out of revenue". This point was elaborated in academic papers:[5] "By 31st March, 1928, the issues from the Exchequer . . . had been paid off" . . . "there is nothing in the financial structure of the schemes that corresponds to the subscribed capital of a company. Nevertheless the balance sheet does include a figure for the capital account. . . . This figure first appeared in the accounts for 1928-9 on the suggestion of the Public Accounts Committee".

Guidance on how to establish a definition of "an acceptable return on investment" for nationalised industries had been set out in April, 1961, in a White Paper, Financial and Economic Obligations of the Nationalised Industries. By 1966, when Conservative M.P. Nicholas Ridley asked in Parliament if there was a specific financial target for the Scheme, this guidance had not been formally adopted. Informed commentary on aspects of the Scheme's running has been mostly positive, such as the conclusion of Talbot:[6] "The populist image of an ineffectual state bureaucracy . . . was demonstrably inaccurate". Carlisle M.P Ron Lewis was clear that the general principle of the abolition was "public enterprise versus private ownership".

Jim Callaghan, later to be the leader of the Labour Party, expressed his suspicion, one he shared with Ron Lewis, that Willie Whitelaw, Conservative M.P. for Penrith and the Borders, was the main instigator of the sell-off. Ron Lewis was quoted in The Cumberland News: "I am pretty sure that the M.P. for Penrith and the Borders was the prime mover behind this rape of the State Management Scheme in the Cabinet". He restated this in his Parliamentary speech: "The bill is in the hand of Reggie [Reginald Maudling, Home Secretary], but behind is the hand of Willie". A written answer given to Parliament[7] confirmed that only three representations had been made to the Home Office for changes to the Scheme. These were from the Carlisle and District Local Advisory Committee, the Magistrates Association, and the Carlisle branch of the Young Conservatives.

Prior to the bill there had been a web of correspondence including a confidential memo of 1967[8] from Carlisle and District Local Advisory Committee to the Home Office. This memo was copied to the M.P's for the area including Mr Whitelaw. In it the Committee called into question the Scheme's monopoly and argued the Scheme should be run as a business concern, with a new image, and that it should jettison disinterested management. Clearly this would have played some part in the attitude to the Scheme of its recipients, whether or not it was in the direction intended by its authors.

A variation of this thinking was that the brewery interests in general, and the Scottish brewers in particular, had driven this onto the government's agenda. Willie Ross M.P. (Labour, Kilmarnock) suggested the instigators were "the big guns behind the scenes in Scotland, the McEwan-Youngers". The private brewing industry journals had over the years consistently carried articles and correspondence challenging the legitimacy of the Scheme. The leader of the Scottish Conservative Party at that time was none other than Sir William McEwan-Younger, former chair and managing director of Scottish and Newcastle Breweries. The Labour Party led a sustained attack on the extent to which the Conservative party had personal ties and financial interest in the brewing industry, and the extent to which Conservative Party itself was funded by the brewing industry. At that time the requirement to disclose interests and donations to political party funds was less stringent than it is today.

The Secretary of State for Scotland argued that the Scheme inhibited the development of the tourist industry in Scotland and implied that this was the impetus behind their manifesto undertaking to remove the monopoly. The financial performance of the Scottish districts had been generally inferior [9] to that south of the border and this may have further enforced the thinking of Scottish Conservatives. Willie Ross M.P. was of the opinion that the Home Secretary did not himself want to introduce the bill, and other M.P's commented on an apparent lack of commitment from the Home Secretary when presenting the bill to Parliament.

Correspondence from Lord Stonham for the Home Office to the Local Advisory Committee in 1968 accepted a need to "gradually adopt a more commercial approach" to "many problems". However, he had not passed the proposals in the memo to the Minister. Lord Stonham went on to add that there was sympathy for greater autonomy for the Scheme's General Manager, but that "no fundamental changes to policy are proposed". Norman Adams, General Manager, told the Cumberland News in 1971 that the civil service rules made it impossible to run the Scheme as an efficient business. These exchanges will have supported a perception that the Scheme's management was more business minded, innovative and sensitive to local needs than the Home Office.

Until 1971 the principle of disinterested management had been accepted as a central feature of the Scheme. However, this coexisted in tension with the need for a surplus to be generated for the Exchequer. Decades earlier there had been allegations of the Scheme training its managers to serve short measure. The Burt Report of 1957[10] found no proof that this had been formally advocated. There certainly were pressures for generation of an "adequate" surplus and the extent to which disinterested management was practiced was the focus of some argument. This was of mere academic interest after Mr Maudling set out his party's attitude. The unsuccessful Conservative Parliamentary candidate for Carlisle was quoted in the Lords in 1971 as extolling the Scheme, and proposing only to relax licensing controls, and transfer control to a local trust.

Parliament were first made aware of the intention to introduce a bill to abolish the Scheme in written answers on 19th January, 1971:

"Intention of the Secretary of State for Scotland to end the State monopoly in Gretna and Cromarty, State Management Scheme, Gretna and Cromarty.

"Mr Gray asked the secretary of state whether he had yet come to a conclusion on the best method to end the State monopoly of the liquor trade in the Gretna and Cromarty districts.

"Mr. Gordon Campbell: I have already made known the Government's intention to end this monopoly; and I have been in consultation with my right hon. Friend the Home Secretary about the best method of achieving this. We have come to the conclusion that State participation in the liquor trade is neither necessary nor desirable. I intend to discontinue the State Management system and to dispose of all facilities or the State supply of liquor. Legislation for this purpose will be introduced shortly."

Requests by Ron Lewis MP (Labour, Carlisle) for a ministerial statement rather than the written answer were not answered. The bill progressed to its second reading on 20th April, 1971, when there was the first opportunity to debate its content. In this session the exchanges were mostly between the bill's supporters, and Labour members of the opposition. It was by no means a good tempered exchange, and at 10 p.m. the division was taken. There were 277 votes for and 226 against.

The committee stage saw a total of 30 amendments and 9 new clauses. Only two of these were from the Government side. These were all voted down by the Commons at the report stage with government majorities of 29 or more. At its final third reading on 24th June, the unamended bill was passed by 286 to 251. Royal Assent was on 29th July 1971. Throughout the bill's passage the Home Secretary retained the role as sole and final arbiter on how the sell-off would progress. Late in the debates he did however concede that he would 'take professional advice'.

In the Parliamentary debates there was scant attention to the effect the sell-off would have on the level of drunkenness, and there was no attempt to enumerate the indirect benefits of the Scheme. The assertion from Mr Maudling was simply that that there was no longer sufficient "Social justification". Findings from the major reviews of the Scheme were referred to only briefly in support of one or two points. While there were those with an ideological stance for abolition, the financial arguments were those given most airing. Financial arguments related mainly to the accounting policies for calculation of trading surplus & return on investment, and to the valuation of the property portfolio. Jim Callaghan MP (Labour, Cardiff South West) however considered it proper to state the Labour intent to re-nationalise the Scheme. Labour's Willie Hamilton went further confirming that his Constituency Labour Party had a motion for their party conference advocating nationalisation of all the big seven breweries. This was mirrored by Ron Lewis who referred to a similar motion from Carlisle Labour Party.

At the committee stage the option to place a time limit on the sales was considered as the bill placed no obligation to complete the sell-off by any particular date. This amendment would have required any property not sold within a year be retained in public ownership for a further five years, that is into the life of the next Parliament. The brewery itself was the asset with the most uncertain future but it later proved the hardest to sell.

The terminology of the debate ranged widely. The bill was variously termed an abolition, a sell-off, a disposal, a transfer of ownership, a divestment, a Dutch

Auction,[11] or a denationalisation.[12] The voting divisions showed less variation. Clear party divisions were the norm, with only Conservative and Ulster Unionists voting consistently for the unamended bill.

The role played nationally by the Liberal Party during the set up of the Scheme was not reflected in their interventions during its abolition. Of course in 1918 there had been 200 Liberal MPs.[13] whereas in 1970 only six. The Commons in 1970 was effectively a two-way split Labour : Conservative,[14] as were its debates.

The Home Secretary contrasted a reported 7% return on investment for the Gretna and Cromarty, and 5% for Carlisle to an industry norm between 9 and 11 %. Interest rates incurred on the national debt were running at 8 - 9%. The Scheme's special nature also required no contribution to the exchequer for corporation tax. Challenging the implication of these figures Jim Callaghan described the Scheme as a thriving business, a state enterprise which ran at a profit. Lord Jacques looked back to calculate a return against the historic capital costs for the preceding 20 years showing a return between 8% and 18%. This intervention simply illustrated the extent to which arguments over capital value affected the claimed rate of return. Both the property valuations and the method of sale influenced the financial case for the sell-off. If the capital valuation was low, the argument that return on investment was inadequate was weaker. Opponents of the sale did however made the accusation of the intentional use of low valuations, charging that a give-away of public assets was planned.

The brewing industry in the late 1960s had been going through a process of mergers and take-overs. This process resulted in "increased concentration of owner-ship".[15] The extent to which the private sector brewers operated as monopolies was a focus of a Monopolies Commission Report of April, 1969. Neil Kinnock elabo-rated, describing brewing in the UK as an oligopoly. The "big seven" dominated the industry: "They own 56% of all the pubs [and] sell about 67% of the beer".

Ron Lewis spoke in favour of retention of the monopoly, but that it should be neither in the hands of the Home Secretary, nor under the ownership of major brewers. Many years earlier, Hugh Gaitskill had advocated that the Scheme be municipalised, rather than allow the profit to go to the Home Office. A further alter-native, the possibility to transferring ownership to a trust, had been raised by Lord Hailsham in January, 1970. The Secretary of State for Scotland, Gordon Campbell, had responded that his department deemed it not viable.

There was no requirement for private sector brewers to disclose the strength of their beers and there was little awareness of the relative strength of beers. This lack of openness and accountability was manifest not only in matters of beer strength but in accounting practices too. Philip Talbot, discussing his findings from the 1930s ,noted: "The uniqueness of the [Scheme's] accounting system lies in its internal publication and its public availability. By contrast the commercial brewers had a traditional aversion to any form of accounting disclosure that went beyond the confines of commercial confidentiality".[16] He concluded: "In financial terms, the SMS remained consistently profitable and as financially efficient as the commercial sector".

Local attitudes to the Scheme were not homogenous. Michael Jopling MP

(Conservative, Westmorland) struck a note of resentment: "Why should the constituents of Westmorland, a few miles down the road, have to subsidise the beer drinkers of Carlisle?" Anecdotal evidence, such as that mentioned in the Journal of the Brewery History Society however set out the "considerable horror" of Carlisle drinkers at the demise of the Scheme. Which Magazine pronounced that the Scheme produced one of the best and cheapest beers in the country. While there was no consensus even on the difference in the price of beer in Carlisle and district and in the adjoining areas, no-one suggested the SMS beer was dearer.

In 1970 there were around 1500 staff employed by the Scheme. They had, up until the sell-off, been enjoying secure employment as civil servants. Continuity of employment for staff and managers, and attention to pension benefits and rights were the major employment rights topics. The sell-off put every one of them in a position of uncertainty for some considerable time and staff had the choice to find other work or see if the new owners would retain them. Anyone who took a job outside the civil service was not eligible for redundancy payments. Tradesmen and associated mainte- nance staff, mostly employees at the brewery, were refused the right to transfer to other government departments.

On 31st October, 1972, over 500 employees from brewers to barmaids received their six month redundancy notices, Mr Marker, then the General Manager, indicated that "After April 30th, 1973, if they are needed, the employees can be retained on a month-by-month basis".

The bill gave considerable leeway to the Minister as to the method of sale: 'On such terms as appear to him expedient in the public interest". At the committee stage a proposed new schedule was debated: "Procedure for Disposal of Property". This amendment had eleven clauses which would have mandated the method of valuation, the method of sale, and the setting of reserve prices. Clauses 7 and 8 set out that for all properties the sitting tenants or public house managers would be offered the option to buy prior to the property going to auction. Clauses 10 and 11 set out to fix a reserve price at auction which took account of the development value of the property. The amendment, including these schedules, was voted down by 134 votes to 166.

The Under-secretary of State for the Home Department, Mark Carlisle, who had rejected the need for the schedules, went on to detail his government's intended procedure: "We will sell the unlicensed premises through independent estate agents, offering them at or near the valuation set upon them by independent estate agents, checked by the District Valuer, to the sitting tenants in the first place. . . For licensed premises, we will appoint two sets of agents - a London firm and a northern firm. . . I have said that 40 smaller public houses would be offered at or near valuation price".

The criterion for "smaller public houses" was a turnover not exceeding four barrels a week. Eight tenant managers who were excluded from the option to buy the freehold by this criterion employed solicitors Bill McKenna to put their case to William Whitelaw, Conservative M.P. for Penrith. These eight were all outwith Carlisle City area. A Home Office letter stated that the Government could not contemplate sale of each of the premises to the incumbent manager or tenant and that their 'Agents' advised there would be "very considerable loss to the Exchequer".

This potential for a large personal profit was bourn out later by the actual auction sale prices. Factors taken into account by the Government in deciding the form of the auction included "the desirability of maintaining some control over the ultimate ownership of the licensed properties".[17] Governance of the disposal by the state was in part reliant on the Comptroller, and Auditor General, as well as the Public Accounts Committee.

The Scheme's assets were to be split into four groups for auction. The question of what constituted an optimal size became an issue. For an integrated brewing, distribution and licensed premises operation, a common view amongst experts was that the Scheme as constituted was about the optimum size. These included Charles Fletcher-Cooke M.P. (Conservative, Darwen) who, as well as stating in a speech that the Scheme was 'manageable' and had "virtue in its smallness", then went on to warn his party leaders not to shy away from the Conservative Party Conference resolution for "a large and comprehensive measure of denationalisation". Fletcher-Cooke had suggested that the bill, and the denationalisation of Thomas Cook were merely heralds or substitutes for the "denationalisation of the commanding heights of the economy". He was clearly an advocate of that policy.

The Attitude of Breweries to outright ownership was not as enthusiastic as expected. A spokesperson for Newcastle and Scottish Breweries indicated their preferred pattern was for them to loan the money to a publican to enable him to buy the freehold, and for his then being contracted to sell their range of beers, with the house becoming a tied house.

It was clear from the size of the lots in the auction that the breweries and not the incumbent managers were the target of the sales pitch The Local Advisory Committee had advised the Home Secretary to offer all licensed premises for sale to tenants. It was Michael Cocks M.P. (Labour, Bristol South) who pointed to the needs of the brewers: parcels of licensed houses need to be made up so that a brewery has a guarantee of a sufficient number to trade with. If auctioned one by one, there would have been a greater risk for the brewers of buying an unviable small number. It is only possible to speculate if this would have yielded a better price for the Treasury. It was decided that the sale should offer the assets in four major groups, with a separate sale for the Scottish assets.

The assets sold, including those in Scotland, included: 23 hotels; 152 public houses; 2 restaurants; 1 brewery; 10 off-sales shops; many business premises, mainly in and around Carlisle and around 200 dwellings. The Home Secretary used those valuation agencies he and his Scottish counterpart judged appropriate. They were the Valuation Office of the Inland Revenue, outside agencies and the Valuation Office of the District Valuer or, in the case of licensed properties, the Regional Licensed Property Valuer. M.P's were not universally satisfied with this and the Home Secretary was challenged to defend the appointment of a remote London firm to "work with" the two local firms. The implication was that there were no suitable firms closer than London anywhere in Northern England. This view was not popular in the locality. While this could be seen as politically clumsy, or at least dismissive of local feelings, greater political dexterity was needed in the valuation process. The need to avoid "an auspicious correlation between valuations of the District Valuer, and those of the agents" was referred to overtly in internal correspondence. A letter from the Superintendent Valuer to Tiffens asked that the District Valuer be "informed of the contents of each group so that his valuations would keep pace with yours".[18] Further still, a memorandum of a meeting of 6th July, recorded: 'It is to be hoped that the two valuations are not too identical so as to avoid a suggestion of any connivance". A significant factor in producing a sound valuation in 1971 was the annual inflation rate of 9.4%. Estimating the Scheme's capital value was not just the reserve of the professionals. It was a popular amongst M.P's and commentators, who came to a wide range of conclusions. The M.P. for Stoke-on-Trent, R. B. Cant, after paying a cursory respect to the professions, described valuation as "the most-non scientific or all the sciences".

The sale included 166 unlicensed premises in the Carlisle District. There was a whole terrace, numbers 6 to 32 in Currock Street, Carlisle, some self contained flats, and many commercial premises. Looking at the value of land, buildings and plant, Jim Callaghan observed that the historical cost was £3.7 million. The assets had been written into the Scheme's balance sheet at their historical value. Tom Boardman, M.P. and a director of Allied Breweries, offered the figure of £2.2 million as their "Book Value", whereas Ron Lewis proposed £6 million. In the Lords debate Lord Windesham referred to provisional valuation in 1970 of £4.7 million for all three Schemes. The sale actually achieved a total exceeding £6 million in Carlisle and District and a further £0.9 million in the Scottish Districts.

The sale of pubs took until 1973 to complete and there was speculation the year long delay was an attempt to avoid redundancies which might result from a failure to sell the brewery.[19] The closing date for English tenders had been 13th November, 1972, with notification of the outcome to the winning bidders due by 31st January, 1973. The Scottish properties were advertised individually for offers.

Trading as the State Management Scheme ceased at different times in the three districts. Cromary was the first to close in June, 1972. Gretna District followed in March, 1973. Carlisle District stopped trading five months later, on 31st August 1973.

The sale for those properties not already sold to their tenants was by auction. The bill had made no provision for a reserve price. The Local Councils such as Carlisle and the County Councils were excluded from bidding. Premises in Scotland were listed and sold separately from those in England. The auction in England was handled by Sidney & Graham Motion of London and in Scotland by Thomas Roddick & Laurie, Annan. The prospectus included audited accounts of liquor sales at each premises. Purchasers were responsible to assure themselves there would be continuity of licensing, but there was provision to allow some return of deposit if licensing applications failed. The Scheme itself was responsible for all staff redundancy payments.

The English sales went ahead with only two minor amendments to the initial lots: The Bowling Green Inn in Carlisle was withdrawn from Group 1 having been sold to Cumberland Probation Service, and Royal Naval Association Club in Maryport withdrawn from Group 2. Bidders for any one of the groups of properties were required to also bid for some related lots, and could possibly obtain one but not the other. In Carlisle and District the four groups of premises were of a similar annual turnover; around 12,000 barrels of beer and 8,000 gallons of wines & spirits. The groups also had a similar divided equally between Carlisle sites and district sites.

The outcomes from sales to existing tenants were very different from the auction sales. For sales to existing tenants in the Carlisle & District the extent to which the two valuations for each property had agreed was within 2%, and the average price paid by tenants was half way between the two official valuations at £6,518. This contrasts to the outcome for the four groups that were auctioned. For the auctioned properties, despite the two valuations being on average within 1%, the auction sale prices were an average 54% above this at £42,128. Similarly the Carlisle and District licensed premises auctioned one by one reached on average 47% above the valuations, at £28,125. The majority of properties were sold to three of the big brewing interests: Scottish and Newcastle Breweries Ltd took group 1, Greenall Whitley & Co. Ltd. took groups 2 & 4, while Group 3 went to John Smith's Tadcaster Brewery Co. Ltd. In addition, the individual lots were divided three approximately equal ways; between the same three brewers, other established brewers,[20] and private buyers. With the exception of the Scheme's own offices in Carlisle's Castle Street, the winning bidders were required to complete the purchase between three and five months from 31st January, 1973.

In the final split less than 4% of properties went to the non-brewing sector firms, less than 4% to incoming private buyers, 22% sold to their existing tenants, and the remaining 70% to the major brewers.

License applications by the new owners in the former Carlisle and District saw 110 new licenses being issued. No objections were lodged. However, many were granted with the condition that the new owners implemented measures set out by the public health authority and the fire brigade. These arose presumably because prior to transfer these agencies had had no jurisdiction to inspect and then to comment on the Scheme's premises.

The sale of the brewery was not as straight forward as the sale of the public houses. UK brewers already had adequate or surplus brewing capacity, and were more likely to want control or access to the licensed premises than to further brewing capacity. There was no assurance to Parliament that the brewery would remain open, nor any provision to ensure it did. Jim Callaghan noted the "discrete silence of the Home Secretary" on this matter. R. B Cant M.P. (Labour, Stoke-on-Trent Central) predicted that the brewery would close. The intended sale date of the brewery was not met. It was at the end of October, 1971, when the first move to buy the brewery came, It was from Vaux and Associated Breweries, Ltd., a company that had supplied a considerable number of pubs in the area prior to the Scheme. The brewery failed to sell at this first attempt.

Much later the Home Office imposed a deadline to find a buyer by the end of January 1973. It was, in fact, two weeks after this date when it was announced that a buyer had been found. The sale to this bidder ,however, a businessman from Alston trading as Lakeland Breweries, fell through around late September, 1973, following protracted correspondence over the permissible effluent output levels.

In May, 1973, the Carlisle brewery ceased production under the Scheme. It was sold a whole year later, in May, 1974, to Thaekstons, and for only £90,000. The valuation had been in the range £147,000 to £190,000. In 1986, not long prior to announcing the brewery's closure, Mathew Brown, having taken over Theakstons some time before, had defended the company against a hostile take-over bid from Scottish and Newcastle. The brewery finally ceased production in 1987, with the loss then of 30 jobs. The buildings have been preserved externally, but now offer residential and student accommodation.

Having developed a unique scheme there was not only local opposition to disbanding it, but also opposition to inappropriate redevelopment of the premises themselves. In 1970 only a very few of the premises had listed buildings status. In the period of the sale, this matter was being redressed, principally by the Carlisle Civic Trust. In the period since there have been many further listings. The bulk of preservation orders were made in the period 1972 – 1974. They were predominantly grade II and indicated buildings of "special" rather than "exceptional" interest. During property sales the onus was on the buyer to discover the preservation status and the vendor refused to enter into any correspondence on this. In the 1970s preservation proposals were progressed through a process characterised by its secrecy. The listing of the Scheme's properties coincided closely with their sale, and buyers were presumably unaware of which properties were in the process of being nominated or listed. There was a noteworthy illustration of this with five properties listed on 13th November, 1972, the very last day for submission of auction tenders. These five were The Board Inn, St. Nicholas Arms, The Blue Bell Inn & Off Sales, Milbourne Arms, and The Cranemakers Arms. In the Gretna District at that time there were only three preservation orders: The Ecclefechan Hotel, The Queensbury Arms Hotel and Bluebell Inn, Annan..

After the initial remodelling or building, premises were maintained in their existing form, with few major changes, for the rest of the lifetime of the Scheme . Some commentators depicted this conservative maintenance as a failure to modernise, the crusading spirit of the Scheme waning. But it was also beyond or against the remit of the Scheme to make changes which promoted alcohol consumption. Preservation of the Scheme's architecture and design was in harmony with the ethos of the Scheme.

The mechanism for listing remains now mostly as it was then, a central government function triggered by proposals from individuals, local authority officials or other interested bodies. The criteria employed when judging the merits of a proposal included its historic importance, and the extent to which the property is in its original condition, such as a pub having its original ground floor layout. Apart from listing by the DoE there has been little or no use of the other major preservation provision, the Building Preservation Notice. This can restrict development but comes with a widely recognised risk to public funds, local government can be found financially liable in cases where their use this power is judged inappropriate.

Members of the National Historic Buildings Committee were engaged in adjudication of preservation proposals throughout England and their attitude in the 1970s strongly favoured listing of pre-1914 properties rather than post-1914 ones. This date separates the premises predating the Scheme from the New Model Inns built for the Scheme.

At the time of the sale the preparation of a list of the Carlisle & District properties for preservation involved almost exclusively the Civic Trust, officers of the local authorities' planning departments, and officers of the Department of the Environment, the 'DoE'. The initial position adopted by the Trust was for the preservation of all the pubs built specifically for the Scheme[22]. The Carlisle M.P., Ron Lewis joined the Civic Trust in rebutting the initial response to this[23] from an officer of the Department of the Environment. The officer was disinclined to even send an investigator, citing that staff were all fully committed elsewhere. The Trust challenged not only this but also the Department's use of 'normal criteria' alone. The Trust stressed the quality of design, craftsmanship and its maintenance as reasons for more careful consideration. They also disputed with them the use of a 1914 cut-off date for listing decisions.

Eventually the Trust were invited to draw up a preservation list, and on it were twenty five pubs from both the city of Carlisle and the remainder of Cumberland, a mix of pre and post 1914 property. Fourteen of the twenty five they gave priority to and five of these were New Model Inns. The response from the DoE of 9th May, 1972, judged that ten of those on the list should not be listed as they were either built after 1914 or were not of sufficient merit. It was only in later rounds of preservation that the New Model Inns were protected. The local Civic Trust wrote to their national Headquarters in less than guarded terms: "The extraordinarily unimaginative response" from the DoE needed Headquarters to intervene. The Civic Trust HQ response was limited to an offer to pass the papers to a journalist at the Daily Telegraph and a suggestion that one named major brewery chain was more "design conscious" than the others. Despite this, the various lobbying led to a climb down by the DoE, in the person of Lord Sanford, and an agreement to send Antony Dale, Chief Investigator of Historic Buildings, as again "all others staff were fully committed".

In June, 1972, Cumbria County Council Planning officers examined all the Scheme's premises in their jurisdiction, paying particular attention to the six[24] prioritised by the Civic Trust in their list. Two weeks prior to the tour by Mr Dale, Cumbria County Planning officials submitted photographs of fourteen premises that would not be easy to visit in the allotted time. Mr Dale led the review. He toured premises both in and beyond Carlisle on 13th July, 1972. His party included Mr Hall for the Scheme's management, and Mr Morton as a delegate for the Civic Trust. He reported his findings to the DoE's Historic Buildings Advisory Committee. Throughout this process there had been considerable correspondence between the Trust, the DoE, the Home Office, Carlisle City Council, and Cumbria County Council. The Trust continued to campaign for preservation of the 25 buildings it had originally proposed. The DoE then issued a 'complete revised list' of 13th November, 1972, but this was later was augmented by its "supplementary list" for Carlisle of 22nd February, 1973. This supplementary list was made public in the interval between tenders being submitted, and announcement of the winning bids.

In the interval, Greenall Whitley's Chief Group Designer approached the Civic Trust proposing he be "identified" with the Trust. The response was an invitation to apply for Corporate Membership of the Trust, which presumably they did.

In April 1973 there were further listings, this time in the Cumberland County area. The Civic Trust went for yet one more bite of the cherry on 7th August, 1973, pressing the DoE to also list the Pheasant Inn, the Howard Arms, and the Sportsman Inn, all in Carlisle, plus The Oddfellows Arms at Caldbeck. The outcome was listing on 22nd March, 1974, for the Pheasant Inn and the Sportsman's Inn. The Civic Trust through this period was chaired by Jocelyn Morton whose father James had been not only a founder member of the Design and Industries association, but of more direct interest, had been active in the set-up of the Scheme itself.

From the point of view of the properties built for the Scheme, preservation in the Scottish districts was of less importance. There was only one New Model Inn in Scotland; the Graham Arms at Eastriggs. At the time of writing this has not been the subject of any preservation order. Of the Scheme's thirteen other licensed premises in the Gretna District, four have been listed, only two of which are Scottish grade B, the other two being the lesser 'C'. Three of these listings were made in 1971, prior to their sale.

Whereas the stated criteria for listing of buildings have remained mostly unchanged since 1972, the criteria provided great scope for different interpretations. Coincident with the growth of tourism in the economy, both nationally and region-ally, has been a greater propensity to grant preservation orders these support the Heritage industry. In this case however it would be brave to say there was a signif-icant Heritage income arising from the preservation of the New Model Inns.

Preservation does not itself inhibit change of use, so for example of Carlisle's ten bowling greens, ironically, the only one in regular use is at the Redfern Inn, Etterby. While the 2005 renovation of the Horse and Farrier included the retention of the bowling green as a feature, the emphasis of the renovation was more towards serving food than encouraging bowls.

Since the 1970s there have been further reviews by planning officials such as those for Cumbria County Council in the early 1980s and the one for Carlisle which reported in 1994. This later review led to the addition of the Howard Arms and the Central Hotel to the properties listed for Carlisle. Where Preservation orders are in place owners may apply for Listed Building Consent to propose changes. Examples of this include the 1996 proposals for the Crescent Inn (more recently known as The White House) to be extended to the rear. This was followed by proposals for a dance floor on its first floor in 2000, which was granted. The Crescent Inn, so different from the other designs, was recognised as having very carefully created interior design. In this case, the original application received comments from English Heritage: the Crescent "imposes an alien design ethos with no acknowledgement to the building". and 'features worthy of retention … the internal layout reflecting the origins of the SMS'. Listed building status may have inhibited drastic rebuilding, but it has not stopped The Crescent suffering periods of disuse. Listing has also not ensured the condition of some of the painted murals.

In addition to the building, Pub Signs are controlled features too. They affect the character of the building, a point the Scheme's architects were well aware of. They had obligingly adhered to bylaws & planning guidance when designing the originals. Such was the case at the Cumberland Inn and the Apple Tree in Carlisle around 1930, when there was heated correspondence leading eventually to compliance by the Scheme's architects.

Changes and proposals often get coverage in the local press, such was the case with unsanctioned changes in 2005 to the windows at the Horse and Farrier, or the 1997 application for creation of a new staircase inside the Appletree (by then 'Pippins') and removal of an original one in order to expand the ground floor area to the rear. That application came just as it was gaining Grade II status. The application was withdrawn. There have been numerous other planning applications including the successful one for significant extension of the Near Boot, Tarraby, with loss of its bowling green

The outcome for the fifteen New Model Inns build under the Scheme has been the grade II preservation of six of them: Cumberland Inn, Apple Tree, Horse & Farrier, Crescent Inn all in Carlisle, and the Spinners Arms at Cummersdale. The last of the six to be listed was Seddon's tribute to Redfern himself: The Redfern Inn at Etterby.

During the Scheme's life pub culture and architecture in the rest of the UK evolved. Lord Inglewood maintained, in 1971, that the Scheme's pubs had "edged nearer and nearer the style of ordinary pub in other parts of the country".[25]

Since 1973, of around 160 licensed premises in the Carlisle & District area ,only seven have closed. The phenomenon common elsewhere the UK of pubs converted to flats is evident in only a few cases, such as the Green Dragon and in 2006 the Cumberland Wrestlers, both in Carlisle. Both The Malt Shovel and The Pheasant Inn have been re-opened as restaurants, and the Duke of York has closed. The Maltsters Arms in Carlisle was demolished.

Since 1973 Planning and Licensing has followed national trends too.

Carlisle City Surveyor John Taylor noted in 2000[26] there will be a reduction in urban pubs and "the boom in . . . nationally themed chains is just one of the factors that could see the end of a few bars on the edge of town".

In 2006, Carlisle District Local Plan, discussing public houses, merely stated, "The Council is keen to see an early evening and late night economy evolve in Carlisle but recognise that this creates potential conflicts".

Much of Carlisle City centre's Botchergate regeneration runs counter to the ethos of the Scheme. Evening drinkers are corralled into this urban hot spot with plenty of stand-up drinking. An absence of drunkenness has not been the outcome, and the role of architecture and décor is more to maximise occupancy than to inhibit over-consumption. The Caledonian in Botchergate, for example, was remodelled as 'CA1', then 'Barcode'. Its manager, talking in 2003, exemplified the change in attitude to architecture and ethos.[27] He claimed that CA1 was "very bright" and that there was "no point having ugly people standing in the pub".

In 2004, Allerdale Council decided to introduce measures to reduce "booze-fuelled violence". These included calls for publicans to abandon cheap drinks promotions. The measuressome were a faint echo of the temperance call for sobriety. The measures included the need for training of doormen, and a ban on drinking in the street. In common with many other UK city centres it is door staff as well as bar staff who now police excessive consumption. The contrast between this approach and that of the Scheme is not entirely one of opposites. The common theme of control is still to be found, but it is no longer one focussed on the encouragement of self control.

There have been other changes in pub culture over the last half century. Alongside, the rise in heavy, weekend drinking, particularly by the young in city centres, has been the expansion of public houses offering bar meals and often restaurant facilities. Women, of course, are welcome, and, in many cases, so are children.

The Scheme was in the vanguard of change in leisure culture during the twentieth century. It led the way in seeking to foster changed patterns of alcohol consumption and did much, by its architecture, management and ethos, to change drinking patterns in Carlisle. The quality of the beer and its price are still remembered with affection by local people.

The interplay between social policy, temperance, wartime imperatives, architecture, design, and politics of the inception and wind up of the Scheme has been explored but the experiment allows no single conclusion. The experiment was only ever allowed one form, that of central control from the Home Office. While this model may have been appropriate during wartime the chance to migrate to a devolved non capitalist model was lost.

There are new experiments in the 21st Century, the prominent ones so far being relaxation of licensing hours and obliquely, the smoking ban in bars. Whereas licensing and our drinking culture remain on the political agenda, across-the-board temperance does not.

Notes to Chapter

1 Replying also for the Secretary of State for Scotland, Rt Hon. Gordon Campbell M.C., M.P.
2 Hansard 612 1185, Mr Nabarro & Mr Vosper.
3 Yorkshire Post, 11th April, 1959.
4 Letter published in Evening News & Star, 26th Jan, 1971.
5 State Management of the Liquor Trade, Dr R.M. Punnett Dept of Politics, University of Strathclyde, Public Administration, Summer, 1966.
6 Talbot, P.,... Journal of Finance and Management in Public Services Vol 5 No2.
7 Hansard for 26 November 1970
8 Carlisle and District Local Advisory Committee, The Case for a Change in Organisation, 10th April, 1967.
9 Paraphrasing R.M. Punnett in Public Administration, Summer 1966 p201
10 Burt Report, May 1957, Cmnd. 168
11 Mr W E Garret (Wallsend)
12 Mr Neil Kinnock (Bedwellty)
13 Coalition Liberals supporting Lloyd George; 127, Liberal Party, followers of Asquith; 36.
14 1970 Commons was split Conservative; 330, Labour; 288, Liberal; 6. Others; 6.
15 Monopolies Commission Report on Unilever Ltd and Allied Breweries Ltd.
16 Philip Talbot, Journal of Finance and Management in Public Services. Volume 4 Number 2
17 Home Office letter of 27th January, 1972, to Hon. Secretary of the Local Advisory Committee from Francis Graham-Harrison.
18 Letter from Ernest Arthur Bullock, Superintendent Valuer, Northern 1 Region, 27th July, 1971.
19 'SMS axing not held up – Govt.' Cumberland Evening News, 25th May, 1972.

20 Whitbread West Pennines, and Jenning Brothers Ltd.
21 Quoted holding in 2005.
22 Letter from Civic Trust to the Home Office, 28th March, 1972.
23 Letter J. O. Thompson, for DoE to Carlisle & District Civic Trust, 9th May, 1972.
24 Greyhound Inn, Burgh-by-Sands; Globe Tavern, Longtown; Oddfellows Arms Caldbeck; Miners Arms, Maryport, Drovers Rest, Monkhill; and Wheatsheaf Inn, Abbeytown.
25 Hansard [Lords] Vol 321, 2nd July, 1971. pp 632
26 Cumberland News, April 14th, 2000.
27 Carlisle District Local Plan 2001 – 2016 Redeposit Draft, August, 2005.
28 Cumberland News, 25th April. 2003.

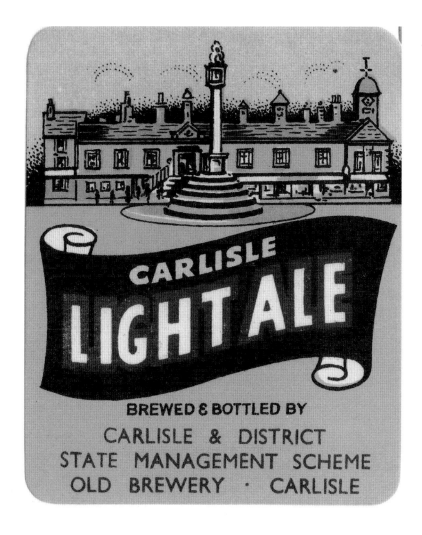

APPENDIX ONE
Royal Commission on Licensing (England and Wales) 1929-31

WITNESSES (Carlisle) who gave evidence before the Commission in 1930: BOYD, John. Clerk, Carlisle. May 23

CHANCE, Robert Christopher. Mayor of Carlisle. May 9

COURTNEY, The Rev. Archibald Jeans, London; formerly of Wigton, Cumberland. May 9

CREIGHTON, Miss Mary Ellen, JP; Member of the Local Advisory Committee, Carlisle and District State Management Scheme. May 22 EVANS, Sidney W. Clerk, Carlisle. November 21

EVENS, The Rev. G. Bramwell, Halifax; formerly of Carlisle. May 23 JOHNSTON, Andrew A. Chief Constable of Carlisle. May 8 LOVE, William W. Machine Printer, Carlisle. November 21

MITCHELL, Albert Ernest, OBE; General Manager of the Carlisle and District State Management Scheme. April 29

POTTS, Councillor John Robert, Member of the Local Advisory Committee, Carlisle and District State Management Scheme. May 23 ROBERTS, Charles, J.P. July 9

ROGERSON, Alderman Thomas. Dairyman, Carlisle. May 23

SANDERS, Sir Edgar. Late General Manager of the Carlisle and District State Management Scheme. April 30

SPENCE, Eric Herbert. Late Chief Constable of Carli'sle. May 8

STEWART, Ernest. Superintendent, Carlisle Division, Cumberland and Westmorland Constabulary. May 8

STUART, The Very Rev. Henry V. Dean of Carlisle. May 9

SYKES, Sir John, CG; KCB. Member of State Management Districts Council (Independent). April 29 and July 29

WILSON, Archibald Kennedy. Chief Constable of Plymouth and late Chief Constable of Carlisle. May 8

APPENDIX TWO
State Management Scheme Acquisitions

Carlisle and District

JULY 1916: Apple Tree Inn, Lowther Street; Bowling Green Hotel, Lowther Street; Malt Shovel Inn, Rickergate; Board Inn. Pasternoster Row. AUGUST 1916: Carlisle Old Brewery; Wellington Hotel, English Street; Golden Lion, Botchergate; Crown & Anchor, Scotch Street; Globe Inn, Bridge Street, Caldewgate; Ismay's Vaults, Scotch Street; Waggon & Horses, Bridge Street; Blue Bell Inn, Rickergate; Earl Grey Inn, Botchergate; Lord Brougham, Warwick Road; Howard Arms, Lowther Street; Shakespeare Tavern, St. Cuthbert's Lane; Crown Inn, Corporation Road; Malsters' Arms, John Street; Woolpack Inn, Milbourne Street; Drove Inn, Stanwix; Lorne Arms, Shaddongate; Edentown off-licence, 28 Eden Street; Saracen's Head Inn, Caldew Bridge; Crown & Thistle, Stanwix; Queen Adelaide, Botchergate; Railway Hotel, London Road; London and North Western Railway Inn, James Street; White Ox, St.Nicholas; Three Crowns, English Street; Royal Oak, Bridge Street; Green Dragon, Newtown; Pheasant Inn, Caldewgate; Globe Inn, Caldew Bridge; Museum Inn, Belle Vue; Cumberland Hotel, Botchergate; Crown Hotel, Botchergate; Jovial Sailor Inn, Caldecotes; Carlisle South End Unionist Club premises, London Road; Duke of York

Inn, Shaddongate; Fox and Hounds, Rickergate; Sportsman, Heads Lane; Linton Holme Hotel, Lindisfame Street; Milbourne Arms Inn, Milbourne Street; Star Inn, Botcherby; Beehive, Warwick Road; Albion Hotel, Botchergate; Black Bull Inn, Upperby; Moulders' Arms, Currock Street; Admiral Nelson Inn, Dalston Road; Horse and Farrier Inn, Raffles; Joiners' Arms Inn, Church Street; Carlisle New Brewery; Currock Hotel, Currock; Caledonian Hotel, Botchergate; Three Crowns Inn, Rickergate; Golden Fleece, St.Nicholas; Denton Inn, Denton Holme; Prince of Wales Inn, Denton Holme; Crown Hotel, Stanwix; Samson Inn, London Road; Cumberland Wrestlers, Currock Street; Drove Inn, Rickergate; Black Bull, Annetwell Street; 19 Castle Street. bought and alterations started; Messrs. Hope & Bendle, Lowther Street; Hole-in-the-Wall, St.Alban's Row, (managed by Hope & Bendle); St.Alban's Spirit Stores; Friar's Hotel, Devonshire Street. SEPTEM-BER 1916 Iredale's Brewery; Turf Hotel, the Sands; Blue Bell, Scotch Street; The bars at Harrison & Hetherington Auction Marts; Goliath Inn, Crown Street; Plough Inn, Caldewgate; Spinners' Arms Inn, Milbourne Street; Petteril Bridge Inn, Warwick Road; Cross Keys, Upperby; Lion & Lamb, Scotch Street; Queen's Brewery (Graham's), Caldewgate; Queen's Head Inn, Caldewgate.
OCTOBER 1916: Longtown: Graham Arms; King's Arms; The Wheatsheaf; The White Swan; The Globe; The Bush; and Monkhouse's Vaults. Crown & Thistle, Rockcliffe; Ship Inn, Rockcliffe; Highland Laddie, Todhills; Metal Bridge Inn, Blackford, Rockcliffe ; Coach & Horses, Kingstown; King's Arms, Kingstown; Graham Arms; The Clift; Robin Hood, Smithfield, Near Boot, Tarraby; The Old King's Head Inn, Fisher Street; Nanson's Vaults, West Tower Street; Deakin's Vaults, Botchergate; Golden Fleece, Corporation Road; Hare & Hounds, Botchergate; The Great Central Hotel, The Viaduct; Pedestrian Arms, Newtown; City Vaults, FisherStreet; Bird-in-Hand, Stanwix; Queen's Inn, Great Corby; Corby Bridge Inn; The Wheatsheaf, Wetheral; The Crown, Wetheral; Royal Oak, Scotby; Lowther Arms, Cumwhinton; The Old Bush, Scotch Street.
MARCH 1917: Blue Bell Inn, Carleton; Royal Oak Inn, Gaitsgill; Pack Horse Inn, Burgh; Drover's Rest, Monkhill; Heilk Moon (Joiners' Arms), Scaleby.
APRIL 1917: Railway Tavern, Botchergate; Wellington, Great Orton; Rose & Crown, Kirkbampton; Tam©O'Shanter, Little Bampton; The Stag, Crosby-on-Eden; Co-operative Inn, Warwick Bridge; Pointer Dog Inn, Bolton-Fell-End; Black Lion Inn, Hethersgill.
FEBRUARY 1918: King's Arms, Dalston; The Crown, Broadfield; The Greyhound, Cotehill; Royal Oak, Moorehouse.
MARCH 1918: Black Lion, Durdar; Bridge Inn, Hawksdale; The Waterloo, Aglionby; Solway Hotel, Silloth.
OCTOBER 1918: Jacob Thomlinson Ltd., Maryport/wine and spirits merchant (purchased); Broom Vaults, High Street, Maryport; bonded stores and The Board Inn, Maryport; spirit vaults, King Street, Maryport; Crown & Mitre Hotel, Wigton; Shoulder of Mutton Inn, Aspatria; Ship Inn, Allonby; Swan Inn, Ellenborough; Birdin-Hand, Papcastle.
NOVEMBER 1918: Fox & Hounds, Aspatria; Sun Inn, Aspatria; Ship Inn, Dearham; Struggler, Dearham; Crown Inn, Ellenborough; Princess Royal, Flimby; Miners' Arms, Fothergill; Artillery Arms; Black Lion; Queen's Head; Royal Oak; Senhouse Arms; Shakespeare; Ship Inn (South Quay); Station Hotel; Sun Inn; Victoria; White Swan; (all in Maryport).
FEBRUARY 1919: Railway Hotel, Southwaite; Spirit Vaults, Wigton; Board Inn, Senhouse Street, Maryport; Sailor's Return, Maryport; Broom Inn, Maryport; Grapes Inn, Glasson; New Crown Inn, Glasson, Maryport.
JANUARY 1921: White Swan, Wigton.

APPENDIX THREE
Table of Preservation Status of State Management Properties

Listed prior to the sell-off, 11-Apr-67

Royal Oak, Wigton II

Scottish Listings, 03Aug-71

Ecclefechan Hotel, Ecclefechan, C   Bluebell Inn, Annan, B

Queensbury Arms Hotel Annan, B

Carlisle First Listing, 13-Nov-72

SMS Offices, Carlisle, II   Cranemakers Arms, Carlisle, II

Blue Bell Inn & Off Sales, Carlisle, II   Milbourne Arms, Carlisle, II

St. Nicholas Arms, Carlisle, II   Board Inn, Carlisle, II

Carlisle Second A Listing, 22-Feb-73

Horse & Farrier, 1929* Carlisle, II   Crescent Inn, 1932*Carlisle, ll

Cumberland First Listing, 19-Jun-73

Stag, Crosby on Eden, II   Bush Inn, Longtown, II

Royal Oak, Gaitsgill, II   Senhouse Arms, Maryport, II

Spinners Arms, 1930*Cummersdale, II Drovers' Rest, Monkhill, II

Broom Vaults, Maryport, II   Greyhound Inn, Burgh-by-Sands II

Near Boot Inn, Tarraby, II   Globe Tavern, Longtown II

Carlisle Third Listing, 22-Mar-74

Gretna Tavern, Carlisle II   Sportsman Inn, Carlisle II

Turf Inn, Carlisle II   Pheasant Tavern Carlisle II

Golden Lion, Carlisle II   Caledonian, Carlisle II

Red Lion Hotel Carlisle II

Subsequent Listings

27-May-77

Board Vaults, Maryport II   Crown Inn, Maryport II

Lifeboat Inn, Maryport II   Station Hotel, Maryport II

22-Sep-83: Corby Bridge Hotel, Great Corby II; Crown Hotel, Wetheral II; Queens Arms Inn, Warwick on Eden, II; Crown and Thistle, Rockcliffe 16-Jan-84. II; Graham Arms Hotel, Longtown. 15-Jun-84 II; Blue Bell Inn, Dalston, 19-Sep-84 II; Bridge End Inn, Dalston, 19-Sep-84 II; Ship Inn, Thursby, 08-Nov-84 II; SMS Carlisle Brewery, Carlisle, 29-May-87 II; Central Hotel, Annan, 12-Jul-88 C(s); The Buck Inn, Annan, 12-Jul-88C(s); Railway Inn, Carlisle, 24-May-93 II; Howard Arms, Carlisle, 11-Apr-94 II; Central Hotel, Carlisle, 11-Apr-94 II; Friars Tavern, Carlisle, 11-Apr-94 II; Apple Tree 1927 *, Carlisle, 06-May-97 II; Cumberland Inn 1930 *, Carlisle, 14-Apr-00 II; Redfern Inn 1940 *, Etterby, Carlisle 17-May-00 II.

Proposed by Civic Trust but never listed

Malt Shovel 1928*Carlisle; Albion Tavern, Carlisle; Harraby Inn, 1949 Carlisle; Oddfellows Arms, Caldbeck; Wheatsheaf Inn 1935 *Abbeytown; Earl Grey 1935 *Carlisle; Coach and Horses 1929 * Kingstown; Miners Arms, Maryport; Bounty Inn, Maryport

New Model Inns neither proposed, nor listed

Magpie Inn 1932 *, Carlisle; Black Lion Inn 1929 *, Durdar; Rose & Crown 1930 *, Carlisle; Cumberland Wrestlers 1938 *, Carlisle; Crown 1937 *, Carlisle; Graham Arms Inn 1934 *, Eastriggs, Dumfrieshire

Denotes the inter-war New Model Inns

APPENDIX FOUR
The Board's Rules for their Managers

1. The Manager shall keep the licensed premises scrupulously clean and the rooms used by the public properly ventilated, and lighted and warmed when necessary.

2. The scheme of charges fined by the Board for the letting of rooms and lodgings shall be strictly adhered to. The Manager shall not let rooms or lodgings unless authorised to do so by the Board.

3, No wages shall be paid on the premises except to those employed in the house.

4. Neither the Manager nor his assistants shall smoke during opening hours.

5. The Manager shall not adulterate or dilute any of the wines spirits malt liquors drinks or food which may be supplied to him for salle to customers.

6. The Manager shall under no circumstances either directly or indirectly receive from any persons supplying goods to or dealing with the Board any gift bonus or commission or benefit of any kind whatsoever.

7. The business carried on at the aforementioned premises shall be cash or ready money business only and credit shall not be given or allowed to any customer.

8. No "ring-paper," "ring-book," or any certificate or warrant for the payment of any pension, separation or any other allowance by the War Office, Admiralty or any other Government Department or by any Public Body, no Army Certificate, advance note, pawnbroker's duplicate ticket or any other document article or thing shall be received purchased or taken as security from a customer or other person.

9. The Manager shall not advance money to customers or cash for them.

10. No gaming and no raffle of any description shall be allowed to take place on the licensed premises or on any ground occupied therewith.

11. The, Manager shall not, without the express permission of the Board, supply to any person who is not an official of the Board any information or give replies to any questions concerning the licensed promises or the business carried on therein or the wages of the Manager or his staff or the terms of his or their service.

12. All letters, books, invoices and other documents received or kept, by the Manager in connection with the business of the licensed promises are the property of the Board and are strictly private. The Manager must carefully preserve all such papers as are not transmitted by him to the Head Office and will be held entirely responsible for their production when required.

13. All moneys received by the Manager in respect of the sale of goods to customers or otherwise in relation to the business shall be banked daily or otherwise or shall be directed by the Board.

14. The Manager shall exercise the greatest possible care to prevent drunken person entering the licensed premises and shall not permit a drunken person to remain on the premises or sell or serve intoxicating liquor of any kind to a drunken person

15. The Manager shall not open or keep the premises open during prohibited hours.

16. The Manager shall use all possible means to prevent excessive drinking by customers and shall carefully observe the demeanour of all customers who remain in the house for a prolonged period. He shall also satisfy himself as to the complete sobriety of a customer before allowing him to be served with any intoxicating liquor. No messenger known to be sent by any person who has been refused drink on the promises shall be supplied,

17. The Manager shall not sell or allow to be sold to any person apparently under the age of eight-

een years for consumption on the premises (i) spirits of any description; (ii) ale beer stout or porter except for consumption with a meal.

18. The Manager shall duly observe and be wholly and solely responsible for the due observance, of the provisions of all Acts of Parliament relating to the sale of liquors and to licensed persons and licensed premises and shall do all things necessary to comply with and observe the same and shall also comply with and observe the Orders of the Board now in force relating to the sale and consumption of liquors and any future Orders which may be made.

19. The Manager shall not give any entertainment or permit any entertainment to take place upon the licensed premises without the consent of the Board and without the requisite legal authority (if any) recognized for the purpose.

20. The Manager shall not permit any trade or other advertisement to be exhibited either in or on the premises without the consent of the Board.

21. The Manager shall not sleep away from the premises nor be absent during business hours on private business without the consent of the Board nor shall he be a member of or become a candidate for any County, Borough, District or Parish Council, Board of Guardians or other public body, corporation or committee or be a director or engage in any other employment or business whatsoever, without the consent of the Board.

22 The Manager shall not be the secretary, treasurer or any other officialof any club, society or other organization which holds its meetings or the meetings of its committee at the premise of which the manager is in charge.

23. The Manager shall not fell nor cut injuriously any of the timber or ornamental shrubs (if any) and trees and the Manager shall not break up or alter the arrangements of the garden (if any) without the consent of the Board in writing.

24. Except with the consent of the Board not more than one dog shall be kept in or about the premises.

25. No person except those employed in or lodging at the house shall be allowed to remain on the premises during closing hours.

26. If the Manager shall accept parcels or goods of any description from customers or others for safe custody he shall do so at his own risk and the Board shall not be held responsible by the owners thereof for any loss or damage suffered in respect of such parcels or goods. Managers of premises to which no livery stables are attached shall not accept parcels or goods for safe custody.

BIBLIOGRAPHY

Aldridge, Meryl. The British New Towns. A progamme without a policy. Department of Social Administration and Social Work / University of Nottingham. Routledge & Kegan Paul. 1979

Bailey-Scott, M. H. Houses and Gardens. George Newnes Ltd. London 1906 Black, Naomi. ed. Celebration. The Book of Jewish Festivals. William Collins & Co. Ltd. London 1987

Boston, Richard. Beer & Skittles. Fontana / Collins. 1977

Bradley, Ian. William Morris and his World. Thames and Hudson. 1978

Braun, Hugh. Elements of English Architecture. David & Charles. Newton Abbot 1973

Brunskill, Ronald & Clifton-Taylor, Alec. English Brickwork. Ward Lock 1977

Capper. W. Bentley. Ed. Licensed Houses and their Management. The Caxton Publishing Company Ltd. London 1948.(first published Nov. 1923)

Carter, Henry. The Control of the Drink Trade in Britain. A Contribution to National Efficiency during the Great War 1915-18. Preface by Lord D'Abernon. Longmans Green & Co. London 1918. Second edition 1919

Coad, Roy. Laing. The biography of Sir John W. Laing, CBE. (1879-1978). Hodder & Stoughton. London 1979

Coulton, G. G. Medieval Panorama. Volume 1. Cambridge University Press 1938 Crook, J. Mordaunt. William Burges and the High Victorian Dream. John Murray 1981

D'Abernon, Viscount. Portraits and Appreciations. Hodder and Stoughton. London 1931

David, Edward. ed. Inside Asquith 's Cabinet. From the Diaries of Charles Hobhouse. John Murray 1977

Durant, Stuart. The Decorative Designs of C. F A. Voysey. Lutterworth Press. Cambridge 1990

Durant, Stuart. Architectural Monographs No. 19. C. F A. Voysey. Academy Editions / St. Martin's Press 1992

Evens, The Rev. G. Bramwell. The Truth about Direct Control in Carlisle. As administered by the Central Control Board (Liquor Traffic). P. S. King & Son. Westminster 1917

Foot, Michael. Loyalists and Loners. Collins 1986

Fried, Albert and Elman, Richard M. Selected and edited by: Foreword by Raymond Williams. Charles Booth 's London. Hutchinson & Co. Ltd. London 1969 George, David Lloyd. War Memoirs. Odhams Press Ltd. (new edition) 1933-4 George, Richard. Lloyd (Earl Lloyd George of Dwyfor). Frederick Muller Ltd. London 1960

Gilbert, Martin. Winston S. Churchill. Volume III (1914-16). Heinemann. London 1971

Gilbert, Martin. Winston S. Churchill. Companion Volume IV, Part 1(January 1917June 1919). Heinemann. London 1977

Gill, Eric. Autobiography. Jonathan Cape 1940

Girouard, Mark. Victorian Pubs. Studio Vista 1975

Gorham, Maurice; and Dunnett, H. McG. Inside the Pub. The Architectural Press. London 1950

Gourvish, Terry. R. and Wilson, Richard G. The British Brewing Industry 1830-1980, Cambridge University Press 1994 (Copyright: The Brewers' Society 1994) Grigg, John. Lloyd George - From Peace to War 1912-16. Methuen 1985 Harrison, Brian. Drink and the Victorians. Faber & Faber 1971 Haydon, Peter. The English Pub: A History. Robert Hale Ltd. London 1994

Hayler, Guy. ed. The Prohibition Movement. Papers and proceedings of the National Convention for the Prohibition of the Liquor Traffic, Newcastle-upon-Tyne, April 1897

Hopkins, Hugh Evan. Charles Simeon of Cambridge: A Biography. Hodder and Stoughton. London, 1977

Howse, Ernest Marshall. Saints in Politics. The "Clapham Sect". George Allen & Unwin Ltd. 1953

Hunt, J. A City Under the Influence. Lakescene Publications. Border Press, Carlisle 1971

Jackson, Michael ed. The World Guide to Beer. Mitchell Beazley. London 1977 Jones, Thomas. Whitehall Diary. Volume 1. Oxford University Press 1969 Laing, Dave and Hendra, John. Beer & Brewing. Macdonald Guidelines 1977 Langhorne, Elizabeth. Nancy Astor and her Friends. (first published in the USA by Praeger Publishers, Inc., New York). Published in Great Britain by Arthur Barker Ltd. London 1974

Longmate, Norman. The Water Drinkers. Hamish Hamilton. London 1968

Luke, W. B. Sir Wilfrid Lawson. Simpkin, Marshall, Hamilton, Kent & Co. Ltd. London 1900

MacCarthy, Fiona. Eric Gill. Faber & Faber Ltd. 1989

Mackintosh, John P. The British Cabinet. (third edition) Stevens & Sons Ltd. London 1977

Macleod, Robert. Style and Society. Architectural ideology in Britain 1835= 1914. RIBA Publications Ltd. 1971

Marwick, Arthur. The Deluge. British Society and the First World War. The Macmillan Press Ltd. London 1965

Marwick, Arthur. Britain in the Century of Total War. War, Peace and Social Change 1900-1967 The Bodley Head 1968

Marwick, Arthur. The Nature of History. Macmillan & Co. Ltd. 1970

Masse, H. J. L. The Art Workers ' Guild 1884-1934. Shakespeare Head Press. Oxford 1935

Monckton, H.A. A History of English Ale and Beer. The Bodley Head 1966

Moon, Karen. George Walton. Designer and Architect. White Cockade Publishing. Oxford 1993

Morton, Jocelyn. Three Generations in a Family Textile Firm. Routledge & Kegan Paul Ltd. 1971

Naylor, Gillian. The Arts & Crafts Movement. Studio Vista. London 1971

Oliver, Basil. The Renaissance of the English Public House. Faber & Faber. London, 1947

Osband, Linda. Victorian House Style. David & Charles 1991

Owen, Frank. Tempestuous Journey. Lloyd George: His Life and Times. Hutchinson 1954

Pevsner, Nikolaus. Pioneers of Modern Design. Penguin Books 1960. (revised and partly re-written)

Pevsner, Nikolaus. The Buildings of England: Cambridgeshire. Penquin Books 1970 (2nd edition)

Pevsner, Nikolaus. Some Architectural Writers of the Nineteenth Century. Oxford University Press 1972

Pratt, A. The Licensed Trade: An Independent Survey. John Murray, London 1907 Punnett, R.M. State Management of the Liquor Trade. The Royal Institute of Public Administration, Volume 44. (reprinted from the Summer 1966 issue of "Public Administration")

Raverat, Gwen. Period Piece. Faber & Faber 1960

Rawnsley, H. D. Harvey Goodwin: Bishop of Carlisle. John Murray. London 1896 Read, Donald. Edwardian England 1901-15 (Society and Politics). Harrap. London 1972 Roberts, Charles. The Radical Countess. The History of the Life of Rosalind, Countess of Carlisle. Steel Brothers (Carlisle) Ltd. 1962

Ross, Kurt. "Codex Mendoza " (commentaries). Miller Graphics. Productions Liber SA.C.H. Fribourg 1978

Rowland, Peter. Lloyd George. Barrie & Jenkins Ltd. 1975

Rowntree, Joseph; and Sherwell, Arthur. State Prohibition and Local Option. Hodder & Stoughton 1899

Selley, Ernest. The English Public House As It Is. Longmans, Green & Co. Ltd. London 1927

Service, Alastair. Edwardian Architecture. A Handbook to Building Design in Britain 1890-1914. Thames & Hudson 1977

Shadwell, Arthur. Drink in 1914-22. A Lesson in Control. Longmans, Green & Co. Ltd. 1923

Spiller, Brian. Victorian Public Houses. David & Charles (Publishers) Ltd. 1972 Stamp, Gavin; and Goulancourt, Andre. The English House 1860-1914. The Flowering of English Domestic Architecture. Faber & Faber 1986 Sutherland, Douglas. Raise Your Glasses. Macdonald, London 1969 Taylor, A. J. P. Ed. Lloyd George: A Diary by Frances Stevenson. Hutchinson, London 1971 Thompson, Paul. William Butterfield. Routledge & Kegan Paul. London 1971 Troup, Sir Edward. (Permanent Under-Secretary of State in the Home Office 19081922). The Home Office. G. P. Putnam's Sons Ltd. 1925 Turner, John. Lloyd George's Secretariat. Cambridge University Press 1980 Vaisey, John. The Brewing Industry 1886-195L (for the Economic Research Council). Sir Isaac Pitman & Sons Ltd. 1960

Vernon, H. M. The Alcohol Problem. Bailliere, Tindall & Cox. London 1928

Ward, W. R. Religion and Society in England 1790-1850. B. T. Batsford Ltd. London 1972

Watney, John. Beer is Best. Peter Owen Ltd. London 1974

Webb, Sidney and Beatrice. The History of Liquor Licensing in England. (principally from 1700-1830). Frank Cass & Co. Ltd. London 1903, reprinted 1963 White, James. The Cambridge Movement: The Ecclesiologists and the Gothic Revival. Cambridge University Press 1962

Wilson, John Dover. Life in Shakespeare's England. Cambridge University Press 1911; Pelican Books 1944, reprinted 1962

Wilson, Trevor. Ed. The Political Diaries of C. P. Scott. Collins, London 1970 Woodruffe, Brian J. Wiltshire Villages. Robert Hale. London 1982

Yorke, Francis, The Planning and Equipment of Public Houses. The Architectural Press. London 1949

1914 The Licensed V ctuallers 'Official Annual

1932 Royal Commission on Licensing (England & Wales) Report 1929-31. HMSO Cmd 3988

1972 Sale Catalogues (England and Scotland). Thomson, Roddick and Laurie Ltd. (Annan and Carlisle)

1978 C. F A. Voysey: architect and designer 1857-1941. Lund Humphries, London in association with Art Galleries & Museums and the Royal Pavilion, Brighton.(copyright 1978 Brighton Borough Council)

1982 Government Control of the Liquor Trade (Carlisle & District State Management Scheme). S. E. Kirby. Group for Regional Studies. Museums Journal No.10

1983 Bricks and Beer. English Pub Architecture 1830-1939. British Architectural Library. London

1984 The Architecture of the Well-tempered Environment. The Architectural Press Ltd. 2nd edition